BASS FISHERMAN'S DIGEST

By Chris Christian

DBI BOOKS, INC.

ABOUT OUR COVER

Zebco has come a long way since they introduced the first spin-cast reel some 40 years ago; today they are the number one manufacturer of fishing tackle in America and enjoy the highest brand awareness among consumers that fish.

Our cover pictures some of their more recent Pro Staff™ offerings that are ideally suited to bass fishing. From left to right: the Model 110 Bait-Cast Reel mounted on a Model PSC50L Graphite Casting Rod, the Model 2020 Spin-Cast Reel mounted on a Model PSC59MH Graphite Trigger Stick, and the Model 20 Medium Freshwater Spinning Reel. Photo by John Hanusin.

PRODUCED BY

GALLANT CHARGER

OUTDOOR GROUP

Publisher
Sheldon Factor

Editorial Director
Jack Lewis

Production Director
Sonya Kaiser

Art Director
Paul Graff

Associate Artists
Denise Comiskey
Gary Duck

Copy Editor
Shelby Harbison

Production Coordinator
Pepper Federici

Lithographic Service
Gallant Graphics

ISBN 0-87349-19-3   Library of Congress Catalog Card #87-073414

CONTENTS

INTRODUCTION

MY GOOD FRIEND, Jack Mitchell, once began the introduction to a book on rifle-smithing by saying, "the most difficult part of writing a book on riflesmithing is getting started. The hundreds of different types of rifles, the myriad of individual tasks necessary to build one almost from scratch and the seemingly endless techniques used to accomplish each task are of staggering proportions. It's like sitting down at the dinner table with a knife and fork and attempting to eat an elephant."

I read that with some amusement, at the time. But, as I finish proofing the last chapter in the book, the distinct aftertaste of elephant clings to my palate.

During the last two decades the bass has risen, with considerable fanfare, to the position of the most popular gamefish in America. It didn't reach that plateau because of its ability as a fighter; there're a lot of fish that'll put a bigger bend in your rod than a bass. Nor because of its table qualities; most serious bass anglers release their fish. Nor because it is easy to catch. In fact, the opposite is more often true.

The bass didn't earn the respect of America's anglers by being a pushover. It did it by being one of the most perverse, unpredictable and challenging gamefish that swims. Locate feeding bass one day and they may cheerfully assault any lure you throw them. The next day, they may reject every lure or even be gone! They'll be in one place during the spring and usually many others during the rest of the year. They inhabit lakes, reservoirs, ponds, rivers, tide waters, creeks and streams. They exist comfortably in some of the wildest and most inaccessible areas of the country, as well as in city park lakes. In each type of environment they can often display different behavior.

Among the bass clan are six recognized species and four distinct subspecies. There are literally thousands of different artificial lures they will take, as well as many live baits. They are among the most sensitive of all freshwater gamefish to daily changes in weather, light levels, water clarity and water levels, any of which can stop their activity, or move them from a specific area.

Challenging, yes. But, their widespread distribution makes them accessible to virtually any angler in the country, and many have taken up the challenge.

Despite the differing species and habitats, expert anglers have learned that "a bass is basically a bass wherever you find him." Once an angler learns how bass relate to specific environments, how to build a basic selection of effective baits, select proper rods and reels, utilize electronic aids — and understand why the bass must do some of the things they do, as well as why anglers must be equally discriminating — he will be in a position to unravel the mysteries of America's fish on virtually any water.

In this book, each aspect of bass fishing is addressed. One term you will often read in the following pages is "professional angler." It is the professional angler who has been responsible for a large part of current knowledge concerning the most effective way to catch bass under a wide range of conditions.

After a decade as a guide, I have seen the difference in the way that most of my customers — basically, average weekend anglers — view the sport and its challenges as compared to an individual who has to catch bass for a living. Those differences are sometimes startling, as are the relative successes of the two groups.

Sometimes a factor as small as selecting the right rod tip action for a specific lure can spell the difference between landing a trophy bass and losing the fish. Professional anglers examine their sport in detail and you'll read the opinions of the country's best anglers on the following pages.

New techniques are being discovered almost daily and, even then, with a creature as inherently perverse as the bass, we may never fully understand every variable that enters the picture.

Would anybody care to join me for dinner? The elephant souffle is marvelous.

Chris Christian,
Georgetown, Florida

CHAPTER 1

MEET THE BASS

The smallmouth bass (top) shows a distinctly different coloration and marking pattern than does the largemouth to which it is compared here. Anglers have little trouble in telling the two species apart, the author insists.

This North American Native Is The Most Widely Distributed Gamefish In This Country

WHEN THE first explorer set foot on the North American continent, he was confronted with a number of unfamiliar and sometimes unique animals and fish. Among these was a pugnacious, broad-shouldered piscatorial predator now assigned the generic name of *Micropterus*.

These fish were found in virtually every major waterway along the Atlantic seaboard in one of its various species.

Even then, its disposition for blasting non-living objects was well known. As early as 1764, John and William Bartram had what might well be the first inter-cultural lesson on "topwater bass'n" when they were shown how to "bob" for Florida largemouth bass by the Seminole Indians.

The bobs were rather crude affairs constructed of bone and feather, but they were assaulted with the same ferocity that modern injection-molded surface lures experience today.

The black bass currently ranks as the most popular gamefish in North America, and few anglers live more than a couple of hours from excellent fishing waters.

One of the reasons for this popularity is the widespread distribution of the fish. It is an extremely hardy and adapt-

A distinctive row of spots located below the lateral line identify this as a spotted bass. Rock, gravel and current are critical to smallmouth populations in rivers and streams.

able predator with a broad range of habitats. They live and thrive in the country's deepest manmade lakes, as well as in backyard ponds. They adapt well to rivers, tidal waters, creeks, streams and natural ponds. Give them a stable, relatively clean environment and a steady food supply and you'll have a fishable bass population.

Although all black bass share common characteristics, they are broken down into six recognizable species. In this book we'll concentrate on the three most common: the largemouth bass *(Micropterus salmoides)*, smallmouth bass *(Micropterus dolomieui)* and the spotted bass *(Micropterus punctulatus)*.

Within each of these these species are sub-species that differ enough to be distinctive.

The remaining bass species: the Guadalupe bass *(M. treculi)* Redeye bass *(M. coosae)* and the Suwannee bass *(M. notius)* are restricted to relatively narrow ranges not readily accessible to a large number of anglers and will not be dealt with in-depth.

However, each of these latter three species share a strong family resemblance to the smallmouth and spotted bass, in that they prefer moving water and the stronger currents.

Largemouth bass: The most widely distributed of the bass, it was originally native only to the eastern sections of the country and some parts of Mexico. Due to intentional and accidental transplantings, it now is available in virtually every one of the lower forty-eight states, Hawaii,

The spotted bass, while not as plentiful across the nation as the largemouth, presents a worthy angling opponent.

some areas of Canada, Southern Africa, Japan, parts of Europe, some Caribbean Islands and areas of South and Central America.

These bass prosper in virtually all types of habitat and environment that will support members of the bass species, making them by far the most adaptable of the bass.

They are also capable of the greatest growth and the current world record for the species is twenty-two pounds four ounces.

Largemouth bass are further divided into two sub-species, or strains. The Florida largemouth *(M. salmoides floridanus)* was first described as a subspecies differing from the Northern largemouth *(M. salmoides)* by Bailey and Hubbs in 1949.

Determining the difference between the two subspecies

requires scale and vertebrae counts and is done best in a laboratory. What is significant for anglers, however, is the fact that the Florida strain grows more quickly and achieves greater size than its northern cousin.

When the two subspecies are placed in the same environment, they will spawn together. Some writers have referred to this as hybridization, but the correct term for the offspring, according to California Department of Fish and Game biologist Larry Bottroff, is intergrade.

"An F-1, which biologists call a first generation hybrid, is not possible between Northern and Florida bass," he explains. "A true hybrid is a cross between separate species, like Florida bass and spotted bass, not subspecies of the same bass."

Bottroff has been heavily involved with the introduction

The stocky river smallmouth is obviously different in appearance from other types. With this species, upper jaw never extends beyond the eye of particular type.

of Florida-strain bass into Southern California lakes and this was the subject of his master's thesis at San Diego State University.

"When integrading takes place between Florida and Northern bass, the Florida strain becomes dominant and the bass grow, behave and develop just like the original Floridas."

A number of states have introduced Florida bass into their waters to help increase the size of their fish and, in many cases, it has worked. In Texas, for example, the state record has been broken every year for the last half-decade; many feel introduction of the larger growing Florida fish is the reason.

Like all the bass, largemouths are spring spawners and they build nests which they guard tenaciously from pred-

ators such as panfish, killfish, turtles, salamanders, crawfish and other egg eaters. Spawning begins to take place when water temperatures (combined with the longer light periods of spring) reach 60 degrees F; and, bass have been observed spawning in water temperatures as high as 80 degrees F. The spawning period for bass in the Northern portions of their range may be as short as thirty days, while the Southern regions may experience a spawning period of five months or longer.

This is one reason why many Northern states close the bass fishing season until after the spawn; the concerted effort can make bass vulnerable to sportfishing pressure. The longer spawning period in the South, combined with the inherently longer growing season, reduces the need for protection of spawning fish.

Smallmouth and largemouth often inhabit the same waters. But unless the environment is ideal for a smallmouth, it will suffer from largemouth competition.

Sexual maturity of the largemouth is related more to the fish's size than to its age. The female bass reaches maturity at about ten inches, while the male may mature at a somewhat smaller size.

Although spawning nests may be constructed in waters ranging from six inches to twenty feet deep (depending upon water clarity), the most common depth range is one to four feet. Although nests may be constructed anywhere within a lake, it is not unusual for them to be grouped on certain shorelines or in specific coves. These areas are usually the warmest and provide protection from strong winds that can destroy the nests. The nests often are constructed to take advantage of the protection offered by rocks, stumps, slopes or objects on the bottom.

Nests are generally placed at least six feet apart. After

the actual egg laying, the female may remain in the vicinity for a few days or may leave immediately. The male will remain with the nest until the fry hatch.

Catching and keeping a male bass from a spawning bed assures the destruction of that bed and the loss of those eggs. This is considered to be an unacceptable fishing tactic by serious anglers.

Bass are reported to do little, if any, actual feeding while engaged in the spawn or the nest guarding. However, they will assault and carry out intruders during this time, making them vulnerable to sportfishermen.

After the bass fry hatch out, the male often continues to guard them, until the fry disperse into cover as individual fish.

The growth rate of largemouth bass is variable and

Smallmouths often choose to inhabit faster-moving parts of streams, rivers where all three species are present. Most often they choose an eddy formed by an object or conflicting streams. (Right) Acrobatic smallmouth has a smaller maw than its cousins, accounting for name.

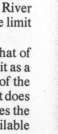

depends largely upon food supply, genetic makeup and length of the growing season. Bass in northern climes do not grow as fast as southern fish, but their life span is increased. Some of the most respected fisheries biologists in the country feel that fifteen years is the maximum life span for a largemouth bass. It is also felt that females live longer than males and it is documented that they routinely reach greater weights.

Smallmouth bass: The original range of the smallmouth bass is second only to that of the largemouth. It shared a large part of the Mississippi River system and the Great Lakes drainage. In many waters, they co-existed with largemouths, although they often showed a marked preference for different types of habitat within the same waters. That is still true today.

The southeastern limit of the smallmouth's native range included all of Tennessee and most of northern Alabama and Georgia, while its western limit was the Red River tributaries in eastern Oklahoma. The northern range limit was Ontario, Canada.

Smallmouth transplanting occurred earlier than that of other bass because of an early general acceptance of it as a sportfish. But attempts to greatly expand the range of the smallmouth did not always meet with success, since it does not prosper in as wide a range of environments as does the largemouth. Today, the smallmouth is, on paper, available

Swift, rocky rivers are the prime habitat of smallmouth bass. Rock, gravel, current are critical to populations.

in every state except Alaska and Florida. But, in many areas it contributes only a minor percentage of the bass catch and often requires annual restocking to maintain populations. The smallmouth has been introduced to Europe and South America, but its status there seems questionable.

The smallmouth bass suffers from competition with the largemouth bass in all but the most suitable environments.

Smallmouth bass occur naturally in large, clear-water lakes and in cool, clear streams having a substrate of rock and gravel and a moderate current. In a typical stream environment, trout would inhabit the cold-water upper sections; smallmouths the middle section, if there was cool water, rocky bottom and a good gradient with large pools between riffles; the largemouth would prefer the lowland

section with a sluggish current and aquatic vegetation.

The importance of rubble, gravel and current to the smallmouth was noted in a study by Reynolds in 1956. He found only scattered clumps of rocks in Iowa's Des Moines River, a stream with a predominantly sand bottom, turbid water and a sluggish current. Smallmouth bass were almost always found over such rock clumps, below a riffle.

Smallmouth bass can live in small ponds and in turbid streams, but these are not always the best environments, especially if largemouth bass also are present.

According to Hubbs and Baily (1938), the best smallmouth lakes are over one hundred acres, more than thirty feet deep and have clear water with scanty vegetation, large shoals of rock or gravel and thermal stratification.

In these waters, they generally inhabit depths of less

The largemouth is hardiest and most adaptable of the species. This has allowed its original range to be increased by transplanting.

than forty feet, although they have been taken deeper. They often are found over rocky bars and ledges, in water five to twenty feet deep. Research being conducted currently on transplanted smallmouth bass in Texas indicates they spend the majority of their time in waters fifteen feet or less.

In streams, smallmouth — like the other bass species — are not commonly found in an area of strong current, but rather in the lee or eddy water created by objects on the edge of the current. Characteristics of cover that might attract the greatest numbers of smallmouth are darkness and quiet water.

Field studies have shown that summer smallmouths often inhabit water depths with a temperature of 61 to 71 degrees (Mile and Juday 1941, Westman and Westman 1949 and Hallman 1959). But in several laboratory ex-

periments, the temperature selected by smallmouths, when offered a choice, was about 82 degrees.

Most smallmouth bass do not move great distances in any environment and have restricted home ranges. In streams they have been observed occupying the same pool throughout the year.

In physical appearance the smallmouth bass differs from all other bass in that it has all the following features: (1) there is no dark horizontal band along the side, but often they are barred vertically; (2) the upper jaw never extends beyond the eye, giving the fish a mouth of smaller dimensions when opened; and (3) there are thirteen to fifteen soft rays in the fin on the back.

Smallmouth bass have been divided into two subspecies: the northern smallmouth *(M. d. dolomieui)* and the Neosho smallmouth *(M. d. velox).* The latter was prev-

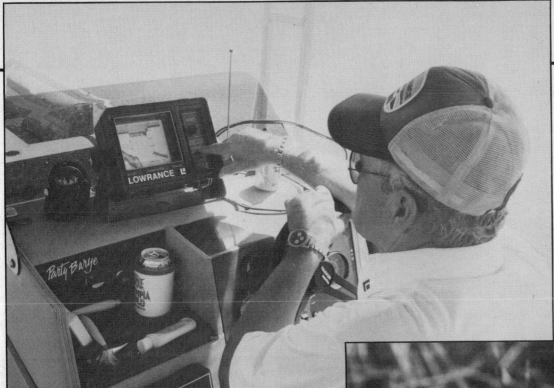

Spotted bass have been taken from 80 feet-plus. Serious anglers tend to rely on sophisticated depthfinders to find them. (Right) Largemouths have affinity for weeds and such beds often are most productive angling spots.

alent in the Arkansas River system in Missouri, Oklahoma and Arkansas. Significant intergrading has taken place between the two subspecies, however.

Smallmouths spawn in much the same manner as the largemouth — making a nest in a sheltered area, utilizing the same depth ranges and performing the same guarding behavior by the male. One difference is that while largemouths often prefer a sand bottom, smallmouths are fond of pea gravel if available. Thus, in the same water body, largemouths and smallmouths may spawn at the same time, but sometimes in separate areas.

Smallmouth bass are more susceptible to nest predation and the fry are more sensitive to sudden temperature changes upon hatching than are largemouths. As a general rule, a smallmouth population suffers a higher annual mortality rate than does the hardier largemouth.

Proper management of a smallmouth fishery, especially one that receives significant angling pressure, is considered by some biologists to include closing the season during the spawning period.

Although the growth rates of smallmouth bass are, like the other bass, dependent upon food availability and environment, smallmouths exhibit a notably slower growth rate than largemouths. Sexual maturity in females occurs at about ten inches in size, but it will take a smallmouth three to five years to reach that size. Males mature at a slightly smaller size and attain this in two to four years.

The maximum life span is generally accepted as fifteen years and the current world record for this species is eleven pounds fifteen ounces.

Few smallmouth bass over ten pounds are taken and a five-pound fish is considered a legitimate trophy.

Spotted bass: Sometimes known as the Kentucky bass, it has become one of the more important sportfishes in the southeastern and midwestern portions of the country. It occurs over a wide area; ranging further south than the smallmouth, but not as far north or west as either the largemouth or the smallmouth.

Spotted bass will gather in areas of steeply sloping shorelines for spawning.

Spotted bass occur naturally in the Ohio River drainage from West Virginia, North Carolina and Ohio through Indiana, Illinois, Kentucky and Tennessee; in the central and lower Mississippi River drainages in Missouri, Kansas, Oklahoma, Arkansas, Louisiana and Mississippi; and in parts of the Gulf Coast drainage in Georgia, Florida, Alabama and Texas.

Two subspecies exist: The Wichita spotted bass *(M. p. wichitae)* which occurs only in the Wichita Mountains of Oklahoma, and the Alabama subspecies *(M. p. henshalli)* which is restricted to the Mobile Bay drainage of Mississippi, Alabama and Georgia.

The natural range of the spotted bass has been extended only slightly through transplanting. The largest success has been the introduction of the Alabama spotted bass to a few California reservoirs, where it has done well. The current world record for the species, nine pounds, was taken recently from one of them, Lake Perris.

Although the spotted bass was first described about 1830, it wasn't until 1927 that the species was readily recognized. Identification still causes problems today for some anglers.

The spotted bass earns its name from rows of horizontal spots regularly arranged below the lateral line of the fish. In addition to these distinctive markings, the species is further distinguishable from the other bass by the following characteristics: a lateral band of dark blotches which tend to merge and form an irregular longitudinal stripe; dark olive variegated markings, often roughly diamond in shape, above the lateral band of blotches; usually a creamy-white

All bass species utilize shallower water to spawn. Each prefers its own type of bottom composition. Knowing what the bass require is one key to locating them during spring season.

color below the lateral band; prominent dark spot on the tip of the opercle and at the base of the caudal fin; shallow emargination between the spined and soft-rayed portion of the dorsal fin; upper jaw extending to a point beneath the posterior part of the eye; head more elongated and pointed than either the largemouth or smallmouth; scales on the cheeks smaller than those on the opercle; patch of fine teeth on the tongue that can be readily felt with the finger; and unbranched pyloric caeca. (Hubbs 1972; Lawrence 1954; Viosca 1931).

Within their range, spotted bass flourish in streams, rivers and manmade reservoirs. They do not fare well in natural lakes or ponds.

In a stream or river environment, the spotted bass generally occupy different habitats than do any largemouths or smallmouths sharing the waters. They prefer areas of more current than largemouths, deeper water and relate more to rock, sand bars and wide, deep pools. However, they often occupy current areas that are too warm or turbid to support smallmouth bass.

In impoundments, they generally select areas of rocky substrate and steeply sloping shorelines, avoiding areas of mud bottom and dense emergent vegetation. In general, they fare best in the same deep, clear lakes that form the proper habitat for smallmouths, but can do so at a more southerly latitude.

In impoundments where all three species are present, spotted bass often utilize deeper waters than either the largemouth or smallmouth, but they tend to make greater depth changes. Although spotted bass have been taken at depths over eighty feet, it is not uncommon to cast to a fallen tree and catch a largemouth on one cast and a spotted bass on the next cast.

Growth rates for spotted bass are similar to those of the smallmouth, although they generally reach the size of sexual maturity — about ten inches — an average of one year earlier in most waters.

Spawning habitat requirements appear to be more specific for spotted bass than for largemouths or smallmouths. In Lake Fort Smith, Arkansas, spotted bass demonstrated a preference for rocky or gravelly substrates for spawning, while largemouths spawned in all parts of the lake.

In Bull Shoals Lake, steep shorelines as well as coves were used by the spotted bass for nesting. Nests along steep shorelines were on solid rock ledges, large flat rocks, and patches of rubble and gravel. Those in coves were on patches of broken rock, large flat rocks, gravel, compacted soil and exposed root hairs of flooded trees.

Nest sites near cover appear to be preferred by spotted bass. In Bull Shoals Lake the fish showed a greater preference for artificial brush shelters as nest cover than did either largemouths or smallmouths.

Observed nest depths differed significantly in steep shoreline and cove habitat. Although extreme depths were similar — five and twenty-two feet on steep shorelines and three and twenty-one feet in coves — the mean nest depth was 12.1 feet on steep shorelines and 7.5 feet in coves. Spotted bass normally spawn deeper than the other bass species and begin their spawn at about the same time as other bass, but sometimes wait for warmer water.

The same spawning procedure of nest building and guarding exhibited by other species is utilized by the spotted bass, although there is some evidence to suggest that under certain conditions the male bass will remain with the newly hatched fry and protect them for longer periods than will the other bass.

CHAPTER 2

Research has shown that bass are most efficient at the predator game when they feed in thin cover or along cover edges. That is one reason why the edges of weed lines are prime spots to seek feeding bass, author says.

UNDERSTANDING BASS

The powerful jaws of a bass make it a formidable predator. Bass consume their prey whole. Size is the determining factor, but due to its belligerent nature, a small bass may attack a lure far too big for it to consume.

America's Fish Is Remarkably Adaptable In Varying Climes And Waters

Big bass swims up to the owner of a private pond to take bread out of his hand. Bass learned this feeding behavior by watching the other fish in the pond perform the same act. Bass also can learn the behavior of avoidance and move out of areas with heavy boat traffic or may reject certain lures, if bombarded with them to any degree.

THE WIDESPREAD distribution of the bass species illustrates their remarkable ability to adapt to a variety of environmental conditions. They are equally at home in waters as massive as the Great Lakes or as small as the one-acre pond behind my house. They flourish in creeks, rivers, tidewaters, natural lakes, man-made reservoirs and virtually any other body of water that offers food and a stable environment.

Within their environment they are one of, if not the, upper level predators among the fish population.

The widely varying environments inhabited by the bass make it one of the most challenging of gamefish to pursue. Unlike many other gamefish that require a fairly rigid environmental and feeding structure, the bass does not. They are true generalists in this respect.

Some anglers have attached "regional behavior" characteristics to the bass, feeling, for example, that bass in the South react differently than bass in the North. There are some slight differences, but not nearly as many as some anglers think. Professional tournament anglers have found that "a bass is a bass, wherever you find him."

The determining factor in the bass' basic movements is the particular environment the fish is in. Bass will respond differently in a man-made reservoir than they will in a tidal river. But a bass in a tidal river in California will show a remarkably similar response to its environment to a bass in a Florida tidal river. Once an angler begins to understand how a bass must respond to a specific type of environment, he will be able to locate bass in similar environments anywhere they are found.

Bass are hardy fish that can survive quite well if handled with some care after being caught. Shaw Grigsby is releasing a six-pound fish that was used in some photos in this book.

Highly sought by the smallmouth bass is the crawfish. Thus, this soft plastic lure from Angler's Pro Specialties has proven itelf as good bait many times! It is an amazingly realistic replica.

In later chapters we'll look at how differing environments affect basic bass movement. For now, though, let's look at the physical characteristics that allow the bass its adaptability.

The bass is a streamlined, highly maneuverable predator that engulfs its prey whole. Smaller bass therefore are restricted to smaller prey, while large bass have a wider latitude in what they can and will eat. Because of the bass' physical make-up, they are not suited for high-speed chases or lengthy pursuits of their prey. They must begin their assault relatively close to their intended victim and finish the task within a reasonable period of time. They have an impressive array of tools to accomplish this.

Senses of the bass: Like most fish, bass have a highly developed sense of smell and research indicates that it becomes more acute with age. However, research has yet to establish just how important the bass's sense of smell is in its feeding. Some scientists feel that the older a bass gets, the more it utilizes this sense; that may help explain why significantly more big bass are taken on live bait than on artificial lures.

Many different "fish scents" have been introduced in recent years to help the angler appeal to this sense. Their effectiveness has yet to be proven conclusively, but many expert anglers feel that adding scent to slow-moving lures

Bright light does not necessarily bother bass. They are members of the sunfish clan and, like the bluegill behind this bass, often bask in the sun close to water's surface. Bass seek shade to hide from prey as well as their enemies.

like worms, jigs and topwater plugs can be beneficial when bass are not feeding well.

Bass are equipped with excellent vision. In physical make-up, their eyes are remarkably similar to ours and they can see and distinguish objects above the surface, see in color and even differentiate between subtle shades of the same color.

The range of vision below the surface is limited by the clarity of the water and the amount of light penetrating the surface. As a result, bass in clear water environments have shown a pronounced tendency to rely heavily upon sight for their feeding, while bass in murkier environments rely less so. This aspect of bass behavior often dictates the tactics an angler must use.

In a clear-water environment, bass often will move considerable distances to take a lure or prey. But given the optimum vision conditions, many anglers have found that most artificial lures look too "artificial" to the bass!

In this situation anglers are wise to use small baits — 1½ to 3 inches — that more closely match the size of the most commonly available forage. Since bass will move a good distance, they also can be drawn or "called" to a bait and topwater lures have proven highly effective in clear water.

Clear water bass depend so heavily upon their sight to feed that a sudden shift to extremely muddy water can cause them to cease moving and feeding completely.

Feeding and light adjustment: Changes in light levels — whether brought on by the normal movement of the sun, by a temporary factor such as a sudden buildup of clouds or a wind that ruffles the surface and reduces the amount of light that penetrates — often can bring on sudden feeding in clear-water bass. In marginal light, bass can seek their prey more effectively and with higher efficiency than in full light.

Bass instinctively know that in order to make a "gain" they have to receive more energy from the prey they ingest than they expended in obtaining the prey. It's a simple fact that they expend less energy under optimum dim-light hunting conditions and they choose to do most of their foraging during these times. When you combine this with the slight limitation to the bass's vision that results from dim light, it's not hard to see why dawn and dusk, clouds or wind are positive factors for anglers pursuing bass in clear water.

Hearing: Of all the senses of the bass, hearing is possibly the most versatile. Even when vision is restricted in stained waters, the sense of hearing remains acute. This auditory system is so precise that it enables the bass to hear sounds and pick up vibrations we cannot. And most of these sounds will trigger some sort of reaction from the bass.

Despite their reputations as indiscriminant feeders, bass consume minnows most often in two- to four-inch sizes. A larger bass prefers larger prey, so lures that offer the favored size, profile and color are good bass choices.

Although bass don't have earflaps protruding from the sides of their heads like humans, their ears are good. They are so highly developed that they can detect the sound of a worm wiggling on the bottom.

These sounds, which are simply vibrations at different frequencies, are transmitted directly from the water through the skin, flesh and bone of the fish's head to the ear. Sound waves travel through the water approximately five times faster than through air: about one mile per second.

In addition to the ears, bass have a second sound-detecting organ called the lateral line. This organ is unique only to fish. It senses strong low-frequency vibrations in the water and is important to the bass in pinpointing the exact source of a sound. Some scientists have referred to the lateral line as "a sense of distant touch." It complements the bass's ears by providing a super-sensitive system for detecting close-range movement. It explains why a bass can unerringly home in on a black plastic worm on the bottom in thirty feet of water on a moonless night.

This hearing system provides the bass with the means to feed effectively under conditions of minimal water clarity, where its vision is impaired.

Anglers fishing stained or muddy waters can make use of this by shifting to larger lures that displace more water and to baits that create strong vibrations (like noisy topwater plugs, rattling crankbaits and spinnerbaits). The more dependent the bass is upon vibration, due to its reliance upon its sense of hearing, the more vibration the angler should provide. Make the bass's job easy!

Forage: It's been said that a bass will eat anything it can fit in its mouth and there could be some truth to this. Bass have been documented to consume a wide variety of forage items, including terrestrial animals like birds, squirrels, mice and such. They also are known to eat frogs, eels, snakes, shrimp, spring lizards, salamanders, crawfish, trout and a wide variety of species of minnows, as well as other items. In short, the bass is far less a gourmet than it is an indiscriminate glutton.

But, what type of forage does it prefer to seek?

In my ten years as a Florida bass guide, I have yet to

Bass tend to utilize a variety of feeding strategies. This largemouth was feeding with a group of five- to ten-pound striped bass in the open waters of Florida's St. Johns River. All the fish were taken on the same type of lure.

clean a bass that showed any evidence of consuming a snake or eel: this, despite the fact that these items are common in the area — and that lures imitating them (plastic worms) are among the most effective artificial lures in Florida.

Nor have I seen any evidence of mice, birds, frogs or other terrestrials. What I have seen is a heavy reliance upon minnows, shiners, bream and crawfish.

Research has been conducted on the subject that lends support to my own casual observations. It shows that the average bass of one to four pounds feeds predominantly upon minnows such as shiners, shad, dace or small bream in the two- to four-inch range, as well as crawfish, which are a highly preferred forage item wherever found. Larger bass have a well documented preference for larger prey and one of the top big bass baits among my fellow Florida trophy bass guides is a seven- to ten-inch golden shiner.

While bass may be opportunistic feeders, taking whatever comes along, they also can display an astonishing degree of selectivity. I have watched bass surface-schooling on shad that would ignore every school of three-inch shad that came along, but rip into every school of 1½-inch shad. Getting a strike from these fish meant not only imitating the color and shape of those shad, but the size as well.

In another example, when shrimp run into Florida's St. Johns River in the late summer, bass seem to pursue them in preference to all else. If your lure doesn't match color and size of the shrimp, you won't get a bite very often.

This selectivity is not uncommon and many researchers feel it has to do with the temporary abundance of a specific prey item. Bass often will key in on the most prevalent forage, ignoring secondary prey. This can happen in any type of environment, from a small stream where small-mouths may be keying in on a mayfly hatch, right up to a major impoundment, where the bass may key on newly hatched shad minnows. This explains situations where one particular size, color and type of lure will produce fish, while other baits won't, even though the bass are actively feeding at the time.

For this reason, experienced anglers often have a large

Bass do not feed effectively from an ambush situation in most cases. However, in rivers or moving water, it often may be the best method for them. This bass was behind piling of a dock and took a plastic worm as it drifted by on current.

selection of baits in varying sizes and colors.

Feeding tactics: The bass has been characterized often as a fish that feeds from ambush. Taking a concealed position, it waits until a prey item swims within range, then engulfs it in a short, powerful rush. Sometimes this is true, but not most of the time.

Research has shown — and experience has proven — that bass cannot feed effectively in heavy cover. The smaller, more agile baitfish can elude the bass far too easily for it to be an efficient tactic. Remember that the bass knows it cannot gain if it expends more energy to catch a prey item than it receives from the item. This is one reason you won't see many ten-pound bass chasing two-inch minnows.

Controlled studies have shown that the bass is most effective and efficient when it does its hunting in thin cover or long open water cover edges. In this situation, the bass's speed and power give it a decided advantage over smaller prey.

Ambush feeding is the least efficient tactic for bass in most cases, but they can be forced into that feeding posture by their environment. One example would be a lake that is covered with surface-matted hydrilla or milfoil, leaving

precious few open water areas and edges. In this situation the bass suffers and research conducted by the University of Florida concerning bass growth in hydrilla-infested lakes shows significantly slower growth than in other environments.

The majority of the time that a bass is in heavy cover by its own choice, it is there to rest and utilizes the cover as protection from its enemies.

One situation, however, where ambush feeding is the preferred tactic is in a small to medium stream or river environment. A bass would expend too much energy battling the current to receive a gain from its prey. So it often will lie behind an object that breaks the flow of the current, providing an eddy for the bass to lie in and wait for the current to sweep food to it. This is one of the few situations where the ambush feeding posture is the most efficient.

The most efficient feeding a bass can do is along edges where it can force a prey item away from cover and into open water. This is one reason the edge of a weedline or some other cover edge is a premier place to look for feeding bass. Bass will move to these edges to feed. In a deep man-made impoundment, they may move *up* from deeper water while a heavily vegetated natural lake may see the bass

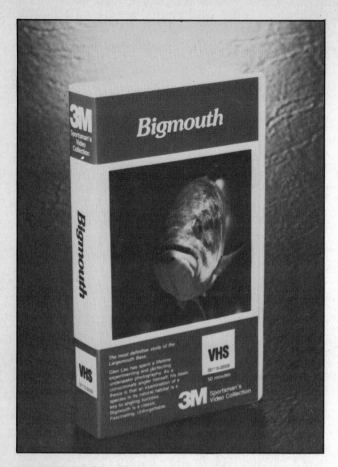 

Anglers seeking knowledge of the habits of bass might do well to obtain some of the excellent videos available on the subject. The greater the angler's knowledge of just how bass respond to their environment, the greater his success.

move *out* to the edge from the thicker inside portions of the weed bed. Move they will, when the dinner bell rings.

One of the most efficient edge-feeding tactics is stalking. Here, the bass positions itself tight to the edge of the cover (using it to help camouflage itself fom its prey) and cruises slowly along, visually sighting its prey and attempting to move close enough to take it in a short rush. Another tactic is flushing. Here the bass will assume the same posture, sometimes within a group of bass, and cruise quickly and erratically along a shoreline or edge. Their quick movements often startle prey that panic and dart toward open water, where they are taken.

In the stalking mode, a slow-moving bait worked along an edge can draw a strike. In the flushing posture, a bait darting quickly from the cover to open water can be deadly. This is one reason why experienced anglers will fish a likely looking piece of cover with several different lures and retrieve speeds. We have no idea how the bass is feeding and only its response to our lure can provide us with a clue.

In deeper, more open waters, where the bass may be holding on channel edges, points or humps, another tactic called habituation often is used. Here the predator seldom chases its prey, but just as seldom attempts to hide from it either. It simply hovers around or over deep structure in an apparent state of inactivity. When a prey fish blunders too close, it gets nailed.

Bass will also stalk and flush crawfish in this situation,

giving a deep water angler a variety of lure presentation options.

Many species of saltwater fish, like tuna, will actively run down their prey. Bass don't, but they use a modified tactic called schooling. Bass will group together to corral a school of baitfish into a tight ball, then charge through the school to break it up, running down the survivors individually. This is common behavior on tidal rivers in the later summer and fall and the "schooling grounds" are often a spot where a large volume of flowing water is compressed into a smaller area. A good example is deeper water flowing over a shallow shoal. This sudden change from deep to shallow tends to disorient the bait fish and make the bass's job of balling them up easier.

Bass also will school in lakes, especially man-made reservoirs. Here they sometimes follow a school of shad until it crosses a compression area, like a hump or channel edge, or they may simply wait at such a spot.

The wide variety of feeding tactics used by the bass allow it to function in an equally diverse series of environments. In some cases, bass may use one or more of these feeding tactics. In others, they may rely only upon the most efficient. In any case, it will be the environment and forage availability that determine which that will be.

Unfortunately, bass do not spend all their time feeding. They exhibit distinct activity stages in that respect. Active bass are those seeking food and they are by far the easiest to catch, since they are conditioned to feed. You'll generally find active fish in feeding areas corresponding to the type of feeding behavior in use at that time.

Neutral fish are those not actively feeding but which will take a bait or lure if it is presented in such a way as to arouse their predatory instincts. Professional anglers call this a "reflex" or "reaction" strike. It is much the same as dangling a thread of yarn in front of a well fed cat. The cat can't resist taking a swipe at it!

Neutral bass may be found in feeding areas, but not always. Most often they will be in a resting position in thicker cover or relating to a deeper water structure; often they comprise the bulk of the catch during a bass tournament, since most such contests are held during hours when bass feeding activity is not at its maximum.

Certain techniques tend to produce this reflex strike more often than others and some examples are: banging a crankbait into the bottom or off a piece of cover, topwater lures, spinnerbaits, worms or jigs dropping suddenly in front of the bass or small, subtle finesse baits worked slowly around the fish.

Negative bass are totally inactive fish and difficult to entice to bite either a lure or live bait. The passage of a cold front often can bring on this state, as can a sudden muddying of the water or a rapid drop in water temperature. This is also common among bass during the week immediately following the leaving of the spawning bed. These fish often move into open water and simply suspend there or bury down into the thickest cover they can find and almost become dormant. They're not much fun.

In most environments, bass can show a wide range of movement, especially in the summer and fall. Moving up from deeper water to feed along a shoreline in the morning, then dropping back to deep water during the midday and repeating the movement in the evening is one example. A change in environmental conditions such as depletion of oxygen or introduction of a pollutant is another. In many cases, however, bass will remain in one relatively small area of a mile or so as long as conditions are favorable.

Tracking studies conducted on some large bass, though, indicate that many of these fish move considerably. In one study, a fourteen-pound bass in a California lake that was closed to fishing four days out of each week would roam the lake during those four days, then move into the "off limits" area when the lake was opened to angling.

This leads us to the fact that bass can learn avoidance behavior. Heavy angling pressure can move them from an area or cause them to become inactive within the area. These fish also can begin to reject certain lures if they are bombarded with them enough.

Bass also can learn positive behavior. I am reminded of one five-pound bass that lived in a private pond in my area. It would approach a person on the shoreline if that person held out a piece of bread — and the fish would take the bread!

One other factor that should be understood by anglers is the gregarious nature of the bass. With the exception of some of the largest members of the species, bass tend to group together and often with others of their own general size. Competitive behavior can be displayed in this situation; it's much like throwing a bone to a pack of yard dogs.

Sometimes, catching or hooking a bass from a group can

Bass found in heavy cover are not usually feeding fish. More often they are neutral in mood, but can be triggered to strike at an angler's bait, if it's presented properly.

excite the others into feeding or active behavior. Injuring a fish within a school, though, sometimes panics the school and stops activity. For this reason, many anglers who practice catch and release will hold the fish in their livewell until they are ready to leave the area, then release them.

This gregarious nature also indicates that, when an angler catches one bass from a small area, there could well be more down there that could be caught, if the angler fished the area more thoroughly.

Adaptable, complicated, often perverse, the bass ranks as one of the most challenging gamefish available. Successful bass fishing is as much a mental game as it is a physical one. And the angler who begins to understand how and why a bass responds to a particular environment is on the road to success.

CHAPTER 3

GEARING UP
FOR BASS

Tendency among today's bass pros is toward rods that are six to seven feet in length for general fishing. Added length offers more leverage, casting distance. (Left) Most professional anglers use both casting and spinning rods. Each has its own advantages in certain situations.

BY THE standards of only a decade ago, contemporary rods and reels are about as far removed from their predecessors as the Concorde is from the DC-3. In those ten short years, the design, construction and materials used in bass'n tackle have made significant strides.

Rods are lighter, stronger and far more sensitive than those on which most of us cut our eyeteeth. Reels also are lighter, feature more precise drag systems and are far more "user friendly." Despite the wealth of quality equipment today, selecting truly effective equipment isn't always easy. There is actually too much from which to choose. Anglers looking for a basic selection of rods and reels appropriate for their style of bass'n and the types of water generally fished can find the task confusing.

Most of the tournament pros — who many anglers rely upon for information indirectly through the pages of the bass periodicals — often carry a broad and diverse selection of equipment. It's not at all uncommon for a pro to have up to a dozen rigged rods in his boat when he competes in a tournament. Sometimes this is done simply to save time in changing lures; it's much easier to just pick up another rod than it is to dig through a tackle box, find the lure you want, then replace the one on your rod with it. Often, though, the reason the pros carry a variety of rods is to be certain they will have the one most effective for a particular fishing situation or lure.

For example, an angler crawling a plastic worm through a fallen tree is going to want a rod that has enough strength and backbone to wrestle a fish out of the tree. Change that scene to a deep, clear Western reservoir where the angler is dropping a Gitzit slowly down a rock bluff and a different set of rod requirements comes into play.

This is not to say there isn't an all-around outfit that could be used for the vast majority of bass'n chores; there are some that would do. But they won't be nearly as effec-

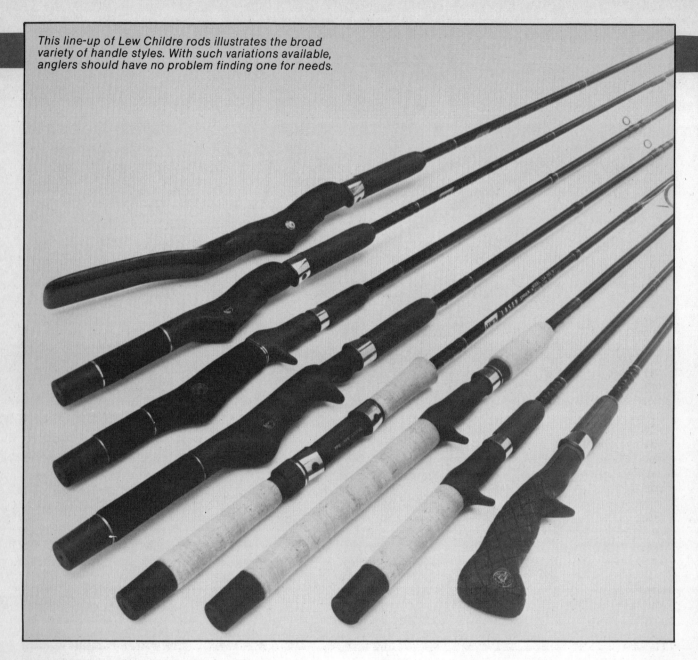

tive in detecting strikes and playing and landing fish, as would be a rod and reel "tuned" to the specific situation at the time.

Setting up an effective selection of rods and reels is easier if an angler understands what each type is capable of accomplishing and where it is applied best.

Casting Reels: Revolving spool baitcasting reels are the most popular choice among anglers using lines ranging from ten-pound test, upwards. The reason for this is the design; since the spool revolves to feed line off of it, diameter of the spool is not a critical factor in how far or easily the reel will cast. A palm-sized eight-ounce reel can handle twenty-pound-test line comfortably.

This is not the case with fixed spool reels like spinning or spincasting models. Here the diameter of the spool largely determines the line size that can be used. A model that would cast twenty-pound line easily would likely have a spool diameter of 2½ to three inches and weigh in the neighborhood of fifteen to twenty ounces. Such a heavy reel

would be extremely fatiguing to use for a full day's casting, as well as being two to three times as bulky as the casting reel.

The biggest advantage to the baitcasting reels is in their small size and weight in relation to the size they can handle. Another advantage is that, in the hands of a skilled angler, they cast farther, with less effort, then will bass-sized spinning or spincast tackle. Surprisingly, once an angler learns how to use casting gear, he will find it more trouble-free than fixed spool reels.

One additional advantage worth noting is the fact that a much broader range of rod lengths and actions is available in casting than in spinning models.

The biggest disadvantage to casting reels is twofold: (1) They cost two to three times that of a comparable quality spinning reel. (2) They are more difficult to learn to use. They do not always have as smooth a drag system as the better spinning reels and, for this reason, are not a good choice for anglers who habitually fish lines in the six- to

Rear drag spinning reels, like this selection from Fenwick, are becoming increasingly popular among bass fishermen, the author feels. This is due to the ease and precision with which the drag can be set when fishing the big ones.

ten-pound range. Many smallmouth and spotted bass experts favor spinning reels, since six- to eight-pound line often is the best choice for fishing the deeper, clearer waters these two species may inhabit.

Most modern casting reels feature a magnetic spool braking system that aids in controlling the speed of the spool on the cast. This system features a variety of settings that will vary the pressure on the spool to account for different weights of lures. New casting reel users should set this control to about three-fourths of full until they begin to master the art of thumbing the spool to control lure flight on the cast. Despite what some manufacturers may say, there is no casting reel that can be used effectively by relying on the magnetic "cast control" alone.

The magnetic control generally is positioned on the left side of the reel. Often, another knob on the right side adjusts the tension on the spool's shaft. This also affects how the reel will cast.

For first-time users, this should be adjusted as follows: Tie on a lure of about three-eighths-ounce and let it hang about six inches below the rod tip. Tighten the spool tension knob until the spool will not revolve with the free spool button pressed inward. Now slowly loosen the tension adjustment, until the lure begins to fall. Make final adjustments to the tension control so that, when the lure hits the ground, the spool stops turning without overrunning or backlashing.

Combined with a three-quarters-full setting on the magnetic brake, this prevents most backlashes while the angler becomes familiar with the reel. As an angler's ability improves, both the tension adjustment and the magnetic brake can be loosened to provide more casting distance.

Most experienced baitcasters will have their tension adjustment loose enough so the spool will overrun when the lure is allowed to fall freely to the ground, the magnetic brake set to one-quarter or one-third of full.

Modern baitcasting reels are remarkably strong and durable. Maintenance is minimal and instructions are to be found in the manual accompanying the reel.

Spinning Reels: Open-faced spinning reels are far more versatile than many anglers think. They can offer casting accuracy equal or better than that of a baitcasting reel, and they can often get a bait or lure into places that even an expert baitcaster might be hesitant to try.

The reason for this is the fixed spool. It does not revolve on the cast, so there is no danger of an overrun that will backlash the line. An angler armed with a spinning reel can easily "skip" lures off the surface of the water (much like skipping a flat rock across a still pond) to place them under overhanging tree limbs or boat docks. Try this with a casting reel and you'll wind up with a mess on your hands. The lure will slow down as it contacts the surface while the spool continues to revolve at the same speed: Backlash City!

Spinning reels are also ideal for fishing in tight quarters where ten to twenty-foot casts often must be made backhand, sidearm or underhand. Without a spool to revolve, anglers can snap more power into the cast, then control lure flight by brushing the forefinger of the rod hand against the lip of the spool as the line plays out. Called "feathering," this is as important to accuracy with a spinning reel as "thumbing" is with a casting reel.

The biggest advantage to spinning reels is in their ability to handle lines in the four- to eight-pound test range more effortlessly than will a casting reel, and for casting lighter lures.

In many clear water situations, lighter lines and smaller baits produce more strikes. This is especially true for anglers pursuing smallmouths, and, in many heavily pressured Western lakes, largemouth bass as well. Lighter lines also allow smaller baits to be worked at greater depths and with a more life-like action than would be achieved with heavier lines. It's a rare professional angler who doesn't have a couple of light spinning outfits available for use.

When selecting a spinning reel, the most important factor to keep in mind is the diameter of the spool. Mini-reels, with spool diameters in the one- to 1¼-inch range will han-

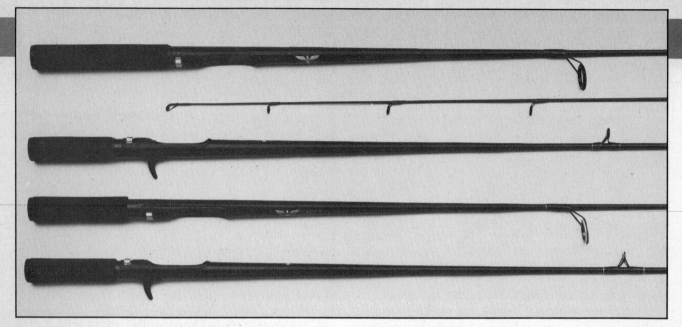

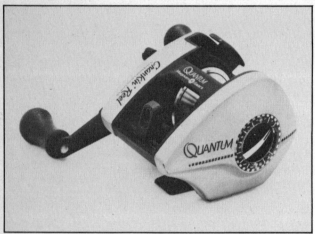

Fat-butted rods like Fenwick's Hooksetters place the angler's rod hand in direct contact with the rod blank. Author prefers these for some applications; says they are among the most sensitive rods on the market. (Left) Quantum casting reels feature low gear ratio that means improved crankbait performance with correct technique.

dle lines up to about eight-pound test without much problem. A loss of casting distance will start with lines of ten-pound and some will become hopeless, if anything over twelve-pound test is used. Medium freshwater models, with spools in the 1½- to two-inch range, will outcast the smaller reels with any line size and function adequately with lines of up to about fourteen-pound test. The larger the spool diameter, the less resistance the line has coming off the spool and the longer the range will be.

The larger reels usually feature better drags, as well as greater line capacity. An angler who intends to use his spinning equipment for striped bass or even inshore saltwater fishing would be well advised to go with the larger models.

I use three spinning outfits for bass. Two of them carry Quantum QD 40 spinning reels, medium freshwater models that spool two hundred yards of ten-pound line. Not only do these rods cast light lures farther than the mini-sized Fenwick outfit I favor for some bass'n, but they do fine double duty in saltwater. The increased line capacity and larger, more heat-resistant drag has allowed me to whip some hefty fish, including one fifty-pound tarpon.

These larger reels are heavier, though, and the angler who intends to use a spinning outfit strictly for bass with

lines up to ten-pound test should be more comfortable with the little Fenwick.

There is a big disadvantage for open-faced spinning reels. Since the bail often closes on a slack line, they can pick up small loops of line and deposit them down in the spool. When this happens, a "ball" of line often comes off the spool within a few casts. Avoid this by feathering the line at the end of the cast. This lets the bail close on a tight line.

If you notice loops in the spool, the easiest way to clear them is to loosen the drag and pull the line off against the drag, until enough line is removed from the spool to clear the loop. Opening the bail and pulling the loop out often results in a tangle.

A tangled ball of line also will come off the spool on the cast, if you have overfilled the spool. Fill to within one-eighth-inch of the lip, no more. Too little line on the spool will decrease your casting distance because of increased friction. Spinning reels are far more sensitive to line capacities than are casting reels.

Spinning reels will cause line twist, if a fish is played incorrectly. Never reel when a fish is stripping line against the drag; you'll twist line quickly. Most experts play a fish on a spinning rod with the pump-and-reel system. The rod is pumped back slowly to bring the fish closer and the line is taken up by reeling the rod back towards the fish, then pumping it back upwards again. This eliminates line twist.

Since spinning reels are used most often with lighter line, proper drag setting is critical. You can get sloppy with a four-pound bass on a twenty-pound casting outfit, but not with the same fish on a six-pound spinning rig.

Most pros set their drag to slip slightly at a point about two-thirds of line breaking strength, then leave the anti-reverse switch on the reel in the *off* position. This allows them to give line to a running fish by reeling the handle

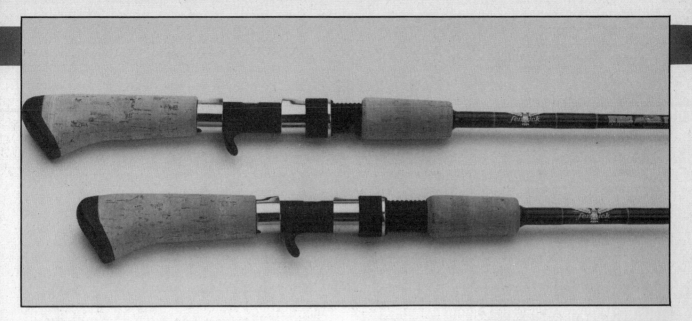

Several synthetics are used on rod handles, but cork is still a favorite. It is lightweight and provides a good gripping surface when wet. (Right) Push-button spincast reels are easy for beginners to learn to use. Zebco 33 has been around for years, has legions of loyal users.

backwards (backreeling), as well as having the drag give a bit on a hard hook-set. It's a double-drag system that works quite well on fish that do not make blistering, high-speed runs and is highly effective on bass.

Spincast Reels: Spincast reels seldom are seen in the hands of a knowledgeable bass fisherman, although some tournament casters like them. They offer every drawback of the spinning reels, with almost none of the advantages. Since this is a fixed spool reel, spool diameter must be large enough to handle lines over twelve-pound test. This results in a large, bulky reel. They will twist line if reeled against a fish taking drag and, since the spool is enclosed, the angler can't see any loop that might be forming and correct it before a problem arises.

To an angler who has had any experience with a casting or open-faced spinning reel, they are awkward to use. However, they can be among the easiest reels for an inexperienced angler to use and, as such, do have some merit.

My personal philosophy is that the beginner should spend a half-hour or so becoming familiar with either a casting or open-faced spinning reel before fishing. Learning to use efficient equipment at the beginning will benefit the angler more than will starting with a type of outfit he or she will step away from as abilities grow. However, as witnessed by sales figures on spincast reels, I'm in the minority in my views.

One point in favor of spincast reels is that they can be used on casting rods, which come in a wider variety of length and action types than do spinning rods. For an angler who "just can't get the hang" of baitcasting reels, this is a plus.

When purchasing a spincast reel, be aware that there is a lot of junk on the market. It's not hard to find a quality casting or spinning reel from makers like Zebco, Shimano, Fenwick, Daiwa, Lew Childre, Ambassadeur, Ryobi, and others. Good spincast reels, though, are rare. The only

models I have had that proved durable enough for bass'n are the metal-framed models from Daiwa and the Zebco 808, 404, and 33 models. There may be others, but I don't know of them.

Most will not handle lines above twelve-pound test with any efficiency. The exception is the big Zebco 808, which handles twenty-pound easily. For the last five years, I've kept two of these rigs, on six-foot casting rods, in the rod box of my Ranger to be used by clients who brought junk equipment with them. They have landed some big bass and I've had little trouble with them.

Accurate casting with a spincast reel is more difficult than with the other two types, because two hands must be used. The rod hand handles the line release button and, as the cast is made, the off hand must be brought to the rod's foregrip ahead of the reel, where it will feather the line coming off the spool. Some anglers try to stop the lure in precisely the right spot with the line release button, but this isn't always satisfactory. The stretch in the line and the spring in the rod can snap the lure back towards the caster when the line is stopped. Accuracy suffers. Controlling line speed during the cast with the off hand is the most effective way to achieve accuracy with a spincast reel.

Some tournament casters like this type of reel, especially

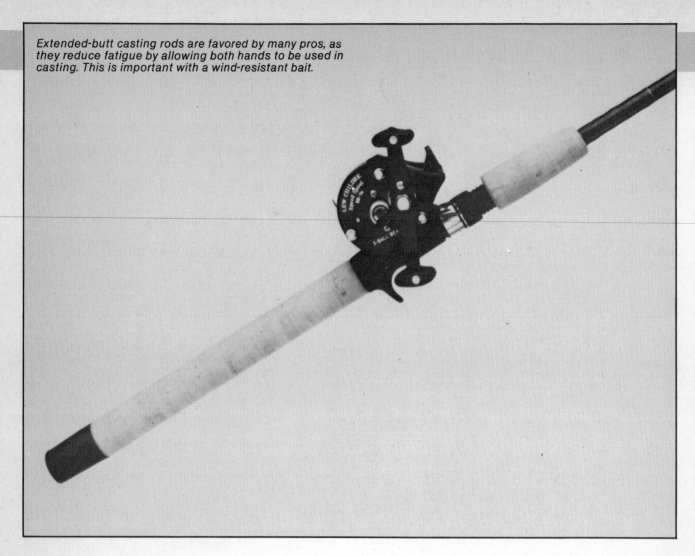

Extended-butt casting rods are favored by many pros, as they reduce fatigue by allowing both hands to be used in casting. This is important with a wind-resistant bait.

when combined with a soft-action rod, because the lure's flight speed is slow enough for them to achieve in-flight control and accuracy. But they invariably do their bass fishing with casting or open-faced spinning outfits!

Mating it with a rod of proper action and length for the lure and line size used is important. A rod and reel must function together to propel the lure accurately to its target, execute the lure retrieve, detect the strike, set the hook, then land the fish. The most expensive and sophisticated reel on the market won't help, if the rod is a piece of junk. The reverse also is true.

Rod materials can be broken down into three major types — fiberglass, graphite and boron — although they sometimes are combined to make one rod. When two or more materials are combined — for instance, fiberglass and graphite, — this is referred to as a composite rod. Sometimes this is done to reduce costs, but in the better composites, it fills a specific bass'n requirement.

Fiberglass began to appear in fishing rods about 1948. And, until a dozen years ago, it was considered the best material from which to make a fishing rod. It since has been eclipsed by graphite, but for some applications fiberglass still is considered superior by serious anglers.

Fiberglass generally is tougher and more durable than graphite and still is the material of choice among many of Florida's trophy bass guides for rough-and-tumble shiner

fishing for big bass. Many favor saltwater popping rods in lengths of 6½ to seven feet.

Fiberglass does not transmit vibrations as quickly as graphite and it has a slower response curve; it takes longer to bend and longer to spring back. A more forgiving material than graphite, many professional tournament anglers favor it for some types of lures. The most common use for glass rods is in fishing crankbaits, where a stiff, responsive rod may cause the angler to strike a bass too soon; the lack of flex in the rod may rip the small treble hooks common to this lure type free from the bass's jaw.

Some maufacturers — Fenwick, for one — now are making composite rods featuring a glass tip section married to a graphite mid and butt section. The benefits of both materials are combined into an effective rod.

The forgiving nature of glass helps play the fish properly, while the inherently lighter weight of graphite makes a rod that is more comfortable to fish. Such rods are becoming standard among professional anglers for fishing crankbaits and some other lures that feature small treble hooks.

Graphite is stiffer, lighter, more sensitive than glass. Boron is said to be slightly better in these respects than graphite. Unfortunately, it is also significantly more expensive. Graphite became *the* rod material of the Seventies, and boron was supposed to become the in-thing for the Eighties, but the latter didn't happen. Serious anglers did

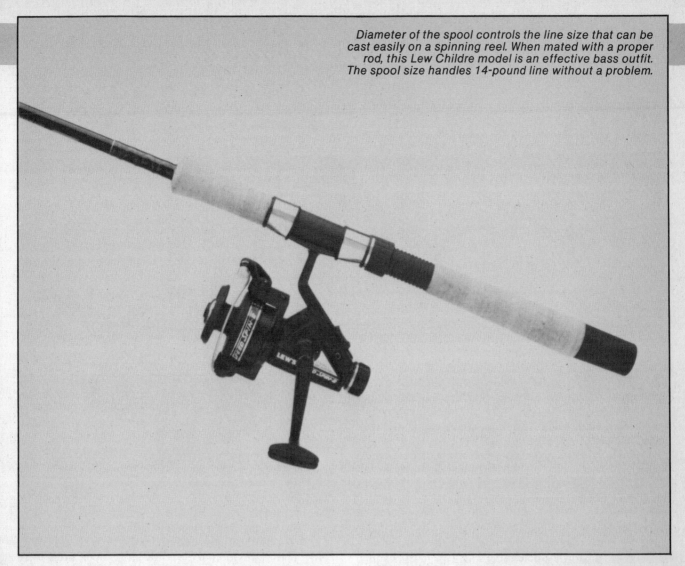

not find enough of an improvement to justify the increased cost.

Today, graphite is the most common choice for most bass rod applications, although boron is still seeing some use. Essentially, among serious anglers, glass or a glass/graphite composite is the first choice when a forgiving rod is needed, while graphite (or a graphite/boron composite) fills the bill for everything else.

Bass fishing rods can be had in commonly available lengths, ranging from five to eight feet. In years past, 5½ feet was considered a standard length, but that is changing quickly.

Due largely to lessons learned on the pro tour, the average bass rod is likely to be six feet. Longer rods provide more striking power, greater casting distance and are no more difficult to cast than the shorter rods. In fact, some pros routinely throw lures on rods of 6½ to seven feet, even in dense, restricted areas.

"Anytime you are able to cast overhand," says Florida pro angler Bernie Schultz, "you'll be better off with a rod six feet or longer. If the cover conditions are such that you have to cast underhand or sidearm, you usually can get by with a six-foot rod, although a 5½-footer is sometimes easier to use. That's the only time, though, that a 5½-foot rod is more effective than a longer model."

Given the lesser weight of graphite, today's six-foot rod is likely to be lighter than the 5½-foot fiberglass type of a decade ago.

The degree of flex in a rod, referred to as its action, plays an important role in how effective it will be. Some lure types require a rod with little flex, while others need a rod with a softer tip. Using the incorrect rod action for a particular lure type or cover situation can result in missed strikes and fish lost during the flight.

Rods generally are labeled by manufacturers in this respect, although there is considerable variation. Most common is to label the rod in accordance with its overall degree of stiffness. "Light," "medium," and "heavy" are common labels, with the heavy rod having the stiffest action. Sometimes mid-actions are denoted, such as a "medium/heavy," with a degree of flex somewhere between the two actions.

This can be a bit confusing when an angler tries to determine the range of lure weights each rod will handle; not all labels are consistent between different makers. One rod company's medium action may have the equivalent of another's light action. There may be variation within different rods in one maker's lineup. For example, the #6 power Fenwick Hooksetter is stiffer and has a faster tip than does the same maker's #6 power Eagle rod.

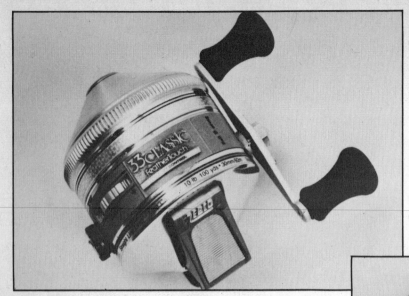

The Zebco 33 Classic is a spincast reel that features what the manufacturer terms a feather touch, an aid to its popularity.

This big spincast reel from Zebco handles line in the 20-pound test range. Most spincast reels are limited to 12-pound. This is due to the diameter of the spool.

Some manufacturers print a recommended line range — say ten to twenty-pound test — on the rod, but this has no direct bearing on the rod's action.

Another labeling system indicates a range of lure weights the rod will handle. It can provide useful information concerning the rod action, although graphite and boron rods usually handle a wider range of lure weights than indicated. A rod with a recommended lure range of one-eighth to three-eighths would be a light-action rod, while one with a range from three-eighths to an ounce would be a heavy action. A better way to select the proper action is to consider the tip action, combined with lure weight range. This provides significant information as to what types of lures will be most effective.

To determine this, hold the rod by the grip and have someone grasp the rod tip at eye level. Pull on the grip to put a bow in the rod and determine where the most bending takes place with moderate pressure. An extra-fast tip will have its action centered in the last one-quarter of the rod tip, fast action is the last one-third, a moderate action in the upper one-half. A slow or soft action will have a fairly uniform bend from tip to butt.

An extra-fast tip rod can be the best bet for casting large, heavy baits or those that are wind-resistant. Among those are big buzzbaits, willowleaf spinnerbaits with blade sized #5 and larger, plus heavy Carolina worm rigs. The stiffer tip also is required to achieve the proper action on some lures, like the Zara Sook and the Pop-R. Combined with a heavy action, an extra-fast tip also is the best choice when fishing lures having one large hook — spoons, spinnerbaits, buzzbaits — in heavy cover.

Serious anglers usually have one or more of these around in the casting configuration spooled with seventeen to twenty-five-pound-test line. Lengths of six to seven feet, combined with a two-fisted "trigger stick" type of handle are popular among the pros.

A fast tip in either a heavy or medium action probably is one of the most versatile of the bass rod actions and a good candidate for the label "all-around."

In either casting or spinning with eight to fourteen-pound line, they will handle most bass'n chores easily. They are ideal for fishing plastic worms, jigs, small- and medium-sized spinnerbaits, most topwater lures and the larger crankbaits.

Many lighter tackle anglers use the spinning models of 5½ to six-foot medium action, spooling six- to ten-pound line. These are good choices for large, open areas with plastic worms, jigs, Gitzits, balsawood topwater plugs and small crankbaits.

For an angler who does not fish heavy-cover waters routinely, a six-foot fast-tip rod in a heavy casting action can be spooled with fourteen-pound line. Combined with a medium-action model of the same length and a spinning model in a medium action and carrying ten-pound line, this would be an effective three-rod set-up for most bass waters.

For such rods, graphite is often the best choice of material, since its lighter weight and wider lure range is an asset. A moderate-tipped rod of glass or a glass/graphite composite is excellent for anglers who routinely fish crankbaits. Many pros like these in a medium, or medium/heavy action and in lengths of 6½ to seven feet. The soft tip helps prevent small treble hooks from pulling free from the bass during the fight. They can, in a spinning configuration, be effective for small, balsawood topwater plugs like Rapalas and AC Shiners for the same reason.

Professional angler Johnnie Borden says, "We try to match the rod action to the lure type we are using, giving some consideration as well to the cover we are fishing in. A big, single-hooked lure needs a stiffer rod to get the hook set properly than does a bait with small #6 treble hooks.

"However, sometimes a rod that has too little tip flex can hurt you. If you find yourself getting strikes but not

Low-profile casting reels are a far cry from models of a decade ago. Graphite and plastic have reduced the weight levels.

Quantum 310MG baitcasting reel has spool tension adjustment on right (below) and on left side (lower right), magnetic brake control to aid in its performance.

hooking the fish, the first impulse is to go to a stiffer rod to get more power into the hook set. You may need just the reverse. If your reflexes are fast, you may be striking before the bass fully has the bait. Many times, a rod that has a slightly softer tip action can give you a momentary "built-in" delay that lets the bass get all the bait before you stick him. This can be a common problem with crankbaits and sometimes with floating lures and buzzbaits.

"Choosing the most efficient rod action for the lure type you are using is extremely important," Borden concludes, "and one of the reasons professional anglers often carry a wide range of rod actions."

One group, referred to as "specialty" rods, can prove beneficial in certain situations. They're intended to handle a specific set of depth and cover conditions that more conventional equipment won't. One good example that's popular in Florida is called a "dock rod."

These are short, stout, open-faced spinning rods with a medium freshwater-sized reel loaded with twelve- to fourteen-pound line. In length, they range from five to 5½ feet and many are custom-made for heavy-action casting blanks.

Their purpose is to allow the angler to move close to a dock, boathouse or other man-made structure and make short, accurate casts underneath it. Sometimes casts need to be made underhand, backhand or sidearm to get the bait to the innermost reaches where the larger bass often hold. Once a bass is hooked, the short, stout blank aids in prying

the critter loose from the maze of wood. They're not good for much else, but are superb tools for fishing docks and win many Florida tournaments.

Another specialty rod is laughingly referred to as a "defensive rod." These are spinning rods in the seven- to 7½-foot range with eight- to ten-pound line. They are intended for long-distance casting for surface schooling bass or when your boat partner doesn't seem to get you quite close enough to the cover being fished.

When an extra spool loaded with twelve-pound line is carried for the reel. This allows anglers to "pitch." This is an extended-range version of flipping. In some clear water situations, anglers may not be able to approach within eight or ten feet of the bass-holding cover without spooking the fish. These rods allow precise, soft-landing lure presentation from distances of twenty feet or more. Often that can make the difference between catching a bass and spooking him away from his cover.

One specialty rod no serious bass fisherman should be without is a flipping rod. First popularized by California angler Dee Thomas, flipping has become a standard tactic

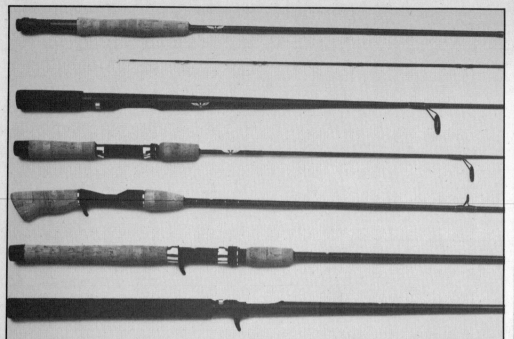

among professional anglers and has won considerable amounts of money on the pro tour.

"What makes flipping so effective," says California pro Gary Klein, "is that it allows you to place a lure in places you never could reach with a conventional cast — and to do it with a soft, natural water entry. I have caught bass from a fallen treetop by flipping after another angler had made repeated casts to it with the same lure."

Flipping is done with baitcasting rods of heavy action in lengths of seven to eight feet. Line ranges in the 20- to 40-pound class, with 25- and 30-pound the most popular. It is a close-range presentation system and often fish are hooked with less than seven feet of line past the rod tip. The bait is not cast in the conventional sense; it is simply flipped into likely looking places with a soft up-and-down motion of the rod. Correctly done, it allows a bait to be dropped lightly into the water and sink straight down through even the thickest cover.

Mastering the flip cast is not difficult. It can be done in the backyard and many pros have done just that; practicing at home until they can drop a jig or plastic worm into a teacup every time at fifteen feet.

To begin the flip cast, hold the rod in your right hand (for right-handed anglers) with about seven feet of line past the rod tip, which is in an upwards position. With the left hand, strip off an arm length of line, moving the left arm straight out to the side of your body. To start the cast (or flip), lower the rod tip slightly, then raise it again. This will make the lure swing out, then back to you like a pendulum. As the lure reaches the backward end of its swing, lower the rod and the lure will swing forward toward its target.

The lure is aimed by pointing the rod at the target. As the lure begins swinging to the target, feed out the line by bringing your left hand back to the reel. As the lure touches down, bring your left hand onto the foregrip of the rod, engage the reel and allow the lure to sink into the cover with just a little slack in the line.

Most strikes will come as the bait falls. Some may be

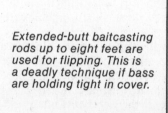

Extended-butt baitcasting rods up to eight feet are used for flipping. This is a deadly technique if bass are holding tight in cover.

Unusual-looking spinning rod by Lew Childre is intended to provide leverage with butt placed along the forearm. (Below) Medium freshwater spinning reels are heavier, so have the ability to handle heavier line with ease.

nothing more than a few slight twitches on the line; the line may move off to the side or the lure may not drop as far as it should. If you're flipping in five feet of water and the lure only falls two feet, it's probably a bass that has interrupted its progress. Sometimes, though, a bass will really slam a dropping jig or worm and the next thing you know you'll be glad you got your left hand onto the rod!

The most commonly used lures for flipping are the jig-and-pig and the Texas-rigged plastic worm, because they can penetrate the thick cover without hanging up. If your lure makes it all the way to the bottom unmolested, jig it up and down a time or two, then gather line with your left hand and raise the bait out for another flip.

Flipping can be deadly in brushtops, fallen treetops, grassline edges or in areas of heavily matted surface cover like hydrilla, hyacinths and milfoil. It can often be the only way to get a lure into such cover. It is often most effective during the middle of the day when bass usually retreat to heavy cover.

Flipping usually is restricted to targets within fifteen feet or so, although skilled flippers can increase this distance by using the thumb of the rod hand to allow the lure to pull line off the spool during the latter stage of the cast, gaining extra distance.

If that still isn't enough distance, some anglers resort to the longer spinning rods and shoot line off the spool, controlling distance with the forefinger of the rod hand by feathering the line. The procedure is basically the same as in flipping, but without the revolving spool to control, distance can be increased.

Given the wide variety of equipment available, anglers won't have much trouble putting together effective outfits. When selecting a rod and reel, though, make sure the com-

bination you choose is comfortable in your hand. Rod grips come in a variety of styles and materials. Reels have different shapes, heights, and widths. The two items may look great, but may not fit your hand when mated. An outfit that is awkward and uncomfortable to use is going to be far less effective than it could be.

When purchasing a rod for a reel you already own, take the reel with you and install it on the rod before you make your final decision. See how it feels. The same holds true when purchasing a reel or buying an outfit.

Anglers who keep these factors in mind add greatly to their enjoyment of the pursuit of America's fish.

CHAPTER 4

All photos and illustrations courtesy of Du Pont

Badly worn or abraided line such as this, shown in a microscopic photo, can have its breaking strength cut by well over half. It is a common occurrence when one is fishing in heavy cover and the line is abused badly.

THE LOWDOWN ON LINE

Monofilament lines are made from a single strand of nylon. This cross-section of Du Pont's "Prime" line shows the new co-filament technology being utilized.

Often Ignored Or Overlooked, This Is Your Most Important Link To The Bass

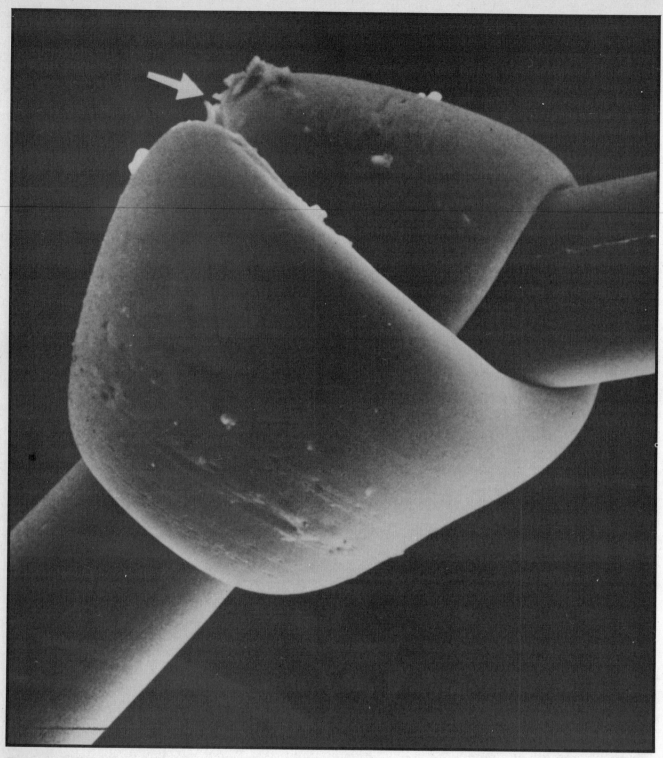

This enlargement of an overhand knot illustrates how monofilament line can cut and abraid itself. This line will break at the knot — or in it — at about one-half of its rated breaking strength because of the abrasion.

IT IS amazing how often we bass fishermen tend to get lost in the forest and forget what the individual trees actually look like. Take the subject of line and knots, for instance.

We all know how important these items can be. But, when we slide out from behind the wheel of a $20,000 bass boat, turn off the $1000 graph we have used to locate bass, ease a $500 trolling motor over the bow, turn on a $400 bow-mounted LCR to more closely monitor our precise position, pick up a $200 rod and reel and cast our $5 crankbait to the fish, we are still placing our ultimate success or failure squarely in the hands of $2 worth of line — and a knot that is free!

And if the solid weight of that first strike suddenly turns into sickening slack, we have only ourselves to blame.

Modern monofilament fishing lines first were introduced

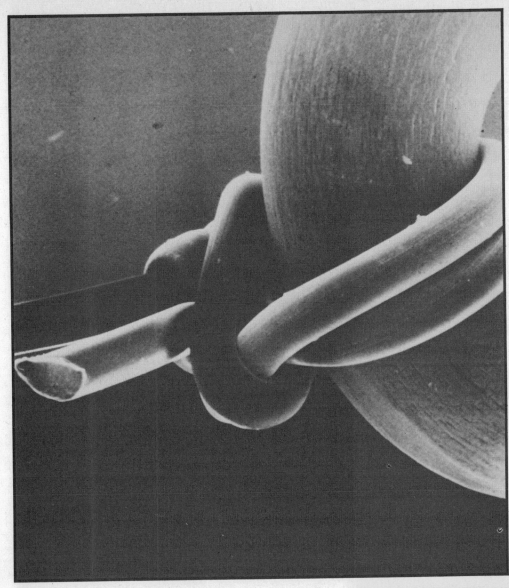

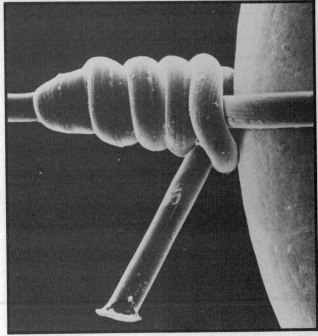

Left: Many efficient knots utilize a double wrap of line around the line tie eye to help prevent any wear, increase strength. (Below) The improved clinch knot provides cushioning effect to prevent line from cutting itself under stress. The knot must be snugged down, not loose.

commercially in 1939 and things have not been the same since for the fisherman — or the fish!

It is the angler who has ultimately come out ahead, because most brands of monofilament line — even the cheapest — are far superior to the natural linen lines they replaced over forty years ago. Monofilament is superior simply because it has better fishing performance qualities and requires much less care than the older lines.

Monofilament is a synthetic product derived largely from petroleum products. Practically all monofilament lines are made from nylon, while some of the new cofilament lines incorporate polyester with nylon.

The manufacturing process is one of the critical variables in modern lines. Each line manufacturer keeps much of his exact specifications a closely guarded secret, but the basic process can be described this way: Nylon polymer resins are poured into a hopper and heated until they are molten. Then, a pump or screw forces the molten resins out a tiny opening or die-hole that establishes the basic diameter of the line. This molten line is immediately cooled and wound on a roller.

It then is stretched between two sets of rollers, the

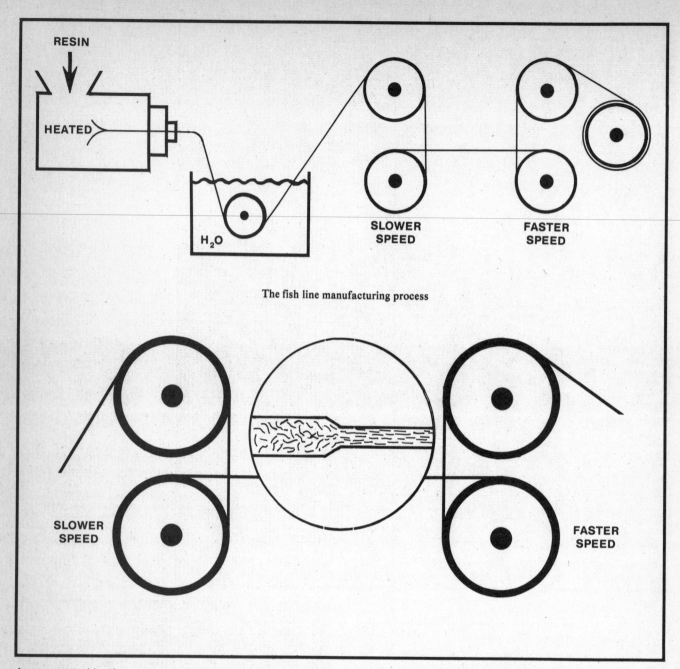

The fish line manufacturing process

As suggested by the sequence in these drawings, modern manufacture of monofilament line is a complicated process.

second one running at a faster speed then the first. The ratio of speeds between the rollers is what is known as the "draw ratio." This is what orients the molecules in the direction of the line, increasing its tensile strength and reducing its diameter.

The two key areas in the production of monofilament line are the exact blend of nylon in the melt process and the draw ratio. Manufacturers differ here and this is why some brands of line tend to perform better and last longer.

It is also why "bargain basement" brands of line are false economy in the truest sense of the word. The machines and ingredients used to make premium quality monofilament lines are not cheap. The skill and care required to properly operate those same machines is not casual.

Major manufacturers go to great lengths to assure consistent levels of quality in their products and, considering the best cost only a few dollars more, premium lines such as those manufactured by Du Pont, Berkeley, Maxima, Cortland, and others are the cheapest form of insurance an angler has against the possibility of losing expensive lures or a trophy bass.

As stated, not all monofilament lines are the same, even among the premium makers. The reason perhaps is summed up best by the folks at Du Pont. Through their market research with some of the country's leading fishermen they have identified seven basic properties required of a monofilament line. They are, in no particular order of importance:

How to Fill Your Reel

Improper loading of your reel can cause line twist which can greatly reduce casting accuracy and distance. Worse yet, it can cause you to lose fish.

You can avoid problems by having your reel filled on a linewinding machine at your favorite sporting goods store. However, it pays to learn how to do it yourself because most line problems occur at lakeside, miles from the nearest winder.

Insert a pencil into the supply spool to allow the fishing line to feed smoothly off the spool. Have someone hold each end of the pencil while you turn the reel handle. Keep proper tension on the line by having the person holding the pencil exert a slight inward pressure on the supply spool.

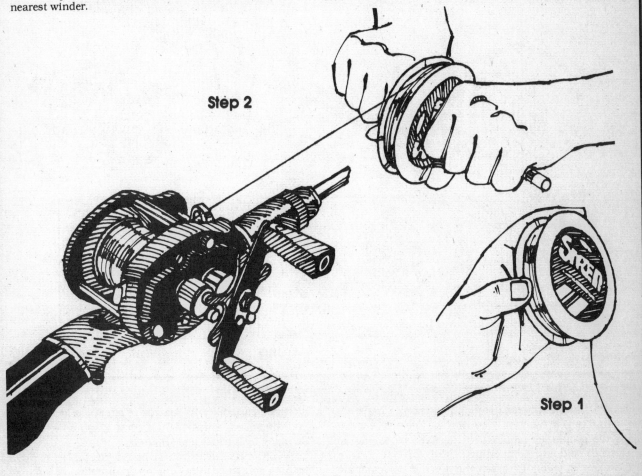

Step 2

Step 1

1. *Knot strength:* provides insurance against break-offs in the knot.

2. *Abrasion resistance:* provides resistance in the line to nicks, scrapes and cuts in use.

3. *Shock strength:* allows the line to withstand a sudden application of force stress such as when setting the hook.

4. *Tensile strength:* expresses the relationship between the breakload and the area (diameter) of the line.

5. *Proper limpness:* is a measurement of the feel of flexibility of the line and most affects castability.

6. *Controlled stretch:* provides the cushion effects in a monofilament line that allows it to give under stress, yet recover.

7. *Visibility:* is imparted by a color system and allows the angler to more readily see the line for control purpose or to detect subtle strikes.

Each of these properties affects the performance of the line and a balanced blend of all is desirable. However, improving the specific performance of one property cannot always be done without limiting one of the others. For example, increasing abrasion resistance can reduce its limpness. Conversely, gaining limpness can reduce abrasion resistance.

Some lines, like Du Pont *Stren,* have been carefully engineered to obtain the best optimum balance between these properties. Other lines, like *Triline XT* and *Maxima,* have been designed with increased abrasion resistance, to aid anglers fishing in heavy cover. *Triline XL* is intended to provide extra limpness, especially for anglers using spinning tackle where stiff lines can cause casting and spooling problems.

When choosing a brand of line, factors like the above should be kept in mind. It would be unfair to criticize a stiff, highly abrasion-resistant line, because it didn't perform

Filling a Spinning Reel

You fill a spinning/open-face reel differently than a bait-cast reel because you must allow for the rotation of the pick-up bail which may cause the line to twist.
Follow these steps:

1. Have someone hold the supply spool or place it on the floor or ground.
2. Pull the line so that it spirals (balloons) off the end of the spool.
3. Thread the line through the rod guides and tie the line to the reel with the bail in the open position.
4. Hold the rod tip three to four feet away from the supply spool. Make fifteen to twenty turns on the reel handle, then stop.

5. Check for line twist by moving the rod tip to about one foot from the supply spool. If the slack line twists, turn the supply spool completely around. This will eliminate most of the twist as you wind the rest of the line onto the reel.
6. Always keep a light tension on fishing line when spooling any reel. Do this by holding the line between the thumb and forefinger of your free hand.

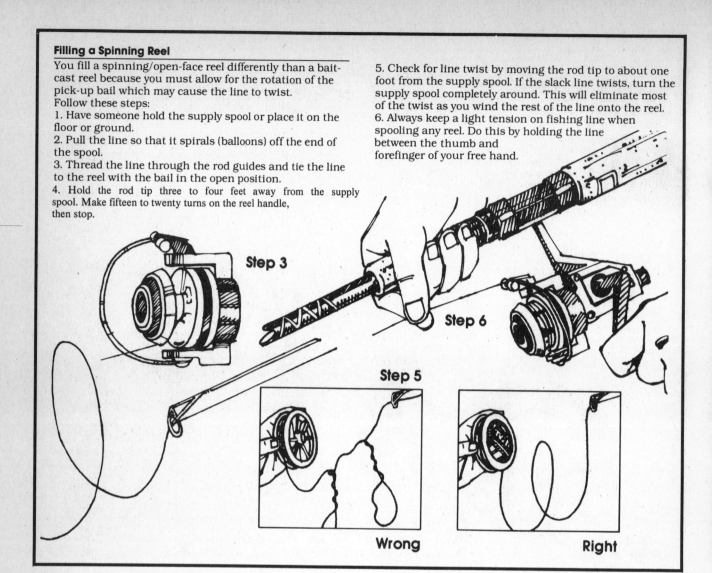

Step 3

Step 6

Step 5

Wrong

Right

well on a small-diameter spinning reel spool. That's not really its intended function. Choosing the line that best displays the properties required for the type of fishing an angler will be doing is important.

Co-filament technology, where nylon and polyester are co-extruded to produce a line with a nylon outer sheath and a low-stretch polyester core, is one attempt to gain in one property without losing another. These new lines can offer decreased stretch and increased sensitivity while still maintaining many of the desirable properties of the monofilament lines. They can be an excellent choice for worm or jig fishing...deep vertical jigging...or in other situations where extreme sensitivity and minimal stretch are required. The best example of this new line technology is *Prime Plus* from Du Pont.

Regardless of the line chosen, it is important for the angler to keep in mind that while one property may be of more importance under a specific set of conditions than others, all will come into play to some degree every time a fish is hooked. A professional angler and the holder of numerous tournament records, Roland Martin explains it like this:

"Accurate casting is important, so the fisherman needs a line with the right amount of limpness for ease of handling and good castability. When you're after bass around cover, your line needs abrasion strength to stand up to repeated dragging over rocks and stumps.

"Visibility is seeing a strike before you feel it, as well as helping you control the length and direction of your cast. When a bass strikes your lure, the line must have the shock strength to withstand the sudden impact of the hook set without breaking. And when you set the hook, your line needs the right amount of stretch — but not too much — to give slightly without breaking, and then recover.

"Now that you're ready to land the bass, tensile strength and knot strength become the important link between you and the fish. You need a line with uniform tensile strength — no weak spots — that will match its pound test and you need a line that won't break when sudden stress is applied to the knot."

It is not the purpose of this chapter to compare one brand of line with any other. Even if that should be done, the reader would only have the personal opinion of the writer. It is far better for the reader to keep these basic properties in mind and to experiment with some of the premium lines made by Du Pont, Berkeley, Maxima and Cortland to determine which suits your needs the best.

The need for each of the seven listed properties is pretty

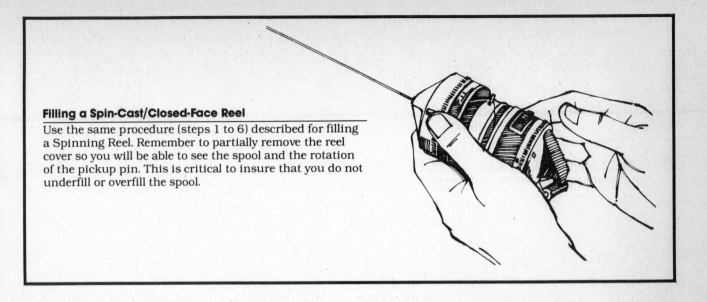

Filling a Spin-Cast/Closed-Face Reel

Use the same procedure (steps 1 to 6) described for filling a Spinning Reel. Remember to partially remove the reel cover so you will be able to see the spool and the rotation of the pickup pin. This is critical to insure that you do not underfill or overfill the spool.

self-evident. But, among many serious anglers there is a controversy today as to just how much of one property — visibility — is really needed.

Being able to see the line is important to any bass fisherman under some conditions. It can be critical when fishing really slow-moving baits like worms or jigs. It can be extremely critical with baits that are commonly used as fall baits, like Gitzits, spoons, grubs and similar lures. It may be of minimal importance when fishing "contact" baits like crankbaits and spinnerbaits, as well as those lures where the strike is evident. These include topwater plugs and buzzbaits.

Manufacturers have made high visibility lines in various colors as well as fluorescents by incorporating dyes, pigments and fluorescence into the nylon melt. Some manufacturers of lower grade lines simply dip their product in dye.

The fluorescence in the line picks up ultra-violet radiation from the sun even on a cloudy day, making the line more visible to the angler. This allows the angler to detect subtle twitches of the line — often indicating a soft take by the bass — that he might not be able to see without the fluorescence.

Three critical questions arise from the use of these lines. Is colored fluorescent line visible underwater under most conditions? If it is visible, can fish see it? And if they can see it, does it spook them and prevent them from striking the lure?

The first two questions have yet to receive a definitive answer. Much of that depends upon the clarity of the water and the amount of light penetrating to the depth of the line.

The third question also is somewhat muddied. Many record gamefish have been landed on fluorescent lines, as shown by the records of the International Game Fish Association. On the other hand, many experienced bass professionals have found their catch rate decreasing in clear water situations when fluorescent lines are used. This is most prevalent when using worms, jigs and finesse baits.

If there was a general consensus among the bass pros it probably would be to avoid fluorescent lines in clear water, while they would not be detrimental in stained or muddy

water. Anglers fishing slow-moving baits in the latter situation might well benefit from fluorescent line, especially if they have difficulty seeing clear lines well.

If controversy exists relative to the amount of visibility a line should have, there is absolutely none over the proper care line should receive. Regardless of the brand of line purchased, without proper care and replacement it will not perform to satisfaction. So important is this aspect of proper line usage that many pros refuse to take any chances and will re-spool their rods with fresh line before each tournament competition day!

Monofilament line is remarkably tough stuff. In fact, it is virtually ageless. The latter fact is pointed out each year when birds and marine animals are killed and injured by becoming entangled in monofilament line discarded in the water by thoughtless anglers. This stuff does not deteriorate and should never be deposited in a waterway. It can be detrimental to fish and wildlife for years to come.

But, how long will it remain in top condition, delivering peak performance, when spooled on your reel?

Line replacement depends on how much the line has been used, not on the age of the line itself. You could store a spool of monofilament on its original spool for years (under the proper conditions) and it would be just as good as the day it was purchased.

The same holds true for line spooled onto a reel. That line would last indefinitely, if never used or it never saw the light of the day.

One of the biggest enemies of monofilament line is the ultra-violet rays of the sun. A few days of fishing has only negligible effect, but continued exposure over a period of several months may weaken the line. Consequently, when reels are not being used, they should be stored out of the sun's rays in a rod box, tackle box or the garage.

New line will stay good for years if left in its original box and stored in a cool, dry place, out of the sunlight.

Other than ultra-violet light, monofilament line appears to have only one other enemy: Battery acid — or the corrosion resulting from it — will destroy line quickly. If you have been handling batteries, it is important to wash your hands thoroughly before touching any line.

Independent test results have shown that monofilament

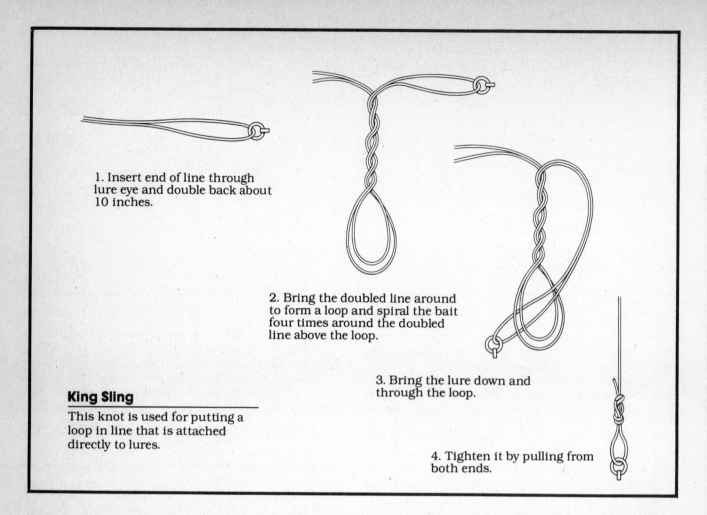

1. Insert end of line through lure eye and double back about 10 inches.

2. Bring the doubled line around to form a loop and spiral the bait four times around the doubled line above the loop.

King Sling

This knot is used for putting a loop in line that is attached directly to lures.

3. Bring the lure down and through the loop.

4. Tighten it by pulling from both ends.

line is not damaged by exposure to salt water, gasoline, motor oil, insect repellants, sun screen lotion, detergents, rust inhibitors or lubricants.

The key to proper line replacement depends on how much it has been fished, and where it has been fished.

An angler fishing four or five days a year might find he can replace his line on a yearly basis. Or if he is fishing in highly abrasive cover, he may have to replace his line every couple of trips. An angler who is fishing deep, relatively unobstructed waters may be able to squeeze dozens of outings from a spool of line. But the angler fishing heavy cover will need to replace more often. Serious anglers will often replace their line after every three or four trips. It may sound like a lot, but line is surprisingly inexpensive.

The most economical way to efficiently replace line is not to completely strip the reel clean of the old line. That's wasteful, because fifty yards of fresh line is all any bass fisherman really needs on his reel. Instead, purchase your line in 250- or six hundred-yard bulk spools and, when it is time to respool, just strip off the top fifty yards, tie on line from the bulk spool with a uni-knot (or similar line-to-line connection) and re-fill the reel.

One 250-yard spool will give an angler five line changes; for many casual anglers, that's a year's supply. A six hundred-yard spool will allow one reel to be re-lined every month. Either of these is a far more economical alternative than purchasing a small, one hundred-yard, spool and completely re-filling the reel from it.

One problem often encountered by anglers, especially those who fish only a few times a year, is line curl on the reel. This is not a serious problem, nor is it always cause to change the line.

Like most plastic materials, nylon has a memory — the characteristic of returning to its original shape. In fishing line, that often results in coils of line from the reel spool. The degree of set the line will take is related directly to the amount of moisture in the line and the degree of tension on the line when it is stored. Nylon is hydroscopic; it absorbs water and, when it does so, both the diameter and the length of the line will increase with increasing moisture content. When the reel is stored, the water evaporates and the line shrinks back to its original length and diameter. This causes tension on the line and sometimes can cause casting problems the first time the reel is again used.

This is easy to solve by simply soaking the line to induce moisture. Stick the reel in the water for a few minutes or just trail the line over the stern of the boat for the same length of time.

This hydroscopic nature can induce other changes in monfilament line, as well. Some of these changes are dramatic and can seriously affect line performance.

Nylon absorbs water quickly and, while some blends take on water more rapidly than others, all nylon lines ultimately will attain the same moisture content. Within about an hour of fishing, the line will absorb from six to eight percent water, depending upon its pound test. Water makes line softer, more limp and easier to handle. It also makes the line thicker and longer — as much as two per-

Knots to Hold Terminal Tackle

Improved Clinch Knot

This is a good knot for making terminal-tackle connections and is best used for lines up to 20-pound test. It is a preferred knot by professional fishermen and angling authorities.

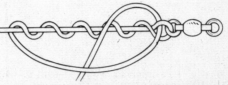

1. Pass line through eye of hook, swivel, or lure. Double back and make five turns around the standing line. Hold coils in place; thread end of line around first loop above the eye, then through big loop as shown.

2. Hold tag end and standing line while coils are pulled up. Take care that coils are in spiral, not lapping over each other. Slide tight against eye. Clip tag end.

cent by the end of the fishing day. In addition, water also will cause changes in other line properties, as shown in the accompanying chart.

Another factor that will alter your line's strength is the knot you tie. Especially, if it is tied improperly.

It is a fact that any knot you tie into your line will reduce

Changes in Line Properties From Dry to Wet

Property	Change
Tensile Strength	Decreases from 15-20%
Abrasion Resistance	Decreases as much as 50%
Shock Strength	Decreases as much as 25%
Knot Strength	Decreases from 15-20%
Stretch	Increases as much as 50%
Limpness	Increases as much as 60%

(Sample ranges determined from laboratory tests of all premium quality lines.)

Now you know why avid fishermen proclaim: "The line you buy isn't the same as the line you fish with."

The Uni-Knot System

Here is a system that uses one basic knot for a variety of applications. Developed by Vic Dunaway, author of numerous books on fishing and editor of "Florida Sportsman" magazine, the Uni-Knot can be varied to meet virtually every knot tying need in either fresh or salt water fishing.

Tying to Terminal Tackle

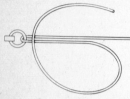

1. Run line through eye of hook, swivel or lure at least 6 inches and fold to make two parallel lines. Bring end of line back in a circle toward hook or lure.

2. Make six turns with tag end around the double line and through the circle. Hold double line at point where it passes through eye and pull tag end to snug up turns.

3. Now pull standing line to slide knot up against eye.

4. Continue pulling until knot is tight. Trim tag end flush with closest coil of knot. Uni-Knot will not slip.

The Uni-Knot System

Joining Lines

1. Overlap ends of two lines of about the same diameter for about 6 inches. With one end, form Uni-Knot circle, crossing the two lines about midway of overlapped distance.

2. Tie Uni-Knot around leader with doubled line. Use only three turns and snug up.

3. Pull tag end to snug knot tight around line.

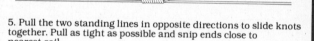

4. Pull knots together as tightly as possible and trim ends and loop.

5. Pull the two standing lines in opposite directions to slide knots together. Pull as tight as possible and snip ends close to nearest coil.

---

its breaking strength from that which the line is rated. Some knots do this more than others.

Most line manufacturers have emphasized this in the way in which they evaluate a knot's strength. Knots are rated according to how much they diminish the strength of the line; that's calculated by a laboratory machine called an Instron Tensile Tester. This machine first meassures the precise breakload of the unknotted line, then measures the breakload of the same line with a knot tied onto it. The breaking point of the unknotted line is divided into the breaking point of the knotted line to produce a percentage measurement. The formula is:

$$\text{Knot efficiency} = \frac{\text{Knotted breakload}}{\text{Unknotted breakload}} \times 100$$

For example, one of the most popular knots among many expert anglers for tying lures directly to the line is the double improved clinch knot. It rates between ninety-five percent and one hundred percent efficient, meaning the line is not likely to break in the knot itself, the knot being almost equal in strength to unknotted line. Not all knots show this level of efficiency, however.

The problem with knots is that monofilament line is tough stuff and actually will cut into itself. I have a friend who will take 100-pound monofiliment line and break it between his two hands. No, he's not Hulk Hogan. He simply curls the line back on itself and uses the line to cut through itself.

Good knots have a cushion against the cutting action. Poor knots do not. The common overhand knot for example, has a rating of about fifty percent. It's a poor choice for any monofilament application.

Improperly tied knots pose the same problem. Careless tying, failing to properly draw up the spirals neatly, not snugging the knot can take a perfectly good ninety-five per-

World's Fair Knot

The winning knot in Du Pont's Great Knot Search

Created by Gary L. Martin of Lafayette, IN, this terminal tackle knot was selected by a panel of outdoor writers as the best new, easy-to-tie, all-purpose fishing knot from 498 entries in the Du Pont Great Knot Search. Martin named it the World's Fair Knot because it was first publicly demonstrated by him at the Knoxville '82 World's Fair.

1. Double a 6-inch length of line and pass the loop through the eye.

2. Bring the loop back next to the doubled line and grasp the doubled line through the loop.

3. Put the tag end through the new loop formed by the double line.

4. Bring the tag end back through the new loop created by step 3.

5. Pull the tag end snug and slide knot up tight. Clip tag end.

The Uni-Knot System

Snelling a Hook

1. Thread line through hook eye about 6 inches. Hold line against hook shank and form Uni-Knot circle.

2. Make as many turns through loop and around line and shank as desired. Close knot by pulling on tag end of line.

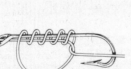

3. Tighten by pulling standing line in one direction and hook in the other.

Line to Reel Spool

1. Tie loop in end of line with Uni-Knot; only three turns needed. With bail of spinning reel open, slip loop over spool. (With revolving spool reel, line must be passed around reel hub before tying the Uni-Knot.)

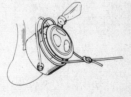

2. Pull on line to tighten loop.

cent knot and turn it into a fifty percent one.

Abrasion generated by snugging a knot also can weaken the line, reducing the knot's effectiveness. Many anglers will counteract this by moistening the knot with saliva to act as a lubricant, before snugging the knot down.

Modern monofilament lines are a far cry from the products of yesteryear. They outperform, outlast and outcast any other type of fishing line on the market. But, they do need minimal care, replacement and proper knots, if they are to achieve their performance potentials.

CHAPTER 5

THE BASS BOAT

The best fiberglass bass boats are those that feature a hand-laid hull. Fiberglass and bonding resins are rolled into place by hand, not sprayed on with a choppergun. Hand-laid hulls are lighter, stronger and will last longer.

THE IMAGE of the modern bass fisherman wouldn't be complete without him sitting behind the console of a gleaming metal-flake monster capable of zipping him down the lake at speeds in excess of sixty miles per hour.

Of all the various gamefish there are to pursue, how many have actually had a specific boat design created expressly for them, and named after them? Have you ever seen a bluegill boat? How about a trout boat? No, and you're not likely to, either.

Actually, there would be no need to design a boat expressly for other species, because the contemporary "bass-boat-type craft" is as close as one will get to the perfect freshwater fishing machine. It is more than adequate for most inshore saltwater applications, as well.

This level of versatility didn't come about by accident. The bass boat is probably one of the few fishing craft that has evolved over the years as a direct result of on-the-water experience and requirements. What we have today is largely the result of years of input from professional bass fishermen who demanded the best possible craft for their needs. In fact, the evolution of the modern bass boat parallels the evolution of bass tournaments.

The earliest bass tournaments were rather unsophisticated affairs and so was the equipment used. For the most part, early bass boats were nothing more than a glorified jon boat to which a 25-50 horse engine was hung. Electric

trolling motors were equally crude, often affixed to the transom. Fourteen to sixteen feet was a common length for these craft and they were quite adequate for the smaller lakes routinely fished in those days.

As purses became bigger, competition became tougher. Savvy anglers knew the importance of getting to a good fishing hole first and increased speed became a requirement. Hull designs were modified with that in mind and engine sizes increased.

As tournaments were held with increasing frequency on larger reservoirs to accommodate the increasing numbers of competitors, seaworthiness and safety became prime concerns. The fourteen- to sixteen-foot boats began to give way to eighteen- and nineteen-foot hulls; their beams were widened to provide better rough-water handling.

Today's modern tournament bass boat is likely to be in the eighteen- to twenty-foot range with a beam of over seven feet. Engines in the 150- to 200-horsepower range propel them at speeds of 55 to 70-plus mph. Plush, padded seats provide a soft ride, while elevated casting decks and pedestal seats afford comfortable fishing. Sophisticated electronics packages allow anglers to literally "see" what lies below them. Trailers that allow the boat to be driven on and off make launching the boat a breeze. Bass boats have come a long way since their humble beginnings and today's anglers have a wide variety of models from which to choose.

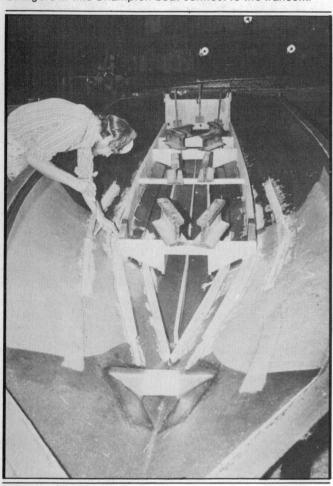
Below: Internal support system helps provide structural strength needed to handle rough water. Note how the stringers in this Champion boat connect to the transom.

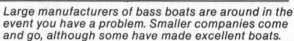
Large manufacturers of bass boats are around in the event you have a problem. Smaller companies come and go, although some have made excellent boats.

The most important factor to consider when choosing a bass boat is to pick a hull size and configuration best suited to your fishing needs, not necessarily what some TV bass pro feels is suited to *his* needs.

For example, if you fish primarily on smaller waters where a thirty-mile run is not needed, where rough seas are not encountered, where launching ramps are not state-of-the-art, you might be quite happy with a fifteen-foot hull and a fifty-horsepower engine. Not only will you reduce your initial cost, save on insurance and fuel, allow yourself to tow with a smaller vehicle, but you'll likely be able to launch and fish in places larger boats cannot.

On the other hand, if you fish tournaments on big reservoirs where rough water is a fact of life, you might well need an eighteen- or nineteen-foot hull for safety's sake.

If the other household members fail to share your enthusiasm for bass fishing, the same bass boat hulls can be had in a family-oriented fish and ski configuration. Distaff members often find an additional monthly payment a bit easier to take if the item is something the whole family can enjoy.

Regardless of what type of hull you choose, there are several factors to keep in mind. The first is to choose a manufacturer that has been around awhile and offers a good warranty, as well as having his product carried by a local dealer. Small companies pop up in the bass boat industry seemingly overnight. Some leave the same way. It's comforting to know the manufacturer is going to be there if something goes wrong and feels confident enough about his product to back it in writing. Always ask about a warranty and shy away from those who don't offer one.

Also ask about the way the boat is made. Many are assembled with the use of chopperguns which spray resin and chopped fiberglass where the operator points it. Some are made by hand, the assembler actually hand-rolling the fiberglass into place. Using the choppergun is cheaper for the manufacturer, but the result does not equal the strength and quality of a hand-laid hull nor will they have the lifespan.

Check the transom, where the engine will hang. It should be supported by braces or stringers, actually tied into the hull. This supporting system provides strength and shock absorption in rough water and extends the life of the transom.

While you're in there, check the interior of the rear battery area. Is it rough and unfinished looking? If it is, the chances are excellent that corners also have been cut in the areas you can't see. Examine the product to see if the obvious signs of care and quality are there. If they're not, go elsewhere. There are plenty of bass boat manufacturers like Ranger, Skeeter, Stratos, Champion and Cajun that make high quality products.

The hull you select will largely determine the engine size range you can mate with it. All bass boats are rated for motors in a certain specified horsepower range. For example, an eighteen-foot Ranger might be rated for engines in the 115- to 175-horsepower range. If you want the max-

Moulded fiberglass hulls are standard for larger bass boats. They offer many advantages over wood, aluminum.

imum performance, in terms of speed, that the hull will offer, then the larger engine would be your choice. If, however, you are more interested in economical operation, a pleasant outing and don't really care whether you can hit 60 mph, the 115 might be a better bet. You might be pleasantly surprised at the difference in insurance premiums should you choose the smaller engine.

One thing that should never be done is to put on an engine larger than the maximum rating size. Not only is it unsafe, but it can void your insurance.

Be sure, too, that you select an engine that has a power trim feature. This is a small hydraulic unit that allows you to change the angle of the motor while running. This gives better performance, saves gas and allows the engine to rev easier. It also allows you to tilt the motor up easily to fish in shallow areas and makes loading and unloading the boat a breeze. A bass boat engine without power trim is like a rifle without a scope. It will still work, but it won't work nearly as well as it could.

The next thing you'll have to do is decide on the propellor you'll put on the motor: whichever type you select will be something of a compromise.

A prop that offers maximum top-end speed may not lift the boat smoothly on plane from a dead stop. One that literally blows you out of the hole may not deliver top-end performance. Your boat dealer is the best person to advise you in proper selection of a prop that will offer all-around performance.

Regardless of the prop chosen make certain it is made from stainless steel and not aluminum. The latter is less expensive, but you'll pay for it in the long run through prop repairs or even lower unit damage caused by a bent prop ear.

My first boat had an aluminum prop and I eventually wound up with three of them: one on the engine, one for a spare, one in the shop for repairs. They seemed to rotate monthly. Now I run stainless steel and have had no problems for years.

Transom to hold the engine is critical in a bass boat. It must be reinforced to be part of hull.

Selecting the trailer your boat will spend ninety percent of its life on is equally important. When your boat is in the water, it is supported fully — almost cradled by the water. It also must be cradled properly on the trailer, because no matter how strong or how well built the hull, it can be deformed and permanently damaged if subjected to prolonged high pressure on the wrong areas.

A deformed hull can cause unpleasant handling characteristics like porpoising or hopping, loss of maneuverability, loss of speed and, in extreme cases, it may crack under stress. An improper fitting trailer also can create a serious towing hazard that could lead to an accident.

If you're purchasing your bass boat from a dealer, getting the proper trailer probably will be easy. Most dealers offer custom-fitted units and can even color-coordinate them to the boat!

To determine the load capacity, add the weight of the

Top level bass boats are plush, with deck carpeting, padded seats and bright metal-flake paint schemes. For fully rigged boat of this particular type, one can expect to pay in the neighborhood of $20,000.

hull, motor, a full fuel tank (number of gallons times 6.6 pounds); the weight of the batteries, then add one hundred pounds for your gear. Add ten percent as a safety factor, then select a trailer that has the next highest load rating above that.

For example, if your total weight is 1495 pounds — including the safety factor — do not buy a trailer rated for 1500 pounds; get the next larger size. The few extra dollars in cost will be repaid many times over in peace of mind. Why someone would pay $15,000 or more for a bass boat, then try to save a few dollars on the all-important piece of equipment that will carry it is beyond me. If anything, it should be the other way around.

If your fishing trips take you over good roads and ramps, a drive-on style trailer with dropped axles is a good choice. It centers the load closer to the ground, improves handling, reduces wind drag and makes loading and unloading the boat easy, even if you're by yourself.

If, however, you must travel backcountry "semi-improved" roads, you may require a straight axle trailer to avoid hanging the rig up on crowns and dips.

The tires should be fourteen- or fifteen-inch and have a C-range rating and four-ply sidewall construction. Many bargain-basement trailers use tires that would be more at home on a go-cart and they will invariably cause problems. Smaller tires have to turn more times to cover the same distance at the same speed as do the larger tires. The increased stress and wear on tires and wheel bearings isn't worth the few extra dollars real wheels will cost. There are few things in life more frustrating than a boat trailer breakdown late on a Sunday afternoon. Anything you can do to avoid it is worth twice what it costs!

Hull support systems fall into two categories: rollers and rails. The rails — carpeted bunks — are preferred, since they distribute the boat weight over a much larger area. Rollers can damage hulls and cause deformities. Most manufacturers use the rails today. Once positioned properly, they not only support the boat, but also serve as a guidance system for loading the boat; hit the center of the rails, apply a little throttle and it's like putting your hand in a glove.

It's also advisable to install Bearing Buddy's on the trailer wheel bearings and pick up a grease gun. Keeping your wheel bearing packed with a good grease is the surest way to avoid a failure.

With a properly set up hull, motor and trailer, you're ready to go boating, but you're not ready to go fishing. There are still some important items you'll need.

Other than the main engine, the single most important piece of equipment on a bass boat is the electric trolling motor. Mounted on the bow and powered by marine deep-cycle storage batteries, a trolling motor gives the angler the means to position his boat precisely in wind current or even a strong surface chop. And it allows the angler to do it while still keeping both hands free to fish.

The ability to move your boat to the optimum casting position for a particular target is so important that one who is fishing for bass from a craft without a trolling motor will automatically double his catch simply by installing and using one.

Trolling motors are available in two major types: those that mount on the bow so that their power can be used to pull the boat and those that clamp onto the stern and push the boat.

This Champion bass boat is on its way to a dealer to be rigged with the outboard, trolling motor and other items. Author says it is most important that one buy his rig from a dealer with good reputation.

The bow-mount system is standard on virtually all bass-fishing craft, since it affords a much more precise means of control. It is far easier to pull a chain in the direction you want it to go than to push it. That analogy pretty well sums up the differences in handling characteristics of the two mounting positions.

While gasoline engines are rated in horsepower, electric motors have their power measured in "pounds of thrust." This figure measures the power of the motor at its highest speed and maximum current draw. Almost all trolling motors, though, allow the user to select a lower rating and draw through a switch. In effect, they offer variable speeds up to the maximum.

When determining how powerful a trolling motor to purchase there are a variety of factors to consider. In no real order of importance, they are:

1. The weight of the boat.
2. The environmental conditions you fish under (river current, windy waters, small calm ponds, etc.)
3. The amount of vegetation you may have to chop through.
4. And, the length of time you will fish before recharging the battery.

Starting with the bare minimum power requirements for a five-hour fishing trip on sheltered waters with little vegetation to chop through or current to contend with, you could fish adequately in a sixteen-foot bass boat with an electric motor producing twenty-one pounds of thrust at maximum. An eighteen-foot boat should have a twenty-eight-pound unit. A lightweight fifteen-foot aluminum bass boat could get by nicely with eighteen pounds.

There are some cute little charts put out by some trolling-motor manufacturers that state you could get by with less power, but after ten years as a guide I feel these figures are the minimum. Usually, you will need more power.

The nice thing about electric trolling motors is that, if you don't need the maximum power, you don't have to use it.

For example, the Motor Guide *Brute* mounted on my Ranger produces forty-one pounds of thrust. This is a 12/24-volt motor which utilizes two batteries to produce full power. When I am fishing for schooling bass in the fast current areas of the St. Johns River, I need every bit of power it offers. However, when I launch at one of the smaller lakes in the area, I can turn it to the 12-volt position (where power is drawn from only one battery) and fish quite comfortably on reduced power. With five speeds in the 24-volt position and another five in the 12-volt setting, I have, in effect, ten different speeds with which to work.

Higher speeds are needed to chop through weeds, fight wind and fish in current. Lower speeds fill the bill on calm waters. By being able utilize lower speeds, I draw less current from the batteries and often can fish for several days before the need to recharge.

When selecting a trolling motor for your boat, always consider your power requirements, then purchase a model that will exceed them by 30 percent. Having too much trolling motor will never hurt you; too little can ruin a fishing trip.

Trolling motors are available in a variety of power ranges and can be had in a 12-volt or a 12/24-volt mode. In the former, one battery is used for all power to the motor. In the latter, two batteries — wired together in series — are used. A switch on the trolling motor control allows the user to

Other than the main engine, the electric trolling motor is the most important piece of equipment. It allows an angler to position his boat precisely for best casting.

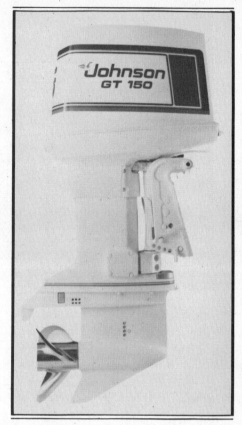

operate the 12/24-volt motor on one battery (12 volt) or both (24 volts).

The maximum amount of thrust available from 12-volt motors is a little over thirty pounds, while the bigger 12/24-volt models can produce as much as sixty. For boats up to and including sixteen feet in length, most 12-volt motors producing twenty-one pounds or better are adequate. Larger boats, though, will require the 12/24-volt motor.

There are some misconceptions concerning the 12/24-volt systems, but they are superior to the 12-volt models. A 24-volt system offers more power when you need it and amperage draw is lower; up to fifty percent of that of a high-thrust 12-volt system. It also is more reliable, because the motor isn't working as hard as in a 12-volt system. If there is a drawback, it is in the extra weight and cost of the second battery.

How your motor is wired can affect performance. Too small a wire can rob power and many bass boat makers now use 6-gauge wire to connect the motor to the battery instead of the previously used 10 gauge. The difference in efficiency between these two wire sizes can be as much as six pounds of thrust if you're running twenty feet of wire to connect the motor to your battery.

The trolling motor circuit should be fused or breakered. The Coast Guard says it must be done within eighteen inches of the batteries. This is to prevent a fire in case of a short or overload within the circuit. Manual reset breakers are a better bet than fuses; they are more effecient and reliable. You should not confuse the circuit breaker with the breaker switch installed in many of the better trolling motors. The latter is intended only to protect the motor head in case of an overload.

The other critical component in the trolling motor system is the battery and this is where most trolling motor problems can be traced. Marine batteries are one of the most commonly overlooked components in a modern fishing rig, but also are one of the most important. Without them, trolling motors don't run, engines don't start, electronics stay silent and, if you need to do a little bailing, you had better have a bucket, because your bilge pump works off them as well.

Considering that the day literally starts and ends with a battery, it's amazing that these devices are so often taken for granted, improperly chosen or incorrectly maintained.

A battery is nothing more than an electro-chemical device used for the storage and dispensing of energy. It does not produce energy, but simply dispenses whatever energy is stored within the case. You could compare it to a five-gallon bucket; put five gallons of water in and you can later take five gallons out. But, when it's empty, you have to add five gallons before you can remove it again.

This storage system works due to the electron flow between two different types of metals when submeerged in a solution of electrolyte — commonly called battery acid — within the battery case. Most often, a 12-volt battery is a

A properly fitted trailer makes launching, recovering a boat simple, even if by yourself. The modern drop-axle trailer allows a boat to be driven on/off by one man. Author insists it's as easy as parking car in garage.

grouping of two-volt cells connected together in series within the case. Each cell functions as an individual entity, but the combined voltage of all the cells produces the total output.

If an individual cell goes bad, the total output of the battery — its ability to deliver and store energy — suffers. The battery is not completely dead, but it won't function to the full capacity that the manufacturer intended. It will be much like a five-gallon bucket that can now only hold three gallons.

This is simple enough on the surface, but for boaters, one more aspect must be understood: There are two different types of batteries commonly used in boating applications. If you choose the wrong battery for the intended task, you can destroy it in short order, no matter how good a battery it was.

The two battery types commonly used are called SLI (starting, lighting, ignition — also referred to as crank batteries) and deep-cycle batteries.

The SLI batteries are exactly like the battery found in your automobile, although the better makers build stronger cases for marine models. Their job in a bass boat is the same; they produce a high-level burst of energy for a brief period to start the engine. They can also be used to power low-drain accessories (the draw of which is measured in milliamps) like depthfinders and running lights.

To generate the power needed to crank over a 150-horsepower engine, the SLI batteries are made with a large number of thin internal plates. The drawback, imposed by the current level of technology used by many manufacturers, is that these SLI batteries must quickly have the energy they expend replaced or the thin plates can warp and buckle.

With bass-boat-sized engines — 70 horsepower and up — the energy used to start the engine is replaced quickly by the engine alternator, just like your automobile. But if this type of battery is used to dispense energy over a long period of time without replacement, as would be the case when running a trolling motor, it will be damaged.

Deep-cycle batteries (so named because they are built to withstand the stress of being continually drawn down to below a fifty-percent charge rate, then recharged) are made with a smaller number of thicker plates.

This type of battery is a true reservoir of energy; put five gallons in and get five gallons out. This is the battery type you want to use to power your trolling motor, which can draw over thirty amps per hour, your livewell pumps (about two amps each) and your bilge pump, which draws about the same as your livewell pumps.

In most bass boats over seventeen feet, a three-battery setup is pretty much standard: one SLI to power the engine and two deep cycles to power the 12/24-volt trolling motor, as well as the pumps. Bass boats of sixteen feet or less can get by with one SLI and one deep cycle for the 12-volt trolling motor.

Chosing the proper battery type for the task will extend its life considerably, but there is one exception:

The AC Delco Voyager battery is a new generation product that can serve both purposes, although Delco may not specifically recommend it. These sealed, maintenance-free batteries utilize a different internal setup than conventional batteries and that allows them to handle both chores. I installed three of them in my Ranger over eighteen months ago — two M-27s for the trolling motor and one M-24 for the engine — and have yet to experience a problem. Considering that battery problems have been a recurring nightmare during my ten years as a guide, it speaks well for the Voyager batteries. In my opinion, they are the best marine batteries currently on the market.

For the angler who fishes from a smaller boat, say fourteen to fifteen feet and powered by a 25 to 35 hp outboard, with a fifteen-pound 12-volt trolling motor, one of the

Professional tournament anglers may travel as much as 250 miles per day by boat. Modern bass boat is largely a result of this need for a fast, stable, safe craft.

Below: Power trim feature makes raising engine in shallow water as simple as flicking a switch; an important item.

Voyager M-27s would handle all the power chores. Batteries are available in varying power capacities — kind of like two, three and five-gallon buckets. The lower-powered models are lighter and less expensive.

Determining how much power you need for your boat is fairly simple. Both crank and deep-cycle batteries have a rating system that will tell you how much power the unit will produce. By knowing how much power you require, you sometimes can get by with a less expensive model.

Crank batteries are rated by cold cranking ampere (CCA). The requirement for this rating is that the battery be cold-soaked until the temperature at the center of the battery reaches 0 degrees C (-18 degrees F). The battery then is discharged for thirty seconds at a rate which will provide a minimum of 1.2 volts per cell at the end of the 30-second test. The rate of discharge required to produce this target voltage is the CCA rating and is expressed in a number. This is the industry standard rating system for SLI batteries.

To determine how large an SLI battery you need, keep this in mind; it takes about one amp of power per cubic inch of engine displacement to provide adequate cold-starting power. In theory, a V-6 outboard could be started with a CCA 150 battery, but that's just the minimum figure and any boater who relies on "the minimum" for anything is going to wind up in trouble sooner or later.

When you add the drain caused by accessories, power trim and the possibility that your engine might be a temperamental starter, it's advisable to at least double that figure. Mercury Marine recommends that all of its engines from 35 hp up use a battery with a minimum rating of 350. Tournament pros and guides often opt for CCA ratings of 500, since it is far better to have more power available than you might need. Trying to rope-start a 150 horse outboard is about as much fun as bobbing for french fries!

Deep-cycle batteries have several rating systems which can cause some confusion. The old "20 amp/hr" rating is considered obsolete and not used by many manufacturers anymore. The "reserve capacity" rating system is more practical. This rating system is expressed in minutes and is a statement of the battery's ability to deliver a constant 25 amps of power at 80 degrees F without dropping below 1.75 volts per cell.

This is a good system for bass boaters, because most of the high-power trolling motors (on the 12-volt setting) will draw about 25 amps per hour at maximum draw. With this,

Large, well designed launching ramps make boating simple. Primitive ramps can handle smaller bass boats. Decision on type of boat to buy depends upon fishing waters.

Automatic livewell switch can assure your catch stays alive. It's indispensible for guides, tourney anglers.

you can tell just about how many hours of maximum draw you can expect from a battery in good condition. Five hours would get most anglers through an average day without any problems.

Hours of usable power (HUP) is the system used on the AC Delco batteries. It incorporates a table on the battery itself that tells the angler how many hours a fully charged battery in good condition will run at various amp draw rates. The Voyagers even have a built-in hydrometer (the Delco "Green Eye") that tells the state of the charge. By knowing that — and how much amperage your gear draws — you can determine whether you have enough power to get through the day.

To select deep-cycle batteries, a good starting point is to measure your power requirements. Add up the draw from your trolling motor on its maximum setting, plus the draw from livewells and other accessories on that circuit, then multiply that by five. Select a battery setup that will equal this power drain. Anglers who fish in rivers or in chronic windy conditions may want to exceed that figure.

How long your batteries will last depends greatly upon how well you maintain them. The worst thing you can do is to fail to recharge them after each trip.

"When a battery is discharged to any degree," says John Owens of AC Delco, "sulfation begins inside on the plates. The longer that is allowed to continue before the battery is recharged, the more difficult it will be to return that battery to its full capacity. If you go fishing on Sunday and wait until the next weekend to recharge it, it won't be long before that battery will no longer accept a full charge. Then you won't be getting all the power you paid for."

A 10-amp automatic charger will bring any battery commonly used by boaters up to a full charge overnight and it's a simple way to prolong the life of your battery.

Other causes of premature battery failure, as they apply to non-maintenance-free batteries, include improper electrolyte levels. Liquid often is lost during charging and, if it is not replaced and kept at the proper level, the plates will be damaged. Corrosion caused by escaping gas during charging also can damage terminals and connections. This must be removed periodically with a mild solution of baking soda and water, exercising great care to see that none of the solution enters the battery where it will neutralize some of the electrolyte and cause further power loss. This is a messy job and one reason why maintenance-free batteries are so popular.

Prior to installing the Voyagers, I never had been able to get a conventional battery to last twelve months. But after 18 months, my Delcos still are going strong. They cost

Even with section of the hull cut away and removed, the Ranger bass boat still is afloat. This manufacturer has been an industry innovator in safety features, as well as in practical areas concerning fishing ease, comfort.

more initially, but since my business requires I be on the water and fully operational, I've found that, in the long run, they are the cheapest batteries I can buy.

Improper storage also can shorten battery life and the biggest culprit here is heat which will cause the battery to discharge.

"For prolonged storage, such as the off-season, we recommend the battery be brought to a full state of charge, then stored in a cool place," says Owens. "Cold won't hurt, since a fully charged battery will not freeze. But heat will accelerate the discharging process and can shorten the life of the battery."

It's also good policy to check battery connections and terminals periodically for corrosion and make sure your wiring, switches and breakers are in good shape. All of these will help ensure that the power you purchase is the power you will get.

There are a few other items you might want to consider installing on your bass boat to make your fishing trips easier and safer. Electronic accessories will be covered in the following chapter, so we won't dwell on them here.

Kill Switch: This is nothing more than a quick release switch connected to the engine control box on one side and the operator of the boat on the other, using a cord. The function of this device is to shut off the engine instantly in the event the operator is thrown from the controls.

Should the driver be thrown from the controls without this device, the boat will invariably begin to run in tight circles because of the prop torque on the motor. Bass boats can — and have — run down and literally chopped to pieces drivers who were thrown into the water because of a collision with an object or just from an encounter with a large boat wake. Most makers of bass-boat-sized engines include this as standard equipment and the cord clips right onto a belt loop or lifejacket D-ring. It's the cheapest and easiest form of insurance you can get. It's also a mandatory requirement in any reputable tournament.

Foot Throttle: This is an after-market accessory that replaces the hand throttle with a foot-activated type. This allows the driver to keep both hands on the wheel and is an excellent safety feature. I personally feel they should be made mandatory on any boat capable of speeds in excess of 55 mph. They greatly improve the driver's ability to control the boat at high speed.

Anchor Reels: These small spring-loaded reels mount inside the gunnels of the boat and hold forty feet of one-

Efficient fishing craft need not fall into high-speed stereotype. This 17-foot Ranger Fisherman is versatile, an eminently practical fishing machine that sells for a great deal less than the cost of a full-blown bass boat.

quarter-inch line. When you want the line, you just pull out what you need. They are great for anchor line and for tying up the boat. They keep loose line off the deck and neatly stowed.

Livewell timers: These are variable switches that can be installed in the dash and allow the angler to have his livewells turned on automatically at predetermined intervals. For guides, who must keep live bait alive, and tournament anglers who will be penalized for dead bass, they're the greatest thing since spinnerbaits!

Rod Tie-downs: Rod Savers are Velco strips that screw to the front deck and allow you to strap your rods down securely when running. A bungie cord and two screw-in eyelets will do the same thing. They're cheap, but if you've ever watched a $150 rod and reel sail over the side after hitting a wake, you'll never be without them.

Automatic bilge pump switch: A float device installed in the bilge that automatically turns on your bilge pump when the bilge water reaches a certain level. A handy little device that can prevent some potentially serious situations.

There is a host of other minor accessories that one can add to a bass boat to make life more pleasent. For that matter, there are enough accessories on the market for an angler to make a comfortable bass fishing craft out of a variety of boats. One certainly doesn't need a bass boat to be an efficient bass angler.

My first "bass boat" was a wide, fifteen-foot skiff with a Johnson 50-horse engine. I purchased a couple of pedestal seats and screwed them onto the deck, added a trolling motor and battery, laid in some marine carpeting, a Humminbird flasher and made a livewell out of the one dry storage compartment with a bilge pump and a piece of drilled PVC pipe for a spray bar. It wasn't fancy or fast, but it caught bass and earned enough money in guide fees to allow me to purchase the Ranger I run today.

Smaller craft of this type, while not quite up to the image of the modern bass boat, often can be ideal for certain situations. In fact, a growing number of my fellow guides now are running two boats. The first is a full-sized bass boat used on larger waters, while the second is a smaller, lighter craft, that allows them to fish small, out-of-the-way lakes where larger boats cannot be launched.

This goes along with the basic philosophy that a bass boat should be a craft that takes you to the fish, then provides a stable, efficient platform from which to catch them.

CHAPTER 6

ELECTRONICS FOR BASS

Modern Technology Provides Anglers
With In-Depth Information

Left: Few pro anglers rely on one depthfinder. Two usually are employed on the console, a third in the bow. (Above) New Fencolor CLC with split screen feature indicates the strength of signal by employing several different colors.

KNOWLEDGE IS one of the keys to bass fishing success. But knowledge by itself is useless, unless the angler has the means to apply it to his or her fishing. It does little good to know bass might be relating to outside bends in creek channels, if one lacks the means to find those channels.

Of all the sports we pursue, fishing can be one of the most complex, because we must enter a foreign environment to do it. We can see what lies above the surface and, with polarized glasses, we can even penetrate the depths to a small extent. By looking at the contours of the above-water terrain we often can even make some educated guesses as to what it might look like below.

But without an effective means of actually seeing what lies in the bass's world, we are just guessing at best.

Determining depth, depth changes, bottom composition, the nature of submerged objects — sometimes, even oxygen levels, water temperature and pH levels — can be advantageous to the bass fisherman. A deer hunter who walked through the woods blindfolded would have little chance for success. So, too, would the angler who has little idea of what lies below the surface.

Serious anglers often rely heavily on electronic equipment. In fact, it has been said in jest (although there may be considerable truth in the statement) that the modern state-of-the-art bass boat sports more sophisticated electronics than a World War II destroyer!

Today's angler has at his disposal a wide range of electronic accessories to aid him in his task of finding bass. Sophisticated depth-finding equipment that not only provides depth information, locates thermoclines and even spots individual bass and baitfish, is as close as the angler's nearest sporting goods store. Available equipment will also determine the oxygen levels of the water being fished, the pH levels, the temperature; it can even determine the color of the lure most visible to bass under the water clarity and light penetration conditions existing at the time.

Which of the current electronic fishing aids an angler chooses to use should be based upon an understanding of precisely what information they will give him and how important that information might be to him. One of the most important pieces of equipment in that respect is a depthfinder.

Depth-finding equipment: Knowing how deep you caught your last bass may help you catch the next one. On the other hand, knowing how deep you didn't catch a fish may help you eliminate unproductive water. With the exception of the electric trolling motor, no single piece of bass'n equipment is as useful as a good sonar unit.

Today's depth-finding equipment is divided into these basic categories: paper graph, video sounders and the grandaddy of them all, the flasher. Each has advantages over the other and disadvantages as well. But, they all operate on the same basic sonar principle.

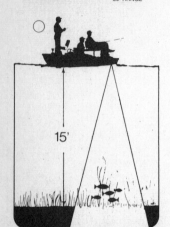

30' RANGE

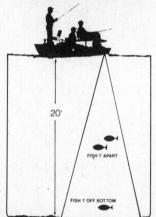

TOO MUCH SUPPRESSION 60' RANGE

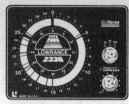
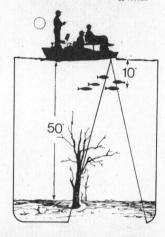

60' RANGE

Courtesy of Lowrance Electronics

Sound waves travel through water approximately five times faster than through air: about 4800 feet per second. This speed can vary slightly with the density of the water — a function of salinity or temperature — but it doesn't vary enough to make much of a difference.

"When a transducer sends a signal through the water at a known speed," explains Robert Choi, vice president of operations at Grace Technology, Incorporated, and one of the designers of the new Fenwick Fencolor CLC depthfinder, "the distance the signal travels to the object and the time it takes the reflected echo of that signal to be picked up by the transducer can be measured. From this, we can determine the precise depth of the object."

Every depth-finding device on the market operates in essentially the same manner; a transducer is mounted (either in the water itself or affixed to the bottom of the boat inside the hull) to shoot a signal straight down below the boat. The transducer both sends the signal and collects the return echo. The transducer is connected to the display unit by a cable and the information received from the transducer is fed into the unit, which interprets the information and displays it on a screen for the angler to read.

The major difference among depth-finding units is in how they display the information and how quickly they do it. Both of these have a direct bearing on how useful the device will be to the angler under certain conditions.

"The paper graph," says Steve Schneider of Lowrance, makers of the X-16 Graph unit, which is considered to be one of the best freshwater units on the market, "has the best ability and capability of any sonar device available to anglers to show individual fish."

Indeed, among professional anglers, the paper graph is considered the most detailed of all depth-finding equipment commonly used by sport fishermen and it's a rare pro that doesn't have one available for use.

The paper graph, as its name implies, uses a carbon-

Electronics are becoming increasingly more complicated, but afford the fisherman knowledge of his situation.

impregnated paper as the display medium. Images are made upon the paper by a stylus, moving in response to the processed information coming from the transducer. These units are more delicate than other types, more expensive to purchase initially and more expensive to operate because of paper and stylus costs. In most cases, they are mounted on the boat's console and not used continuously. Another type of unit, either a flasher or LCD, is used as the basic depth-finding tool, with the graph being turned on only when a more detailed look at submerged structure is desired.

30' RANGE   30' RANGE   60' RANGE

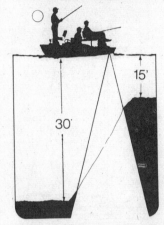

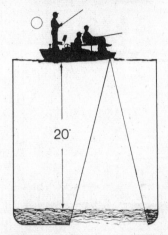

Lowrance 2330 gives readings as to situation at depths.

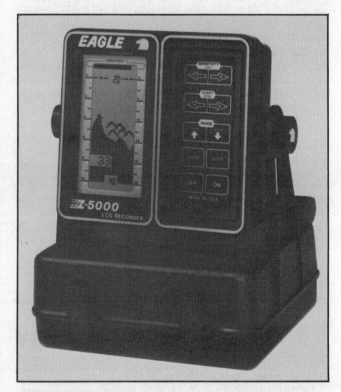

Eagle 5000 is another of those depthfinders that affords a pretty good idea of what kind of bottom is beneath you.

Many anglers feel the detailed information the paper graph supplies is not needed, if your fishing is confined to depths of ten feet or less. However, once an angler starts probing deeper water, the graph can be indispensible.

Getting the most from your graph, though, requires the angler to set it up properly.

"Regardless of the depth you're going to be in," says Schneider, "the first thing you want to do on any graph is to turn the sensitivity up to about the 2:00 position or about three-quarters of full strength.

"Getting the proper amount of sensitivity is critical. If you don't have enough, you will probably get a bottom reading. The bottom is almost always going to give you a good echo, even with low sensitivity. But, you won't know what you're missing if you only have enough sensitivity to read the bottom.

"The tendency," Schneider adds, "is to assume that, if you are getting a bottom reading, you have the unit set up right — and that's not correct. This is one of the biggest problems with new graph users and one reason why some of them become disenchanted. There are lots of things down there for them to see — far more than they might imagine — but they won't pick them up without the right amount of sensitivity."

The easiest way to be certain you have cranked in enough power to pick up individual fish and baitfish schools is to use what is called the second bottom echo or "double echo" as a guide. Turn the unit on and establish a bottom reading on the depth scale appropriate for the depth you are fishing. Then set in a lower depth limit twice that of the present depth and increase the sensitivity until you get a bottom reading at twice the real depth. This means there is sufficient signal strength to be reflected off the bottom, then off the bottom of the boat, back to the bottom, then back up to the transducer. Once the double echo is achieved, you can return to a shallower scale and be certain you have enough sensitivity set in to pick up anything between the boat and the bottom.

"The gray line feature is another one that is not always being utilized properly," feels Schneider. "Here, you want to start at the lowest possible power level and increase the power until you just get a distinctive differentiation in the

60' RANGE

30' RANGE

60' RANGE

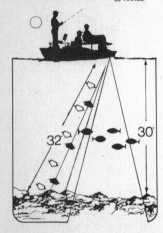

32' 30'

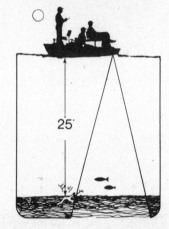

25'

30'

60' RANGE

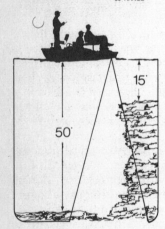

15'

50'

60' RANGE

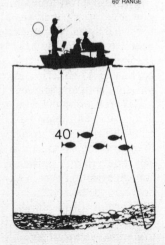

40'

gray line. You want a clear dividing line between black and gray at the top and bottom of the paper, but not a wide line.

"Once you have a clear but narrow gray line, you can use it as an indication of bottom composition. The gray line will get thinner with a soft or mucky bottom because only the strongest signals will be reflected from this. Rock, hardpan, or hard sand will reflect much more of the signal and the gray line will get wider.

"The gray line also can be used as a relative size indicator of gamefish or the degree of compactness in a school of baitfish," he continues. "A fish arch that has gray in it is a large fish. For a signal to gray line, it must be significantly stronger in its return strength than a standard signal and that means it must be reflected from a dense object. If a school of baitfish gray lines, it then is known to be a tightly compacted school of bait."

The graph's ability to show individual gamefish has made it a favorite for anglers who routinely fish deeper off-shore waters. Experienced users also can get an idea of how large the fish is and whether or not the fish is active enough to be caught!

"Graphs have the best ability to show fish," explains Schneider, "and that seems to be what people want to see. But, people shouldn't let the fish arch become an obsession, because in many cases, the unit will not display fish as the classic arch.

"In order for the unit to show fish as distinct arches, the fish has to be stationary and the boat must pass over it. Fish are seldom stationary. And they may be at the outside edge of the cone angle of the transducer or moving in and out of the signal that's transmitted as the boat passes over them.

"Actually," Schneider adds, "one of the most exciting pieces of graph paper isn't the classic arch, but rather a long 'streak.' This indicates a fish that is moving quickly and probably is feeding. Many deep water anglers won't

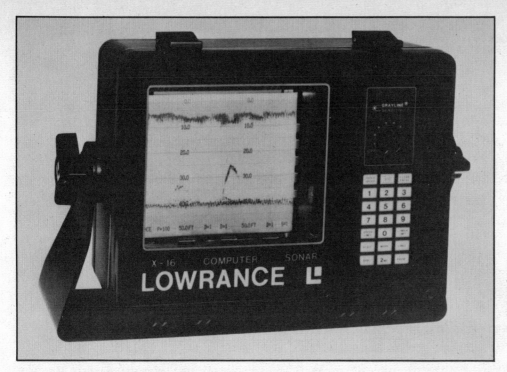

Paper graph on Lowrance's X-16 locates fish and, in many cases, indicates the size and whether they are actively feeding. Many of the pros favor this model.

waste time on a bunch of fish that are holding stationary on deep structure, but will look for active schools, since they are much easier to catch."

Determining the difference between active and non-active fish requires some experience with the graph, as does determining the fish's size.

"There are ways to tell the sizes of the fish from the arch," notes Schneider, "under some circumstances, but not all. The width of the arch from right to left on the paper isn't important in this respect. That's a function of boat speed and how much of the fish is in the signal cone. For example, a ten-pound striper at ten feet may only be in the signal cone for a second and the image is recorded in that time. A bluegill at twenty feet, though, may be in the cone for much longer and it will naturally show as a bigger, longer arch.

"You get your best size information from the up-and-down size of the arch and any gray line that might be present in it. The width of the arch from top to bottom is a close measurement of the depth of the fish from dorsal fin to belly. Here's where the zoom feature comes in handy. Suppose you mark some fish at twenty-six feet. You can zoom into the twenty-five- to thirty-foot range, divide your depth markings down and actually measure the thickness of those fish to within one inch. Another important factor is how much gray line is in the arch. A big bluegill may have the same measurements (depth) as a three-pound bass, but because it is thinner (less dense), the chances of having any gray line in there are remote.

"Familiarity with the water and the fish species also plays a role," concludes Schneider. "Depending upon the structure, time of year, et cetera, it won't take somebody long on his home water to get an idea of the size of the fish he's seeing on the paper."

The paper graph has become an indispensible tool for angers who regularly ply deeper water. Its ability to dis-play fish and draw an accurate picture of the bottom structure is among the best of any depth-finding equipment and it's easily interpreted with only a little practice. It is, however, being challenged by a new breed of depth-finding equipment.

Video recorders: A fairly recent innovation, the new video units offer many of the paper graph's advantages, without some of the disadvantages. These units fall into two distict types: liquid crystal displays and CRT (cathode ray tube) displays. Reasons for their widespread acceptance are ease of operation, durability, lack of moving parts to clean or break and no need for paper or stylus replace-

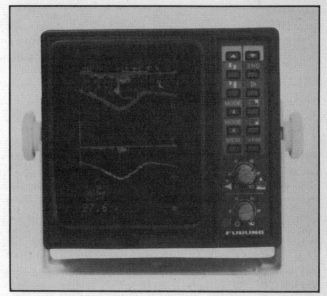

New generation of video sounders like this state-of-the-art Furuno model are sophisticated depth-finding devices that use amber-color displays visible in bright sunlight.

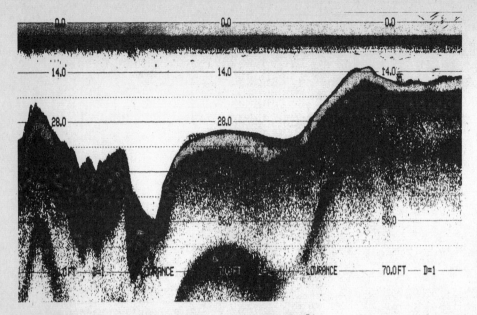

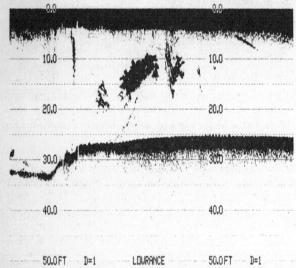

A loosely packed school of baitfish — in this instance, shad — is shown on graph made on Lake Mead, Nevada.

"The key to getting graph-quality resolution," says designer Robert Choi, "is in getting the size of the individual pixels (or light sources) small enough to give that resolution. There's a point of diminishing returns there as well; if too small, they're hard to read."

Another problem that has plagued these units is that a pixel only has one level of illumination; like a light bulb it is either on or off. While a paper graph can print intermediate shades of gray to denote the strength of the signal, a black and white LCD cannot. When shooting through submerged vegetation, the unit often will display the top of the vegetation in the same signal strength as the bottom, making differentiation difficult.

Determining fish size can be equally tough, since large pixels and lack of gray line tended to show fish of widely varying sizes in the same manner. Despite these drawbacks, however, they remain viable tools for the angler and are being improved rapidly.

One of the greatest enhancements has been the introduction of liquid crystal units incorporating more than one color in their display. The new Fencolor CLC is one such unit. Bottom contours are displayed in green, while anything not attached to the bottom is displayed in yellow. I have one of these bow-mounted on my Ranger bass boat and am pleased with its performance.

Another color unit is the Humminbird 41D, which uses red dots within the black display to highlight larger fish. All of the current units of this type feature automatic operation. The user simply turns on the power and the unit selects the sensitivity settings. Manual operation is a feature available on the better units, as well, allowing the user to control the sensitivity himself.

I often leave my Fencolor in automatic for normal use, switching to manual when I want a more detailed look at bottom structure. You will also find such features as zoom ranges, depth alarms, bottom tracking, and more on the better models.

As stated, CRT units are standard equipment on many commercial saltwater boats and have been for years. Using a cathode ray tube, just like your TV, they can paint a detailed picture of what is below your boat. Their biggest

ment. Also absent is the need to interpret the signal, as is required with the flasher.

Although CRT units have been in common use among saltwater anglers for years, the first of these new video units to make a hit on the bass market was the liquid crystal display. They painted a graph-like picture that was easy to understand and, while they in no way matched the fine detail resolution of the graph (and even the newest, most advanced liquid crystal units still don't), they were easy to use; for many applications, an improvement over the flasher.

They met with mixed emotions among professional anglers. In effect, they bridged the gap between the graph and the flasher, but failed to equal performance in several key areas. That's still true today, although video technology is advancing so rapidly that it may not be true in three or four years.

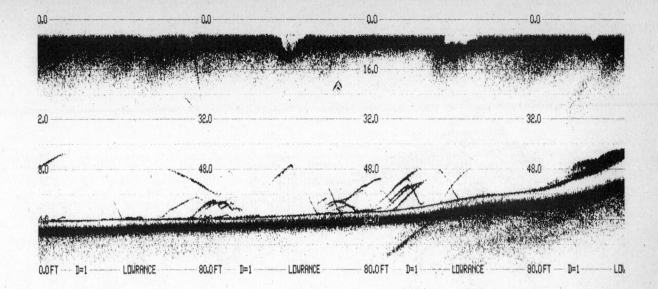

A paper graph does not always show fish as distinct arches. These 'streaking' fish are highly active stripers. The elongated streaks on the graph indicate moving fish. Five stripers were taken from school by author, companions.

drawback for use in freshwater fishing is that the CRT, just like your TV set, is not easy to see in bright, direct sunlight. One manufacturer, however, is changing this.

Furuno long has been a leader in sophisticated depthfiner equipment for the saltwater market. In fact, the first fish ever "found" on a sportfishing depthfinder didn't show up on Carl Lowrance's first flasher; it was marked on a Furuno paper graph in 1946! Since then, the firm has concentrated heavily on the commercial saltwater market, but is now bringing their technology to the bass fisherman.

I have a Furuno FMV-602 video mounted on the console of my Ranger and have found it an astonishing piece of equipment. Targets are shown in distinct amber shades to denote return signal strength; a bright Echo feature enhances targets lying close to the bottom and the six-inch CRT screen makes an easy-to-read display. The unit has a wide variety of depth ranges from 0-15 feet down to 2000 feet and a quick-zoom feature to get an even closer look.

One of the most advanced features on the unit, though, is the ability to use a wide beamed 50 KHZ signal, or the more detailed 200 KHZ signal from the same transducer! The unit also has a split-screen capability.

With this, you can program it to look into the bottom structure on the lower one-third of the screen — display either 50 KHZ or 200 KHZ on the upper two-thirds of the screen — split the screen into two equal parts and display both 50 and 200 KHZ signals or program them to display almost any combination of six different modes.

Furuno claims there has never before been a depthfinding device like this and I'm inclined to agree with them. It is quite a piece of equipment. And while its definition isn't quite equal to that of a paper graph, it's more than close enough for me.

Some video CRT models from Furuno are priced about the same as a quality liquid crystal unit and other manufacturers can be expected to enter the CRT field with comparably priced units.

The first commonly used electronic depth-finding unit

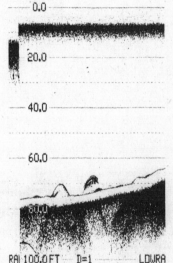

Gray line immediately to right of small hump on the bottom indicates a large fish. Dense object is required to produce such a gray line effect.

was the little Green Box flasher introduced by Carl Lowrance. Today, they are made by Lowrance, Humminbird, Sitex and others.

These operate like any of the previous units, with the operator setting in the sensitivity required to achieve a solid reading. Unlike the others, they display their information in a series of colored bands of varying widths: the thicker the band, the larger the object.

This requires interpretation on the part of the angler and, unlike the other units, there is little time to study the display. The flickering bands are here one second and gone the next. Of all the depth-finding equipment on the market, the flashers are the most difficult to become proficient with.

One would think these factors would spell their doom when compared to the other units, but they haven't. In fact, among many pros, the flasher still is considered the most important piece of electronic equipment in the boat!

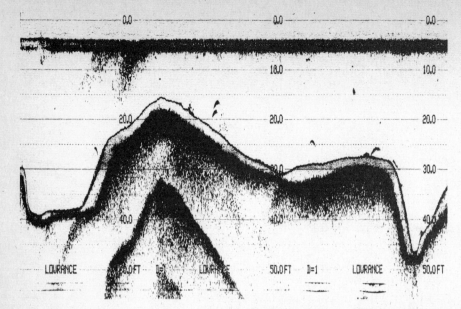

The paper graph can offer an amazing amount of info. This section, made on Lake Mead, shows baitfish school at upper left; several small fish that may be bass at bottom of the structure; one larger fish is near small bottom object in the lower right-hand corner.

Classic "fish arches" suspended over the bottom structure don't always indicate active bass. For a fish to show as arch, it must be stationary as the boat passes over it. Stationary fish may be inactive.

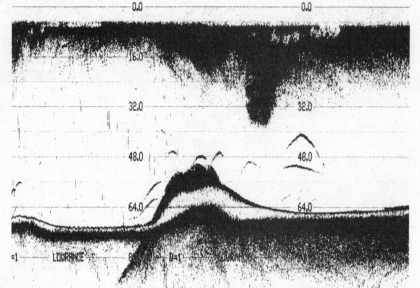

The presence of gray line in the baitfish school at upper left indicates it is most compacted. This is response to a threat to baitfish. Streaking fish are at lower right, arched fish below the baitfish. This may be what fish are fearful of.

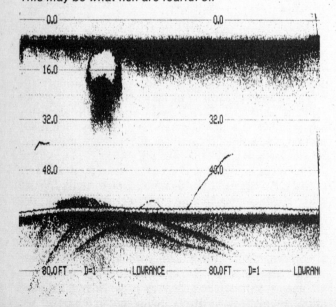

The reasons for this are fairly simple. First, flashers are inexpensive when compared to even the least costly liquid crystal unit. Secondly, they are the fastest of all units when it comes to displaying information. While a good liquid crystal unit may send, receive and display ten pulses a second, a flasher may do 120!

The sudden drop-off you passed over at 50 mph may be twenty or more yards behind you by the time an LCD or CRT unit gets around to displaying it, but the flasher tells you right then and there.

As well, all flashers have the ability to shoot through submerged vegetation to give a true bottom reading and show the height and density of the vegetation. Only the better videos like the Fencolor and Furuno will do this. This has made flashers an indispensible tool for anglers fishing lakes loaded with hydrilla or milfoil.

Because of its ability to immediately display depth changes, the flasher is one of the best choices for navigating strange water. For example, I have a Humminbird Super Sixty flasher mounted on the console next to the Furuno. Most

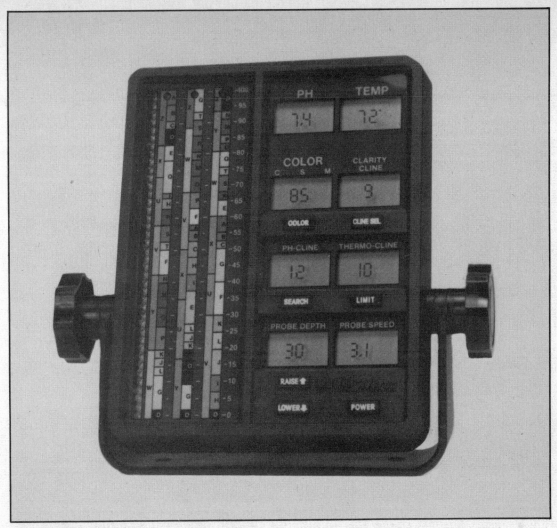

Lake Systems Multi-C-Lector combines the functions of pH meter, temperature gauge and Color-C-Lector into one compact package. The unit provides info at the touch of a button.

often I run the Humminbird, using the Furuno when I want a detailed look at specific bottom structure. When fishing from the bow deck, I operate the Fencolor, which also displays water temperature by means of the temperature probe built into the trolling motor-mounted transducer. It's an effective information system.

Many anglers operate with several sonar units on the boat; some using a graph on the console, a small in-dash flasher there as well and another flasher on the bow. For an angler who just wanted to get by with one unit, a good choice would be a quality liquid crystal unit mounted on the console on a swivel base that could be turned to the bow for viewing while fishing.

Regardless of the type of unit being used, they all operate on the same sonar principle and it is critical for the performance of the unit that the transducer be mounted correctly. Given the variety of transducer types and mounting positions available — as well as the differences between fiberglass and aluminum or wood-hulled boats — this is a step that should be done by an experienced marine dealer, although detailed transducer mounting instructions are included with virtually every type of unit sold.

It is also important that the angler understands precisely what portion of the water his transducer is showing him.

"Regardless of the type of unit used," explains Steve Schneider, "they all use a transducer and there is only a certain angle of coverage, depending upon the depth. For example, at ten feet you may only be looking at a three-foot circle and, at five feet, you see only half of that!"

To figure out what you are looking at, divide the depth by a factor number. For a wide-angle transducer (variously called 16-, 20- or 32-degree transducers, referring to the angle of the signal beam), use a factor of three: in thirty feet of water divide the depth by the factor to arrive at a ten-foot circle of coverage beneath the boat. At fifteen feet, it would be a five-foot circle. A narrow-angle transducer (about eight degrees) will use a factor of seven: at the same thirty-foot depth you would be reading a 4.28-foot circle.

Wide-angle transducers are generally the most effective in the depth ranges normally encountered by bass fishermen, but some anglers who regularly fish deep water will mount both a narrow- and wide-angle transducer with a switch box to determine the one in use. When trying to pinpoint the exact location of a drop-off in forty feet of water,

The simple flasher is considered important by professional bass anglers. Speed of its info processing with ability to shoot through submerged vegetation warrants continued use despite recent advances in other depthfinder types.

in relation to the boat, shifting to the narrow angle in effect gives the angler a "second zoom" feature. This can be important when vertical jigging, since it can pinpoint the exact spot the boat must be to put the lure on the structure.

"One of the most useful pieces of equipment you can have on a bass boat is a temperature gauge," says Rick Clunn. His thoughts on the subject are echoed by most pros.

Water temperature is a factor that affects bass activity levels throughout the year, but it can be highly critical in the winter and spring. Water temperatures across a lake are not constant. For example, shallow, dark-bottomed areas will often warm faster in the spring and tend to hold more heat in the winter. Bass in an area like this will tend to be more active and catchable than bass in cooler areas.

Outside influences, such as inflowing tributaries or underground springs, can create small pockets of warmer or cooler water that may spark increased activity from the bass present. Short of continually trailing your hand in the water over the side of the boat (which does make fishing awkward), the only way to become aware of these situations is with a temperature gauge.

The most common type is a dash-mounted unit that utilizes a probe attached to the transom. Digital readouts are the trend in these, making temperature levels quick to determine at a glance.

I can recall many times where my Lowrance gauge led me to good catches of bass during both the spring and mid-summer seasons by pointing out the presence of underground springs in a particular area. On one occasion, I was idling across a grassy flat on Florida's Lake Toho during the late fall when the gauge dropped from 83 to 72 degrees. In Florida, that indicates an underground spring, since most exit at that temperature. That temperature change wasn't important during the fall, since cooling waters already had scattered the bass. But I marked its location on my map and returned during a February tournament to land three big bass from that small pocket of what was now "warmer" water.

One of my favorite summer schooling bass holes was located in a similar manner. It's a sand bar in Dunn's Creek that has a spring flowing from it. Many largemouth and striped bass stack up there during the scorching summer months because of the cooler water. Without a tem-

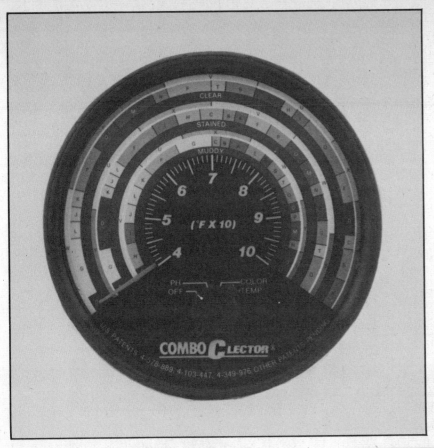

Left: This combination meter measures pH levels, as well as the colors most visible to bass. (Below) Color-C-Lector meter functions like a photographer's light meter. Measuring light levels below the surface, it determines what lure colors will be most visible to the bass under light and clarity conditions.

perature gauge, I probably would never have found it.

PH Meters: Utilizing a meter to measure the pH levels of the water to determine its suitability to hold bass is a relatively new development in bass fishing. As such, it has its proponents and detractors. I will be the first to admit my experience in this area is limited, but some excellent material on the subject has been prepared by Lake Systems Division (315 E. South Street, Mount Vernon, MO 65712). This explains the basic concept far better than I can.

FACTORS INFLUENCING FISH BEHAVIOR

Many fishermen ask about pH; wanting to know what it is, is it important, is it constant in most lakes, what causes it to change, how does it affect fish, will it cause fish to "turn on" or "turn off," and will it cause fish to move.

PH is a measurement of the acid/base relationship of liquids. The scale goes from 1 to 14, with 7 being the neutral point. Anything below 7 is acid and anything above 7 is basic, or alkaline. The farther away from 7 the reading is, the stronger the acid or base solution.

PH is important in any lake, though most lakes do not have a constant pH. All species are affected, although some slow-moving bottom-feeding fish, such as catfish, seem to have a wider tolerance for extremes than more active species.

The sun has a significant influence on pH by causing photosynthesis in aquatic vegetation. Light causes the vegetation to take carbon dioxide (which in solution is a weak acid) out of the water and put oxygen and calcium carbonate (a base) into it. This causes the pH to go up fast in the local area where the vegetation is concentrated. That is why most fishermen think fishing is good early in the morning and late in the evening, but not good during the day. That is because most people fish cover along the shoreline. If there are shoreline mosses or grasses, the big fish may be there feeding early and late, but when the sun gets up high, the pH

goes up and they head for deep water (usually following migration routes like old creek channels, bar ditches, etc.). So, to be effective during the day, take up structure fishing. Yes, some small fish will stay near the shore because they are not as affected by pH fluctuations as the more mature, bigger fish are, and they are not as brave about leaving their home turf.

The sun also causes algae and plankton to photosynthesize, which runs the pH up in large areas, possibly all over the lake. The fish will move away from it if they can. If algae or plankton is thick on the surface, the fish will probably go deep.

Rain also has a quick influence on pH. Moisture condensing and fall-

Modern bass boats are required to have more electronics than a World War II destroyer. (Right) Basic pH meter from Lake Systems helps anglers determine whether the waters they are fishing can hold bass activity. This can be an asset when angler is choosing a lure.

ing through the air picks up carbon dioxide and forms a weak carbonic acid. Normal rainfall will have a pH of 5.3 to 5.6 without the influence of industrial or auto pollution. Polluted air has sulfur dioxide in it which mixes with water to form sulfurous acid (acid rain) which can have a pH as low as 1.5, although it is rare that it would be that low. Rain falling directly into the water has its effect, plus the runoff water coming through all sorts of watershed areas can have an even greater impact. Freshly fertilized farmland, limestone deposits, forest land, etc., all have significant influence on pH in either direction

Another influence on pH is decaying vegetation. It is not only acidic, it is oxygen depleting. However, too much importance is given to oxygen levels by many fishermen, when the real key to fish behavior is pH.

Fish, like man, have a blood pH of 7.4. We air breathers are not so easily affected by the air, it doesn't have a pH. But fish get their oxygen from the water and live in this medium. Minor changes in pH affect the fish's ability to take oxygen out of the water. It affects the hemoglobin of their blood. If the pH is right, fish can get all the oxygen they need from oxygen-starved water. If the pH is too high or too low, they can't get enough oxygen from oxygen-rich water.

Fish prefer and are most active in pH ranging from 7.5 to 8.5 and will be active and aggressive between 7 and 9. Below 7 or above 9 they will be difficult to catch, if they can be found at all. Lures will have to be presented slowly and right to them.

The Environmental Protection Agency defines an oxygen level of five parts per million (ppm) or less as "polluted water." However, laboratory test have shown that, if the pH is between 7.5 and 8.5, fish can survive for over six hours in oxygen levels of less then one ppm, but if the oxygen level is five ppm and the pH below 7 or above 9, the fish will die in fifteen minutes. When you hear about fish kills because of low oxygen levels, you can bet the pH was bad, too.

Fish will move if the pH changes and they will stop, as if hitting a glass wall, if they encounter an unattractive pH change. If they cannot avoid bad pH water, they will become dormant (turned off), and if it doesn't improve, they may die.

A fourth factor affecting a pH change is season of the year. In winter the sun is lower, the water colder, algae and other aquatic vegetation are dormant, decay rates are low, farmers are not fertilizing fields — pH is relatively stable (photosynthesis stops at 47 degrees). Spring brings rain which washes nutrients and silt into the lakes. Since the lake water is still cold and the rainwater warm, the less dense runoff water flows out on the surface of the lake, hence the muddy-looking lakes in the spring. This causes a layering of water. You get the opposite layering in the summer, when water temperatures are reversed. Cool rain runs under the warmer surface water causing a murky layer at a low level. Surface water looks clear. The sun shining on different water clarities, plus

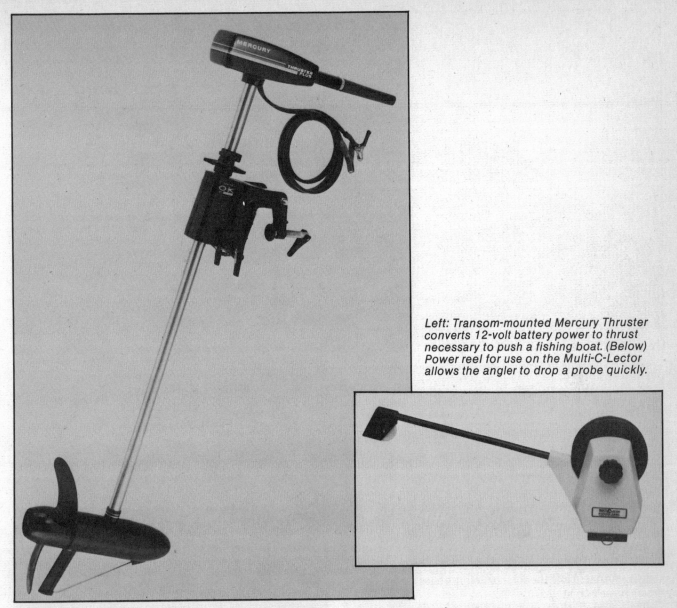

Left: Transom-mounted Mercury Thruster converts 12-volt battery power to thrust necessary to push a fishing boat. (Below) Power reel for use on the Multi-C-Lector allows the angler to drop a probe quickly.

algae blooms, also cause layering. With the Multi-C-Lector, this layering can be measured as a pH cline (breakline), clarity cline or thermocline. These various clines may or may not be at the same level.

Scuba divers report that a favorite place to hide, to ambush rough fish with their spear guns, is in thermoclines (one degree centigrade per meter, or roughly 2.5 degrees F per yard). The water above the thermoclines may be clear, but the water in it murky. Thus the body is hidden, only their mask is showing. This murkiness is probably because silt particles, at or near neutral buoyancy, settle on the more dense, colder water. In this example, a clarity cline and thermocline are together, although this isn't always the case. Big fish also hide in clarity clines so they can ambush their prey swimming above it. Thermoclines are usually found in the summer months and will yield good catches, if you fish at the upper levels. Knowledgeable fishermen often look for breaks between clear and stained or muddy water. Why? Because they hold fish.

PH clines are also horizontal layers where the pH change is significicant (two-tenths of a point per foot). Fish may be seen on a graph recorder below a pH cline, but they will be inactive and hard to catch. If you find a pH cline — and they are most common in the summer — you should fish at the upper level of it or shallower. Eliminate all of the water below it. PH clines are often fairly shallow — three to fifteen feet — while thermoclines are usually deeper — thirty feet or so.

An explanation for the presence of the pH cline and its value as a fishing location or depth, is that the penetration of sunlight, which is affec-

ted by the water clarity, causes photosynthesis in layers of phyto plankton. The photosynthesis causes the pH to change. The baitfish are there feeding on the plankton and the active gamefish are there feeding on the baitfish.

The order of priority for clines is pH first by a mile. If you can find a pH cline, that's the place to fish. Second choice would be a clarity cline and, if you can't find that, look for a thermocline. The new Multi-C-Lector will find and show you the depth of a primary or secondary pH cline, clarity cline and thermocline. It will also alert you to the presence of shears or vertical changes in pH, clarity or temperature, if your boat is moving forward with the probe down. These shears will probably be found if you move past a spring or a stream flowing into the lake or where there is a current within a lake.

The best way to look for an area of a lake that might have the best pH conditions is to give some thought to the factors that affect it as outlined above. Consider the weather, season, recent rain, surrounding area, sunshine, water depths, bottom conditions or materials, aquatic vegetation, algae, age of the lake, etc., then consider whether you are likely to find the best conditions near a shore or out a bit, at the lower end near the dam, at mid-lake or in the shallow upper end of the lake if on an impoundment.

PH will nearly always be a little higher at the surface than it is below. Use your pH guide to eliminate poor, unproductive water below 7, above 9, and below the pH breakline. If the entire lake is below 7, look for the highest pH you can find and fish there. If the entire lake is above 9, look

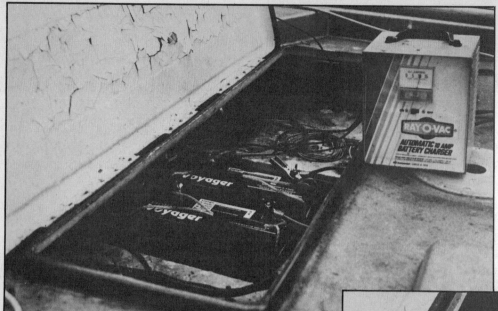

Left: Prompt recharging of marine batteries will aid in extending their life, bass authorities claim. (Below) Powerful 24-volt trolling motors require batteries be rigged in proper sequence.

for the lowest you can find and fish fairly deep because it is probably lower deeper.

Obviously, the factors that affect fish behavior are interrelated, and complicated. That's what makes fishing fun. It takes you away from all the other complications in life and gives you a new puzzle to solve.

Lake Systems is an industry leader in the manufacture of pH meters. They also caused one of the largest stirs the tackle industry has ever seen with the introduction of yet another meter: the *Color-C-Lector.*

This device functions much like a photographer's light meter in that it measures the amount of light available. It does so underwater, taking into account the water clarity levels existing at that time and place. This information then is translated into the color or colors a bass can see best under these conditions.

Being a relatively new tool, reactions have been mixed. Some swear by it, and some swear at it. My experience with the Color-C-Lector — which stays in my Ranger at all times, although it may not be frequently used — indicates it can be a valuable tool.

I particulary like the meter when I'm exploring new water, since it gives me a starting point in determining what colors might be most effective there. I developed some confidence in the meter the first day I got it by taking it out to some of my favorite spots on the St. Johns River. The day was cloudy and overcast and the two lures I had decided to fish where a spinnerbait and a plastic worm. My previous experience told me that, in the shallow cover I was fishing, a chartreuse spinnerbait — which would be fished at about two feet — and a red/shad worm — crawled over fallen trees in four feet — would be the most effective colors. They had worked well for years in similar situations and they caught fish that day.

Interestingly, before I started fishing I used the meter to see how it felt about my color choices. It agreed completely.

I spent the next few weeks trying to prove the meter wrong and I succeeded in doing so only once. It suggested a yellow plastic worm in the shaded area below a boat dock that I knew was holding fish. I rigged one up, fished for twenty minutes without a hit, then changed to the black and blue flake worm that had been producing for me under the dock. A few minutes later, I caught a four-pound bass, but that was the only time the meter let me down.

The meter is simple to use; just lower the probe over the side to the desired depth, flip the switch and read the color scale.

For some, it may be too simple. I recall a conversation with one outdoor writer who considered himself an expert on scientific bass'n. He stated that the meter was totally

The use of a trolling motor allows the fisherman to put his boat in proper position without frightening away the fish. But, to be certain all of this is going to work out to his advantage, he must be certain batteries are good.

useless. He based his statement on the fact that any quantitative measuring device that could not be calibrated by the user prior to use would not accurately measure. I thought about it for a minute and almost agreed with him, until I remembered that the light meters in my 35mm cameras have been delivering perfect exposures for years with little help from me.

The following from Lake Systems better explains how users can get the most from this new tool.

ADVANCED USE OF THE COLOR-C-LECTOR

Nine years of intense research by Dr. Loren G. Hill, chairman of the zoology department at the University of Oklahoma, went into determining that fish see much better than do humans. Their eyes gather more light and amplify it, allowing them to see over forty feet in relatively clear water, where we could see only ten to twelve feet. In stained water, where we can see two to four feet, fish can see to sixteen feet. In muddy water, where we can only see six inches or so, fish can still see three to five feet. They use sight almost one hundred percent in their selection of food. They may be influenced by sound, smell, texture and taste, but sight is their dominant sense.

Fish also see colors quite well and differently than humans. And they see colors differently in different water clarities and in different light levels. He found that some colors are completely invisible to the fish at certain times of day and/or in certain water clarities.

This is nature's way of protecting some species of forage fish; although

they are often highly visible, they become completely invisible or camouflaged during certain times of the day, in certain water clarities or during certain seasonal changes in their own color. If they remained visible to predator fish all of the time, they would have been consumed eons ago.

Dr. Hill also discovered which colors fish see best and which are more likely to trigger an aggressive, attack response. The culmination of Dr. Hill's research was the development of the Color-C-Lector by Lake Systems. Other devices have been marketed that claim to show fishing lure colors, but they are based on what the human eye sees. Obviously, the results cannot be effective because fish simply don't see the same colors the same way we do.

Since the operation of the Color-C-Lector is apparently simple, it is easy to overlook the subtleties of its use which can greatly expand its effectiveness in the hands of a skilled fisherman.

LEARN TO READ THE METER — The Color-C-Lector dial shows three scales — clear, stained and muddy. Each scale has a fluorescent band and a solid-color band. There are six fluorescent colors and twenty solids which are identified by the twenty-six letters of the alphabet. The last six letters (U,V,W,X,Y,Z) are the fluorescent colors. Becoming familiar with the colors in the three clarity scales will expand your knowledge of the Color-C-Lector. Take several minutes and simply look at the face of the meter and compare the positions of various colors on one scale with colors on the other two scales.

What the observant eye will see is some interesting combinations that show up more than once. For instance, silver (F) is found in combination with fluorescent yellow-orange (V) on both the clear and stained bands. Even on the muddy scale, silver (F) is not far from yellow-orange (V) and directly in conjunction with fluorescent orange (U). Similarly, the red hues (A,B,C) are almost in perfect alignment on the muddy and stained bands with a three-band matchup occurring in very low-light conditions for black (D) and in high-light conditions for fluorescent blue (Z). A fisherman learns quickly just which combinations of colors are most likely to turn up during a normal fishing day.

Bass Master Classic winner Charlie Reed knows that battery problems can be the cause of losing valuable fishing time in tourney.

GETTING THE RIGHT READING — *The most critical piece of information needed to use the Color-C-Lector is the depth where the fish are, which is the depth at which you should be taking your readings. With sonar, temperature and especially pH measuring instruments, anglers are able to depend on skill, not luck, to find the most likely depth for fish.*

Identifying the most productive fishing depth becomes even more crucial in muddy water where the primary (most visible) color can change quickly over relatively small changes in depth, due to rapid changes in light intensity. At times when it is difficult to establish a specific depth range for fish, using fluorescent colors is more important than it might be in clear water. Fluorescents radiate more light energy than solid colors and are visible to fish over a much broader range of light and clarity conditions, giving a built-in visibility "fudge factor."

Lower the probe slowly to take a reading. Occasionally, a clarity cline (an abrupt change in clarity) in deeper water can fool a fisherman. Instead of fishing in the clear water conditions indicated near the surface, you could be fishing in stained water at twenty feet. This clarity cline is indicated by a quick change in the rate of needle movement. As the probe is descending through clear water, the needle will move slowly to the left. But if it drops off rather quickly — at, say, 15 feet — you probably have entered a stained or muddy layer.

For example, if the needle points to the fluorescent yellow-orange (V) in clear water, and suddenly drops to fluorescent green (Y), most likely you have entered a zone of stained water where suspended sediment or an algae layer has changed the water clarity. In this situation, it is best to observe the position of the needle on the stained scales and change to fluorescent orange (U).

Another key technique when taking readings can be overlooked. To learn the best lure color to use you should lower the probe where you intend for your lure to land, not a long cast away. In other words, move up to the shoreline, cover or structure to be fished and take a reading there. If sitting in the sun, throwing your lure into the shade, take your reading on the shady side of your boat rather than the sunny side. If fishing surface lures, lower the probe to about three feet for your lure color reading. The fish will see your lure even in muddy water. Keep the probe off the bottom even in shallow water. The bottom may be silty and, if your probe stirs up the silt, it will get an erroneous light reading. Or, if it is on the bottom, it may fall over and get an erroneous reading.

COMBINING COLORS — *One of the best ways to enhance the effectiveness of the Color-C-Lector is to combine several colors on one lure. However, it is wise to combine the right colors.*

With only limited experience using the Color-C-Lector, the needle swings up to the right as light intensity increases during the morning hours and eventually holds in a general area on the scale throughout most of the day, (assuming, of course, that the water clarity and light conditions remain more or less consistent.) As a result, a number of color combinations show up frequently, regardless of which color band you may be using. This can make lure purchases much simpler.

During Dr. Hill's research, several colors were within mere percentage points of being as effective as the primary or most visible color. One test in muddy water showed bass could see non-fluorescent green (R) most clearly, correctly identifying this color ninety-eight percent of the time. The real eye-opener was that non-fluorescent red (A) and gold (E) rated just one percent behind green (R), the bass correctly identifying these colors ninety-seven percent of the time. On the Color-C-Lector, red

The smaller boats carrying 12-volt trolling motors and engines up to 40 hp can use a single deep-cycle battery.

(A), gold (E) and green (R) are adjacent to one another on the muddy scale for good reason.

Looking at the meter, imagine the needle is pointing to gold (E) on the muddy scale. Although fluorescent colors are visible over a broader range of light conditions, in this case, it is better to use the non-fluorescent. Why? Because fluorescent chartreuse (W) is just becoming most visible to the fish and does not reach optimum visibility until the needle points to the middle of the chartreuse color block (near the letter W). Similarly, when the needle is positioned at the other end of the color band, the fluorescent is becoming less visible and non-fluorescents should be used. In other words, the fluorescent color is preferred when the needle is near the center of the fluorescent band. When near the edge, the solid color should be the dominant lure color. However, a dash of the appropriate fluorescent color, regardless of where the needle is pointing on the band, should be included on most every lure.

CHANGING WATER CLARITIES — you may find it difficult to choose between two clarity scales or be working an area with changing water conditions. In such cases, combine the primary colors from both scales on the lure being used. While these situations may not arise frequently, there are times when it may be necessary to combine colors from all three clarity scales.

KEYING COLORS TO LURE TYPE — Another important consideration when choosing color patterns on factory lures, or when painting lures, is determining the most likely angle of attack of the fish. For instance, the key areas on surface plugs for the primary (most visible) color would logically be on the sides or belly where the fish attacking from below could see it best. On structure-bumping crankbaits, the primary color would be most visible on the back or on the sides, assuming the fish are picking the lure off as it scuttles along the bottom. A fisherman needs to visualize how it appears to the attacking fish and which parts of the lure are most visible under prevailing conditions.

Also, there is something to be said for subtlety. One school of thought holds that just a touch of the primary color on a lure provides added visibility without appearing too unnatural. Reasoning is that because of natural camouflage, predatory fish often get only a brief glimpse or flash of the intended victim. But there are times when gaudy baits make the difference by improving lure visiblity under poor conditions or triggering reaction strikes from otherwise inactive fish. Some personal experimentation is in order in deciding which situations demand a subtle approach and which ones call for "bells and whistles."

PLANNING AHEAD — As you gain experience with the Color-C-Lector, you will be able to forecast with surprising accuracy the most visible colors at lakes where you are familiar with the water clarity and fish-holding depths. At this level of expertise, you are combining solid fishing knowledge with the information gained from the Color-C-Lector to actually formulate an angling game plan. For instance, if you expect some first-light topwater and spinnerbait action to be followed by a plastic worm bite in deeper water, these lures (in appropriate colors) can be rigged up in advance. This saves valuable fishing time, adds more casts to your day and improves your overall angling efficiency. Of course, there will always be those times when abrupt changes in water or light conditions can invalidate even the best educated guesses.

When possible, it is wise to rig up lures, like spinnerbaits, without skirts. Then, should conditions be different than expected, it only takes an instant to choose a skirt in the proper color or colors.

The sophisticated array of modern electronics equipment provides the angler with a quick, accurate means to see and understand what is happening in the bass's world.

Of course, you can catch bass without it. Folks have been doing it for years. But, these tools can certainly make the angler's task easier.

CHAPTER 7

ACCESSORIES FOR BASS ANGLERS

A LOT of anglers don't pay much attention to accessory items when they consider the overall aspects of bass fishing. Rods, reels, lures and boats usually get a lot more attention than do such mundane items as line clippers, rainsuits and sunglasses.

But as professional guides and tournament fishermen have learned, these overlooked accessory items, as well as many others, can be of critical importance in the pursuit of their livelihood.

If it rains during a bass tournament, with thousands of dollars possibly on the line, they seldom call the event off and go to brunch! You fish it, even if it's snowing. And a cold, wet, shivering angler is not likely to be nearly as effective as one properly protected from the elements.

The same holds true of an angler who must spend ten minutes dipping through a poorly organized tackle box to find a specific lure. Professional anglers choose their tack-le boxes the same way a top-flight mechanic selects a tool box: a quality product with enough room to store items in an organized, easy-to-find manner.

Most good bass'n accessories fall into one of these two classes: They either allow the angler to function properly in a less than friendly environment or they help him utilize his time more efficiently. In either case, choosing the proper accessories can help make you a more effective bass fisherman. Here are a few items you might want to consider.

Tackle Boxes: Leading manufacturers of hard plastic tackle boxes are Fenwick/Woodstream, Plano and Flambeau. All make quality products and each has a varied product line. Each tackle box they make is "worm-proof," meaning the plastic used in the box's construction will not react adversely with the materials used in the manufacture of plastic worms to create a lumpy, fused mess if plastic worms are stored. This wasn't always the case, but those

Gauntlets, motorcycle helmet, snowmobile suit may keep the angler comfortable, but author recommends against the suit. See page 91 for explanation. (Right) Plastic battery boxes protect and prevent battery acid spills.

problems have been licked by the better manufacturers.

Tackle boxes can be had in a wide variety of sizes, capacities and compartment configurations. In general, they can be lumped into about eight different categories:

1. Satchel boxes are briefcase-type boxes that open to expose a compartment section that allows the angler quick access. Most feature adjustable internal compartments through the use of movable dividers. They can be single-sided or double boxes. These are popular boxes, since they are relatively small, compact and inexpensive, yet hold a large number of lures. They are excellent for plastic worms, jigs and Gitzits, since a large number of individual baits of a certain size and color can be in their own compartment, aiding in organization.

2. Multi-layered satchel boxes usually have a double lid, with smaller individual compartments within the lid, large main compartments below. These are for anglers who want a "travel" box that will carry a small selection of each lure type to fish in a variety of waters. My own travel box, one of the new Plano 1466 Phantom models, neatly stores a wide enough variety of lures to let me fish anywhere in the country, yet packs easily in a suitcase.

3. Drawer boxes are much like a chest of drawers, although a good bit smaller. These boxes feature a dropping front panel that allows access to a number of compartmented pull-out drawers. The number of drawers and

This weedless trolling motor prop helps electric motors slice through underwater vegetation. Author has found they can be utilized on many different electric motors.

arrangement of the compartments varies among manufacturers. For example, my Fenwick box has four large drawers, while other makes may have six or seven more shallow drawers. These are excellent for storing hard baits like crankbaits and topwater plugs and, depending upon drawer arrangement, can make a good all-around tackle box. They are handy in a boat, since it requires little space to open and get at the contents.

4. With hanging boxes, opening the lid affords access to a series of indented partitions where baits are hung, instead of stored on their sides. Originally made to hold spinnerbaits, this storage arrangement allows a far greater number of these baits to be carried than would be the case if they were laid on their sides, as well as helping to keep the rubber skirts separated. The larger models have become popular for hard baits as well. They're a good choice for these applications, but are not a good choice for the angler who wants only one tackle box to carry all his lures.

5. Hanging combos feature indented partitions, but also have one or more compartment trays that fold out with the lid. More versatile than the straight hanging boxes, they still can come up short as an all-around tackle box, but make superb spinnerbait boxes. My Fenwick 85 not only

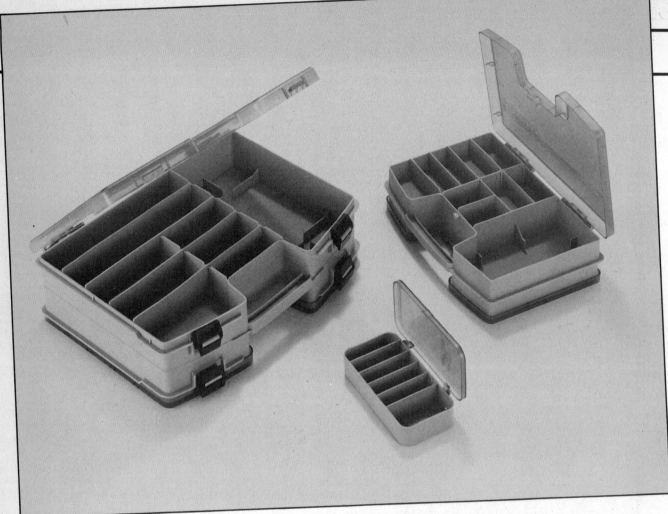

These Fenwick satchel boxes offer the angler a great deal of versatility for minimum investment. The compact size has made them a favorite with many pro fishermen.

allows me to store spinnerbaits neatly, but has room for trailers, spare skirts and other items often used with this type of lure.

6. Hip roof or "possum bellies" are the largest tackle boxes made and can store an astonishing amount. Most feature a number of compartmented trays that fold out with the lid, as well as a large bottom compartment to hold spare reels, line tools or other bulky items. They take a large amount of deck space to open fully, but they can carry the neighborhood tackle shop, and then some.

7. Soft tackle pouches are a fairly recent development. These generally are made of heavy-duty canvas and feature individual plastic compartments inside. They're not a bad choice for the traveling angler or one who wants to travel lightly.

8. Mini-boxes are tiny satchel-type plastic boxes that can be slipped inside a larger box to hold sinkers, hooks and other small items. They offer an excellent way to organize a hip roof box or a large hanging box.

Anglers selecting a tackle box — or boxes — first should consider how much tackle they have to carry and how much room they'll have to do it in. As a guide, I frequently provide lures for my customers as a part of the service. Given the fickle nature of St. Johns River bass, I need a wide variety of lures. My solution is to carry five tackle boxes in my Ranger bass boat: one Fenwick drawer box for hard baits; one Fenwick 85 for blade baits; one Fenwick Magnum (double-sided satchel box) for plastic worms; and two single-sided satchel boxes to hold jig-and-pigs and Gitzits, respectively. That's a load, but my old Ranger has a lot of room.

It's impossible to tote those five boxes if I'm flying to the fishing site, as I often do. That's where the smaller travel box — also called a tournament box — comes in handy. The little Phantom is compartmented to allow me to carry a little bit of everything but not a whole lot of anything. Since I'm the only one fishing out of it, it works out well. During one recent travel spate, I fished in the gin-clear waters of Lake Mead (where Gitzits and topwater plugs proved the key); in Lake Chickamauga (worms caught fish); the Savannah River in north Georgia (where a spin-

nerbait was all I could get the bass to hit); nearby Clark's Hill reservoir (buzzbaits); and the grungy Ohio River (where buzzbaits caught what few bass there were to catch).

A month later, I was deep jigging bass up from sixty feet in Bull Shoals reservoir. A week after that, I was flipping bass from matted hydrilla in five feet of water on Florida's Orange Lake. The box isn't big, but I never found myself needing a lure I didn't have with me.

A tackle box that carries the required bait and allows the bass angler instant access can save considerable time and frustration. It's worth the angler's time to consider this purchase carefully.

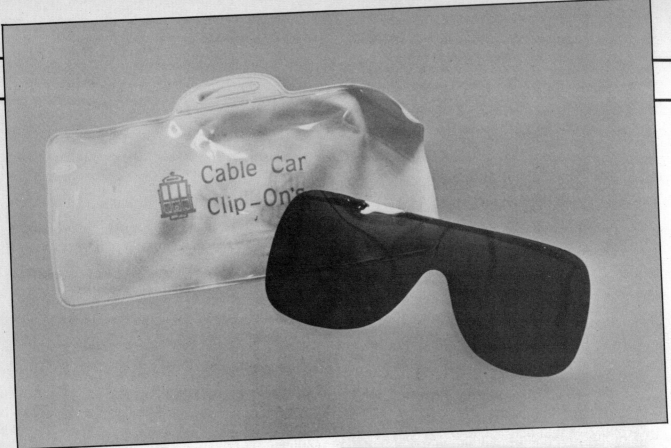

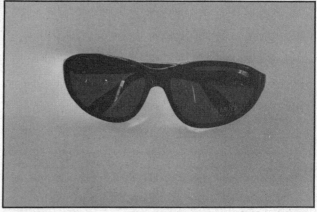

Prescription eyeglass wearers can enjoy the advantages of polarized sunglasses with clip-on models. (Right) A set of polarized glasses helps the serious angler see into the water to locate objects that may hold big bass.

Life Jacket: A personal floatation device (PFD) is required equipment in any tournament and Coast Guard-required equipment on boats over a certain size. This also is an item plain, old common sense says we should have.

Type III PFDs are the most common for bass boat use. These are relatively lightweight, vest-type jackets that slip on and off easily and store flat in most dry storage compartments.

Price range is in the $12 to $30 range — and this definitely is not the place to try to save a few bucks. In any type of bass boating mishap, chances are that an angler thrown into the water from the boat will suffer some form of impairing injury. A life jacket that does not stay securely in place and hold the angler into position so his head is held above the water is useless. Some inexpensive life jackets can actually be "fallen out of" if the wearer does not keep his arms locked at his sides or across his chest.

A quality life jacket should feature a large-tooth nylon zipper that will not bind, grab fabric or corrode. It also should have a strap or clip arrangement that allows the lower portion of the jacket to be attached to some part of the wearer's clothing, like a belt or belt loop. This assures the jacket will not slip off in the water.

There are many good models on the market, but my favorite is the Bass Mann Life Vest. In addition to the two above-mentioned features, it has sturdy shoulder straps that can be used to help rescue you from the water and a blaze orange hood that stores in a Velcro closure compartment behind the neck.

Should a fisherman find himself a swimmer, he can easily slip the hood out of the compartment and over his head. This will help prevent heat loss and hypothermia, also providing a highly visible target for rescuers. The jacket slips on and off quickly, with a minimum of straps and fasteners. This is important to tournament anglers who must wear a jacket while running the boat, but often prefer to fish without the garment.

Inclement weather clothing: Most fishermen don't go

Creating your own lure patterns is easy with modern lure paints. This type dries in minutes to make on-the-water artistry easy. (Left) Hook sharpening devices can be as simple as a small tackle box stone, but they're important. Many hooks aren't sharp enough as they come from factory.

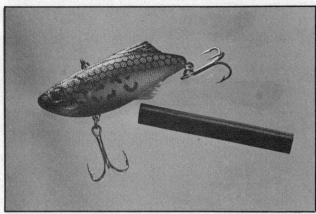

out if the weather is terrible. Exceptions are guides and tournament anglers who have no real choice. While many anglers may not pay a lot of attention to their outdoor clothing, these guys do.

A good windbreaker can go a long way toward making your day on the water more pleasant. They're invaluable during long chill morning runs, when rough water and spray is encountered, and they help reduce fatigue caused by being buffeted by wind during lengthy rides. It takes a well designed jacket to stand up to a tough day's fishing.

Unfortunately, there aren't that many good jackets around. Most of those intended for anglers are built more with style in mind than function. Here are some points to keep in mind when selecting a windbreaker for boating:

1. It should be water resistant. Spray is inevitable on the water and, if it soaks through your jacket, the wind will chill you quickly. Many popular jackets get wet and stay wet.

2. Choose a rolled collar. Conventional shirt-type collars will beat you to death in a fast boat as the wind catches the collar points and slaps your face repeatedly. A twenty-minute high-speed run can leave you feeling like you went ten rounds with Sugar Ray!

Most good boating jackets have rolled collars and include a hood that fits neatly into the collar. The really good jacket has a hood that is waterproof and secures with Velcro straps in addition to drawstrings. Trying to tie a neat bow knot under your chin with cold, wet, semi-numb fingers at fifty miles per hour is a trick few mortals have mastered. Velcro makes it easier.

3. Stylish, waist-length windbreakers look great ashore. But as soon as you climb into a bass boat, zip up a life-jacket and sit down, they ride up. This exposes a portion of your midriff to chill winds, which is precisely what you

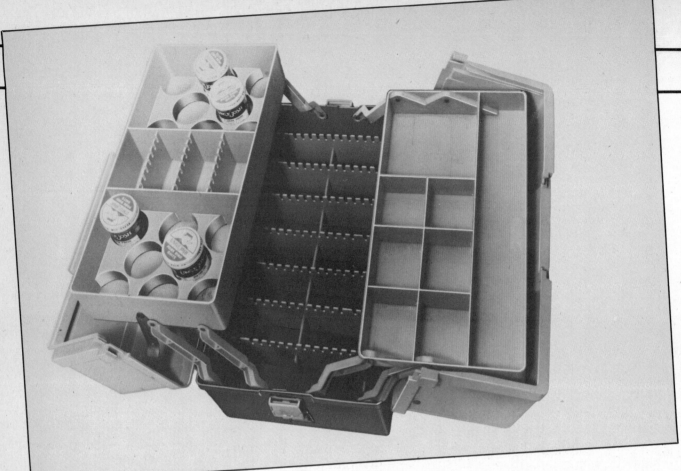

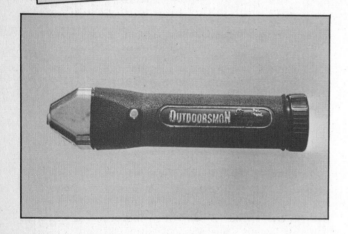

Lightweight travel boxes are popular with anglers who want to have some of everything close at hand. (Left) The Berkley line stripper makes quick work of stripping old line off the reel. It can save a great deal of time.

bought a windbreaker to avoid. Only a few makers cut their jackets to a length long enough to prevent this.

4. Small, fine-toothed nylon zippers will invariably catch jacket fabric and jam. Large nylon zippers won't. Nylon zippers are the only way to go on a boating jacket, so avoid any with metal zippers or, worse, metal snaps. They will corrode.

5. Your hand will get wet while fishing, if from nothing more than water running off the line as you reel it back onto the reel. Commonly used raglan cuffs collect this water the way little boys collect dirt and, once wet, they tend to stay

wet. This creates a chill factor. The best boating jackets have cuffs made of the same waterproof material as the jacket.

Also, see whether those cuffs are adjustable. Velcro closures allow the cuffs to be tightened — to keep cold air out while running — and loosened to provide freedom of movement when fishing.

6. Zippered pockets provide a safe place to store small items you don't want to lose. They should have the same large zipper as the jacket closure. It's also beneficial to have an inside breast pocket on the jacket to store maps and other items.

A good windbreaker should be much more than just "whatever old jacket you don't mind getting dirty." The one I use is the Buck Angler. I'm a bit biased in its favor, because I was one of the designers. In addition to the features listed earlier, it has expanding elbows and back panels for freedom of movement, D-rings, handwarmer pockets and other handy features. It was built by people who have a lot of experience in making jackets for the auto racing crowd and was designed by professional guides and tournament anglers who know what they want in a wind-

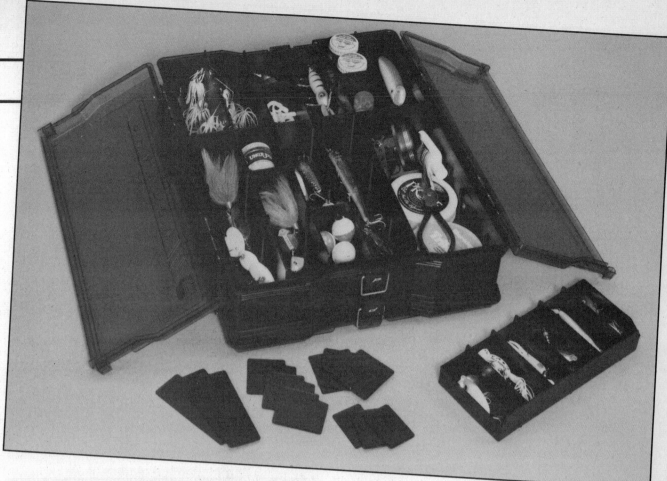

Double-sided satchel boxes are good choice for carrying plastic worms, jigs and other single-hook baits. It will store flat in a boat. (Right) For traveling, a good rod case is a worthwhile investment. Current compact sizes have made them favorites with many professional anglers.

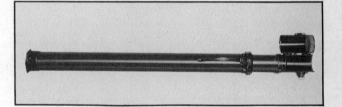

breaker. They're sold through Buck Apparel in lined and unlined versions.

If you spend much time bass fishing, you'll get caught in the rain. A good rainsuit is something you would kill for then.

It's not hard to find a good rainsuit as long as you're willing to pay $30 and up for it. Bass Pro Shops, of Springfield, Missouri, carries a good selection. I favor those made by American Clearwater, but there are many others. Avoid the $5 and $6 "disposable" models sold in many discount stores. A couple of garbage bags will keep you drier than most of those — and last longer.

When looking for a rainsuit, check for large zippers (avoid metal), sturdy construction and, in general, signs of quality. You'll be glad you did the first time you get caught in a thunderstorm.

Cold weather clothing is of vital importance to many anglers, since prolonged exposure to cold weather can sap your strength, affect your preformance and even bring on hypothermia. In the past, snowmobile suits have been popular, but fortunately that is on the wane. These garments can be dangerous in and around the water.

A friend of mine drowned while wearing such a suit, even though he was also wearing a good life jacket. The suit soaked up water so quickly it overpowered the ability of the life jacket to support him. These suits also lose their insulating qualities quickly when wet, making them a poor choice for boating applications.

Far better are the newer Gore-Tex garments, especially those designed for duck hunters. Two-piece outfits featuring pants and parka are preferred, since either can be shed if the weather should warm or you become overheated in them. For the last eight years, I have used an insulated rainsuit made by American Clearwater. It's a two-piece suit that has handled temperatures in the 20s (and wind chill factors a good bit below that) without problems.

You'll also want a good pair of motorcycle-type guantlets for running in cold weather. Those with a Gore-Tex shell and Thinsulate insulation are excellent. Find those with a small clip that allows you to clip them together for

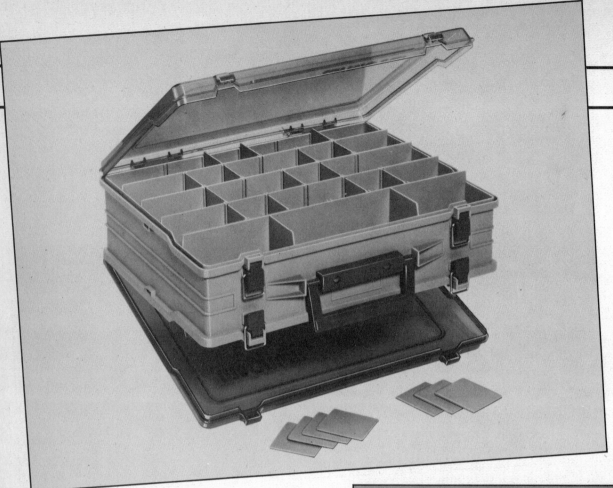

Many double-sided satchel styles feature partitions that can be removed or switched around for your needs. (Right) Mini-boxes can help angler organize his tackle, storing hooks, sinkers, small baits that are a clutter.

storage. I usually clip mine onto my life jacket D-ring to keep from misplacing them.

A motorcyle helmet may look odd in a bass boat, but it is one of the most comfortable ways to run in cold weather and one of the few safe ways to run in a rainstorm. Most pros have one equipped with a clear plastic face shield for such occasions. At 60 mph, raindrops hurt.

Polarized glasses: A good pair of polarized glasses are an invaluable aid when fishing in relatively shallow water. By cutting through surface glare, they allow you to spot underwater objects, determine just which way a laydown log lays and, in short, allow you to be a more efficient angler.

In relatively clear water, dark gray lenses seem to offer the best underwater visibility. In tannic or stained water, amber is a better choice. The best models are those that have side panels to block out as much sunlight around the glasses as possible.

If you wear prescription glasses, you can have a pair made up with polarized lenses, although they are expensive. I just use "clip-on" models that slip over my regular

glasses. These are inexpensive, store easily in a tackle box and work quite well. Avoid buying those models that flip up. The first time you turn your head in a moving bass boat, they invariably flip off!

Measuring board: Essentially a metal ruler with an L-shaped lip at one end, this is used to measure the length of your bass. In a tournament this is critical, since fish below the size limit carry a hefty penalty. As more and more states adopt various size and slot limits, it is something all anglers should carry.

An additional item often carried by tournament anglers is a balance beam. By clipping a fish on either side they can

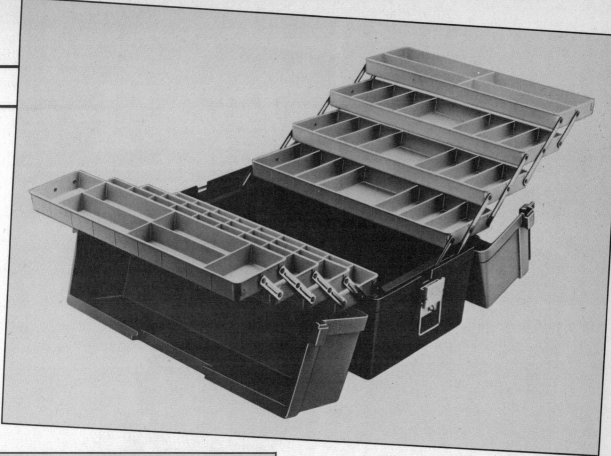

Hip-roof boxes are the the largest currently available and hold an astonishing amount of equipment, but take up a lot of room in a boat. (Left) The Fenwick 85 is author's choice for spinnerbait box. Interior can be customized.

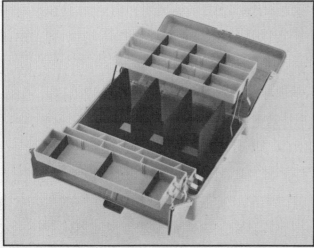

quickly determine which is the heaviest, which makes culling a limit far easier than trying to estimate weight by feel. Angler's Pro Specialties is one tackle company that offers these, although there are others.

Line stripper: This handy little gadget makes short work of stripping old line from a fishing reel. A battery-powered motor picks up one end of the line and zips it off the reel in seconds. Made by Berkley, this tool turns a lengthy chore into a quick one and I don't know of a single tournament fisherman who doesn't have one. It also features a small hook sharpening stone on the top of the unit that turns with the motor.

Hook sharpening tools: Most factory hooks are not nearly as sharp as they could be. Serious anglers sharpen them up themselves. There are a variety of tools to do this.

The cheapest and most convenient is a simple stone tucked away in your tackle box. It allows you to touch up a hook point right on the water. These are available in most tackle shops. Ignition point files and other small files also work quite well.

Many anglers use large units mounted on a workbench at home to keep their hooks sharp. The Point Maker, a power-driven disc grinder, is an excellent tool, as is the Razor's Edge sharpener. The latter unit features a jig that precisely positions a hook in relation to the stone and assures that the correct cutting edge angles are maintained. Worm hooks sharpened with this tool are among the best around.

Regardless of the method used, any angler who does not have a means to properly sharpen a hook will miss fish that he should have caught.

Line cutting tools: I wince every time I see someone cut monofilament line with his teeth. It may work, but there are better ways.

Common fingernail clippers are excellent for precisely cutting line, especially the tag end of knots. They're small,

Above: Combination boxes are an all-around choice for an angler who can fit his gear into one box. This one has large compartment for bulky items. (Below) Protection against harmful effects of too much sun is important.

cheap and some models come with a little twine cord to allow you to loop them around your neck so they'll always be handy. I keep two pair in my tackle box in case one is lost or broken.

A good pair of stainless steel scissors is even handier. Several companies make these especially for fishing, a good choice for cutting line and for trimming rubber skirts and plastic trailers, as well.

Another handy tool is a pair of needlenose pliers with a sidecutting feature. Not only are they good for wrestling hooks from fish, but for straightening bent hooks, cutting hook points off practice lures, tightening nuts on reels and a host of other chores. Avoid the cheap, imported versions. They're sloppily made, rust quickly and don't last long. Invest in a good stainless steel set and you'll have them around for years.

Sunscreen: People who did not consider the effects of prolonged exposure to the ultra-violet rays of the sun years back are paying for it now with skin cancer. Many professional anglers and guides suffer this problem currently,

Hanging boxes, if compartmented, are good choices for crankbaits and for topwater plugs, aiding organization.

This product keeps pork rind baits from drying out too rapidly, makes them easier to get on and off hooks.

and most of them now use a good sunscreen. Choose a lotion with a protection factor of 15 or above and you'll avoid some serious problems in the future.

I favor a product sold by bass pro Bobby Garland, called *Shade Tree*. Its protection factor is 18 and, unlike most sunscreens, is not greasy. Aside from being uncomfortable, greasy lotions do not contribute to a firm grip on your rod. This product comes in a four-ounce bottle that slips easily into a tackle box.

Some form of lip protection also is an excellent idea. During a recent trip to Nevada, I neglected to apply a little Chapstick and wound up with chapped, split lips that took three weeks to heal. I could have saved myself that discomfort by remembering to tuck a small stick of lip balm into my tackle box.

Marker bouys: Small floating marker bouys often get overlooked. Not only are they handy, if you drop an expensive rod and reel over the side, but they are important for those fishing offshore structure. When prospecting a channel edge, submerged island or other potential fish holding structure, dropping a few marker bouys along the edges of the structure gives the angler an easy-to-follow reference point that will allow him to work the area thoroughly.

Lure paints: Some people are never satisfied, and this holds true of anglers who don't necessarily agree with the lure patterns and colors provided by their makers. Adding your own color patterns to topwater baits, crankbaits and other lures is easy with any of the modern lure paints on the market; sometimes it's productive. I usually add a strip of fluorescent orange paint to the belly of the topwater baits I use in the winter months and to most of my crankbaits.

I use Catchin' Colors, which come in small bottles with a built-in brush applicator. Stored easily in a tackle box, these also are handy for painting worm weights and for touching up the heads on spinnerbaits and buzzbaits.

Color Master 7 is a nifty paint product that utilizes a small spray can to apply the paint. With a little practice, one can create some complicated, but effective color schemes right on the water.

Being able to add a small splash of color here and there can be important. On one trip, my boat partner was out-fishing me at least four to one, despite the fact that we were using the same plastic worm. The only difference was that he had painted his sinker in a shade that matched the worm. I hadn't and borrowed one of his painted sinkers. Then things began to even out.

On another occasion, I was working over schooling bass with another fishing friend and doing quite well with a chrome and blue Sugar Shad to which I had added a strip of fluorescent orange on the belly. He was using the same bait without the strip and not doing nearly as well. Once I put a strip on his, he began to pick up fish. Sometimes, small color differences can count and the angler who is equipped to take advantage of them can come out on the long end of the stick.

There are numerous other items on the market that often come in handy. Anything that makes my days on the water more pleasant or more efficient is well worth having.

CHAPTER 8

Above: Willow leaf spinnerbaits are becoming popular among pro anglers, as they produce more flash than other blade types. (Right) Florida pro Cliff McKendree boats bass taken on spinnerbait.

WHAT YOU SHOULD KNOW ABOUT BLADE BAITS

Weedless, Flashy And Noisy, They'll Take Bass Virtually Anywhere

Geography doesn't seem to matter. This bass was taken on spinner in Illinois. (Below) Open-bend styles of line-tie eyes — left and top — are less likely to cause line damage that could cause a break-off and the loss of a big bass.

SPINNERBAITS, BUZZBAITS and weedless spoons comprise one of the deadliest and most versatile lure groups an angler can use. Dubbed "blade baits" because each of these lure types features either a polished metal body or attached metal blades that produce a bait fish-like flash and vibration, they are at home almost anywhere. It makes no difference whether the bass are buried in vegetation thick enough to walk on or if they're lying on the bottom in sixty feet of clear water, there's a lure in this group that can handle it.

These baits are pretty weedless, feature one large hook that takes a solid bite on a bass and can be fished rather quickly. That has made them favorites with professional tournament anglers; these baits have made their way into the winner's circle in many national tournaments and world championships. It's a good bet they've won more tournament money than any other lure type.

They are also one of the easiest of all bait types to use, especially when fishing in, around or over vegetation. In ten years as a Central Florida bass guide, I've found that even anglers with minimal skills can catch good fish on these baits. In fact, the current world record spotted bass was taken on a spinnerbait by a teenage boy who was on one of his first fishing trips!

Success with these lures is sometimes as easy as just "casting and reeling." You will, however, do even better with these baits if you understand the differences between the three types, how to select the most appropriate model for the depth and cover conditions at hand and how they are best rigged for fishing. While the three different lure types in this group often are lumped together under one general name, they are distinctly different in their appearance and even in their uses. One cannot always do the job of the others.

Spinnerbaits: By far the most versatile of the three, the safety pin-style spinnerbait can be effective under the widest range of conditions. With the possible exception of the plastic worm, it is one of the best candidates for the title of "All-around Lure."

Spinnerbaits are available in what would appear to be a staggering array of sizes, types and configurations. In truth, there is a variety of different models from which to choose. This has caused some confusion for many anglers when it comes to selecting the best model for the task at hand. This confusion can be halted, if the angler understands that there are five basic categories of spinnerbaits; each has proven most effective under certain conditions. Once these categories are understood, there won't be any problems determining which lure to use under different conditions.

These five categories are: (1) single spins; (2) tandem spins; (3) long arm; (4) short arm; and (5) flexible cable arms.

The single-spin spinnerbait has only one blade and it may be of any size and type. Basically, these are not quite as weedless as tandem-spin baits, so they are generally best in more sparse cover. They run deeper and produce a distinct vibration that the angler can feel through the rod.

Big willow leaf spinnerbaits have been found deadly on lunker bass in spring months. Bass are territorial at this time and often will attack a large, flashy bait, when they might tend to ignore any smaller size bait.

This makes them the best choice for deeper water, slower retrieves and when used as a drop bait.

The tandem spin features two blades mounted in line; a smaller blade in front and a larger one in the rear. It is more weedless than single spins and therefore the best bet for heavy cover.

They are also a more shallow running lure, since the additional "lift" provided by the second blade tends to keep them closer to the surface. Most experts do not try to fish these baits much deeper than seven or eight feet.

A long-arm spinnerbait is one on which the upper blade-holding arm extends back at least as far as the point of the

The author has found that spinnerbaits are most effective in situations where shallow water, heavy cover are the norm.

A properly rigged weedless spoon has an impressive reputation for bagging outsize bass in shallow, weedy waters. (Below) Shown are the three effective ways to rig a weedless spoon. Each of the trailers gives the spoon different action. Thus, one may prove to be more effective at times than others.

hook. This protects the hook and makes it more weedless. They can be either a single or a tandem spin, but most pros use this arm length only with tandem blades — and only in heavy cover.

A short-arm bait is simply one on which the arm doesn't extend to the point of the hook. They can be single- or tandem-spin models; the biggest difference between the short and the long arm is the bait's ability to hook a fish and be weedless. Short-arm models are not as weedless as long arms, but since the blade arm doesn't cover the hook point, they are easier to hook fish with. Short-arm models are best reserved for sparse cover — single or tandem spin — or when fished in deep water with a single spin.

The flexible cable arm is a fairly recent development that replaces the rigid upper arm with one made of flexible cable. This bait is more weedless in thick, clinging vegetation, but not as weedless as a rigid-arm bait in "hard cover" like fallen tree tops. Pros love these around hydrilla, eelgrass and moss, but usually leave them in the tackle box when "fishing wood."

One other thing that helps make spinnerbaits so versatile is the fact that you can put together a wide variety of blade combinations with them. Changing blades on a spinnerbait is as simple as removing one from the split ring that holds it, installing another. You can switch blade size and blade style. Each change you make will change the running depth and speed of the lure.

Armed with a few different size spinnerbait bodies and a handful of different blades, an angler can make instant

A properly rigged bass boat adds a great deal to making fishing for respectable-size bass easier. (Right) The buzzbaits are made in various sizes, but the serious angler stays with large-bladed models to take big bass.

adjustment to the lure's running characteristics in order to fine tune it to whatever combination of depth and cover he is fishing.

The easiest formula to remember about changing blades is: With the same size spinnerbait body, putting on a larger blade will give the lure more "lift." This will keep it closer to the surface and it can be fished more slowly. Changing to smaller blades makes the bait run deeper and faster.

Spinnerbait bodies are available in sizes from one-eighth ounce right on up to a full ounce. Blades run from a size 1 — about the size of a dime — up to a #8 — about the size of a 50 cent piece — with a Colorado style blade, approaching the size and shape of a good-sized pocket knife blade in the willowleaf style.

The round Colorado style blades produce more vibration that the angler can feel through the rod and are often favored in the single-spin configuration. A one-half-ounce single-spin bait with a #4 Colorado blade is a tough combination to beat, if you want a bait to run deep and slow.

Willowleaf blades produce considerably more flash and tend to make the bait run more shallow. If you want bait to run at a steady clip, about a foot or so below the surface, a three-eighths-ounce tandem spin with a #1 Colorado blade in front and a #5 willowleaf in the rear is an excellent choice.

Another type, the Indiana blade, is similar to the Colorado blade, but is more oval in shape. It's not commonly used,

except by some savvy professional anglers who want to show the bass something "different" than the rest of the competition.

The combination of body and blade configurations is almost endless. The best depends on how the lure is being fished at the moment. However, there are some specific retrieve techniques that are effective under certain conditions and certain body and blade combinations that perform them well. Here are a few to serve as a starting point:

Slow rolling: This is intended to fish a spinnerbait through submerged cover, like logs, pilings and hard reeds. The bait is cast beyond the target and retrieved slowly along the bottom and kept in contact with the cover. Each time that bait "breaks free" of the cover, it is allowed to fall downward until it contacts the cover again and the retrieve is continued.

In water shallower than five feet, a one-quarter-ounce tandem long-arm bait with a #1 and a #3 Colorado blade

This scale-bending bass was taken on a buzzbait in an impoundment with many stick-ups. In thick cover, smaller bladed models often are used to avoid fouling. The 1/8-ounce buzzbait is effective in surface-matted hydrilla.

is a good choice. If more flash is desired, a three-eighths-ounce body with a #1 Colorado and a #5 willowleaf blade is a good bet. In water much deeper than that, many experts will shift to a three-eighths- or one-half-ounce single-spin with a #4 or #5 Colorado or willowleaf blade.

Waking: This is intended to fish the bait fairly quickly over submerged vegetation for active bass. It's deadly in the spring and early summer. A five-eighths- or one-half-ounce tandem with a #2 or #3 Colorado blade in front and

a #6 or #7 willowleaf in the rear is cast and retrieved quickly near the surface to produce a distinct wake or bulge on the surface. Strikes can be explosive! If a faster retrieve speed is required, shift to blades one size smaller.

A variation of this is *skipping*. Here a one-quarter- or three-eighths-ounce tandem bait with #2 and #3 Colorado blades is cranked quickly to the surface and retrieved fast enough to make the blades break the surface every five or six feet. It looks surprisingly like a shad minnow fleeing

Serious professional bass anglers on tournament circuit learn what type of bait to use in a specific set of circumstances. It doesn't always pay off, but a broad range of blade-type baits is carried by most of them.

Wading anglers find blade baits ideal, since the single large hook takes a solid hold on heavy-cover bass, yet it makes the chore of landing the fish a great deal more safe than when using lures that carry treble hooks.

across the top of the grass and can be deadly when bass are seen feeding on minnows in thick cover. Long-arm baits are a good choice for this type of heavy-cover fishing.

Buzz and drop: When fishing a specific point on a cover object where you think a bass might be holding — the end of a log, a dock piling or a stump, for example — you often can trigger a strike by "waking" a large spinnerbait right up to the exact point, then stopping the retrieve to let the bait plummet down on the bass's nose. I read about this one day a dozen years ago while browsing through a bass fishing magazine during a lunch break at a small Florida fish camp on Orange Lake. After lunch I went out and tried it and promptly caught a ten-pound, six-ounce bass! It has worked well over the years, especially when probing cuts, points and indentations on grasslines.

Yo-yoing: Intended to cover sharply sloping banks and points, the bait is cast to the shallow end, then worked back to the boat in a series of pumping motions...much like fishing a plastic worm. The bait will leap off the bottom, then flutter back down, until it again makes contact with the bottom. A one-quarter- or three-eighths-ounce short-arm single spin with #3 or #4 Colorado blade is a good choice. This is an excellent technique for smallmouth and spotted bass in rocky reservoirs.

Or you can just cast the bait out and retrieve it steadily in and around cover. Spinnerbaits are "user friendly" in that respect. In fact, as long as the bait is moving and the blades are turning, it's an effective fish catcher, no matter how you use it.

Selecting a quality spinnerbait should be a simple affair, but it's not. It seems everybody who makes lures makes spinnerbaits. Even some people who don't know anything about making lures make spinnerbaits — and there lies the problem. Some spinnerbaits on the market today are of "less than adequate quality." That's a nice way of saying, "junk!"

When you're choosing a spinnerbait, look for the following features:

1. Stout, quality 3/0 to 5/0 hook that can be resharpened. Soft, small, poor-quality hooks have no place on a bait intended to catch big bass.

2. Blade swivel; if the blade doesn't turn freely, the lure will not be as effective as it could be. The mark of a quality spinnerbait is a top-quality swivel, like a Sampo, on the blade.

3. Line tie eye; there's a big variation here. Some use a twisted wire eye, some a rolled loop, others a form of open bend. The latter is more preferable and here's why: A spinnerbait can turn over in the air on the cast. It's even common for this to happen when using large, wind-resistant blades. With the twisted or rolled loop eye, the line can be forced back into the crevices created by the wire and be pinched and severely weakened. The next big strike, you can break it!

The open bend solves this problem, since there's no built-in crevices for the line to catch. It's really a simple solution to a real problem and, for years, I

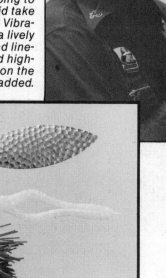

Left: This bass isn't going to take any prizes, but it did take buzzbait. (Below) Stanley Vibra-Shaft spinnerbait has a lively skirt of rubber, open-bend line-tie eye, stout 5/0 hook and high-quality ball-bearing swivel on the rear blade. Trailer may be added.

never understood why every spinnerbait maker didn't use it. One day I was in conversation with an executive from a major lure company and he explained why. It seems you can't use a snap swivel with an open-bend line-tie eye; they wanted to make a lure for the "weekend" angler who connected all his lures to his line with a snap swivel.

I've never seen a serious fisherman yet who would use a snap swivel on a bait intended to run through heavy cover. That may be why most pros favor the open-bend line-tie eye.

4. Skirt; Vinyl skirts are inexpensive, durable and don't "fuse up" in a tackle box. Unfortunately, they also don't have any lifelike action. The best quality spinnerbaits will use a lively rubber skirt.

5. Any spinnerbait intended to run through soft vegetation needs a tapering head with no sharp angles for vegetation to cling to. It should be streamlined in shape. If you don't fish in soft grass, any head style will do.

Spinnerbaits can be had in almost any color imaginable, but the pros have found one can get by with only a few of them. For the most part, they favor skirts in white for clear water, a combination of white/chartreuse/blue for general use, chartreuse or the same color mixed with blue for stained or muddy water or plain black.

The Stanley Jig Company caused quite a stir when they discovered how to make a spinnerbait skirt in the same colors as plastic worms and even how to add sparkle flake

to those skirts. Their new skirts in a clear material with silver flake, chartreuse with gold flake and clear with gold flake became instant best sellers, especially for anglers fishing clear water. They're worth looking into.

The pros like to experiment with blade colors. In times past, it was considered "traditional" to use nickel blades in clear water, gold blades in stained water and copper or fluorescent-painted blades in muddy water. That still works, but it is becoming far more common to use two different colored blades; a gold and a nickel, for example, in a tandem spinnerbait. Many feel that the combination of flashes produced by two different colored blades produces more strikes than using blades of the same color.

Adding a plastic or pork trailer to the rear of the spinnerbait is a popular technique. Most professionals do it when fishing in shallow water, since they feel it makes the bass take the bait with more authority. Many, though, feel it is unnecessary when the bait is crawled slowly in deeper water.

Curly-tailed plastic grubs or split-tailed eels in the three- to four-inch range are the most commonly used trailers. White or a clear with silver glitter is an excellent choice for clear or slightly stained water, while chartreuse is one of the overwhelming favorites in colored water.

Buzzbaits: If spinnerbaits are varied and versatile, buzzbaits are noticeably less so. They're intended to accomplish just one task: bubble their way across the surface of the water where their propeller-shaped blade creates a flashing, frothy disturbance. This noisy bait can draw some awesome strikes from bass and has proven to be one of the best big bass lures ever made! There's something about a big gurgling buzzbait that can make an outsized bass meaner than an NFL linebacker.

These lures can be had in the safety pin-style, the blade mounted on a wire arm above the hook in the same manner as a safety-pin spinnerbait or as an in-line bait, where the blade is mounted on the same shaft and lies in line with the hook. As a general rule, the in-line models can be used in heavier cover, since they're a bit more weedless. But, they do not do as good a job of hooking fish as do the safety-pin models.

Below: Long-arm tandem spinner (right) is a good choice if one is fishing thicker cover. Short-arm bait (left) allows easier hooking of the lunker, but is not nearly as weedless. (Left) Youngster took a first bass on this type of spinner.

These baits are made commonly in one-half-ounce, three-eighths-ounce, one-fourth-ounce and one-eighth-ounce sizes. Some have one large blade, while others have two tandem-mounted blades of smaller size. The larger the bait, the more slowly it can be worked on the surface, since the larger blade provides the same additional "lift" factors that occur with spinnerbaits. The larger baits are not quite as weedless as the smaller lures, however, and sometimes really thick cover dictates that the smaller baits be used.

Most anglers will start with the largest, noisiest model they can work through or over the cover they are fishing, since these have proven most effective at triggering strikes from bigger bass. If the bass respond to the bait by rolling under it or boiling up behind it — instead of really belting it — savvy anglers will switch to a smaller-sized buzzer.

In use, the buzzers are simple. Once the cast is made, the angler quickly cranks the lure up to the surface and gets it running on top. After that, the retrieve speed can be slowed a bit. The most effective retrieve speed with a buzzbait is the slowest speed that will keep the lure on top and making a commotion. It's also advisable to use a steady, unvarying speed, since this allows the bass to home in on the noise more easily. There are times when a quick, erratic retrieve might prove more appealing, but normally a slow, steady retrieve is most productive.

When presenting a buzzbait to a target, one general rule to follow is: The longer the bass has to look at the buzzbait, the less likely he is to hit it.

Buzzbaits are most effective when used in areas of mixed or heavy cover, where the cover itself shields the lure from the bass's view until the bait reaches the fish.

Picture this: A bass in a large grassbed has become active and ready to feed. But the fish cannot feed effectively in the thickest areas of the grass, since the more maneuverable baitfish could easily elude it in the heavy cover. The bass instinctively knows this and adopts the role of an ambusher, its speed and power making it a deadly predator. Moving to an open pocket within the grassbed, the bass conceals itself along one edge of the hole and is all set to make life miserable for the first little critter that swims through that opening.

Suddenly, from one side comes the steady sput-sput of a buzzbait. The fish can't yet see the lure because of the intervening vegetation, but the noise makes it alert. The noise grows louder as the lure approaches and the bass is suddenly confronted with a flashing, frothy "something" scooting quickly through its ambush zone.

It doesn't take Rick Clunn to figure out what's going to happen next!

However, in more open water, where the bass might have been able to see the bait from a distance, the outcome could well be different. Given a good look at the bait, many bass will simply follow it out of curiosity, then turn away when they see the boat.

When fishing a buzzbait, the bait should be cast well beyond the target and the casts planned to take maximum advantage of this "shielding" factor.

These lures can take bass anytime of the year, but are most effective from spring to fall, when warmer waters make the bass more active. They are often at their best during periods of dim light such as dawn, dusk and the overcast days, when bass are more likely to be active in shallow water. They can bring bass charging up from fairly deep water, but many pros feel they're of limited value, if the bass are not positioned within seven or eight feet of the surface.

Because noise and surface disturbance are the strike-triggering factors of this type of lure, the color of the bait

This bass is evidence that the big ones are taken, under proper circumstances, with a bait of spinner type.

isn't considered that important. White is a popular all-around choice, while some anglers carry chartreuse-skirted baits for stained or muddy water.

One problem plaguing beginning buzzbaiters is striking too soon and actually taking the bait away from the fish. It's easy to get keyed up when watching a buzzbait froth its way across the surface and strike as soon as the bass explodes on it. This will result in some missed fish and the easiest way to cure the problem is to watch the bait out of the corner of your eye while you search for your next casting target. This provides a slight "built-in" delay that often allows the bass to get a solid hold on the bait before the angler pulls the trigger.

Weedless Spoons: Unlike buzzbaits, spoons are deadly quiet baits. They have no blades to create vibration or added flash. They slip through even the thickest cover with a seductive wobble that sometimes can be far more effective than noise.

Spoons are often more effective during colder weather, when bass seem to prefer quieter baits. They also can be fished in cover that would foul most spinnerbaits and buzzbaits. This makes it a valuable addition to any angler's

Casting into heavy cover such as the type that surrounds this impoundment calls for a careful choice of baits. (Left) Versatility of spinnerbaits lies in its ability to alter depth and running speed by changing blades.

tackle box, especially if your fishing often takes you to weedy waters.

While some weedless spoons come equipped with a rubber skirt attached to the rear, the grandaddy of them all, the Johnson Silver Minnow comes unadorned; it must be properly rigged to be effective. Spoons should not be fished without a rear trailer of some type.

The most popular trailer is a plain rubber skirt slipped over the rear hook. This gives the bait a medium side-to-side wobble, while the skirt breathes as the lure falls. When retrieved slowly through thick grass, moss or lily pads and allowed to fall freely into each open pocket in its path, it's a deadly winter and spring bait for largemouths.

Replacing the skirt with a five-inch pork strip or a curly-tailed plastic worm gives the bait a "snakey"-looking, tight wobbling action. It also allows the bait to sink a bit deeper. This often can be more effective in scattered, deeper cover like reeds, logs and tree roots.

Installing a pork frog or a plastic trailer like the Ditto Chunky or Mann's Auger Frog causes the bait to ride with the hook pointing up, offering only a slight side-to-side wobble. This is deadly when retrieved quickly over the top of matted vegetation, lily pads or other surface-floating cover. It's exceptionally weedless and can bring fish crashing through vegetation too thick to work with any other bait.

Spoons can be had in a variety of colors, but four combinations have proven very effective. A gold spoon, with a chartreuse pork strip or skirt, is an excellent bet in stained water or in areas where shiners form the dominant forage. A silver spoon, with a white strip or skirt, is a good all-around choice, as is a frog-patterned spoon, with a green skirt or pork frog. When fishing as a surface bait, a black spoon and frog is hard to beat.

Regardless of the type of blade bait chosen, hooks should be sharpened carefully before use. The large single hooks on these baits will not hook fish if they are dull.

A medium/heavy action rod of 5½ to six feet and spooled with fourteen- to twenty-pound line is a good general-purpose rod for any of these baits. Graphite or boron should be used for sensitivity, since bass often can take spoons and sometimes spinnerbaits very lightly. Anglers fishing a lot of big-bladed spinnerbaits will find shifting to longer rods — 6½ to 7½ feet — will make casting these wind-resistant lures easier.

Because of their versatility, especially when fishing in water containing a fair amount of vegetation, this is one lure group you'll want well represented in your tackle box.

CHAPTER 9

Action tail plastic worms are top bets for an angler who is flipping in heavy vegetation areas.

PLASTIC WORMS & JIGS

The jig-and-pig bait can be more effective during the colder seasons than is the plastic worm, author says.

These Versatile Bottom Bouncers Go Just About Anywhere For Big Bass

x

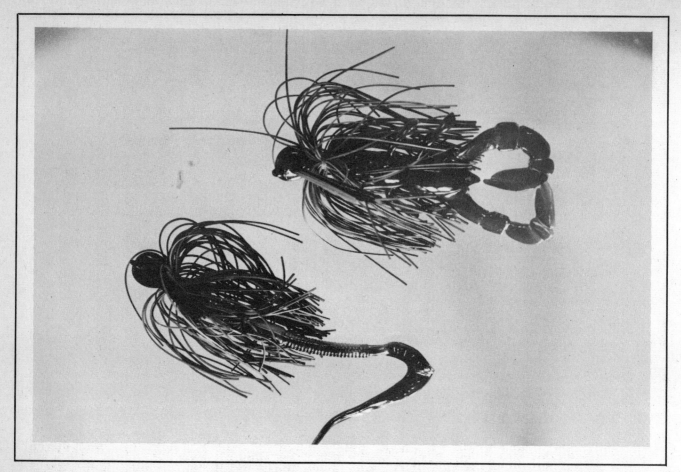

These Stanley jigs show some of the various trailers that can be used to change their speed of fall. Bulky plastic crawfish at top will slow the jig; swimming tailed worm beneath will produce a faster fall and more violent action.

THEY'RE NOT the most glamorous lures in an angler's tackle box. They don't sport a fancy paint job, scintillating flash or pulsating vibration; most don't even have a built-in action. They simply lie soddenly on the lake bottom until the angler brings them to life with clever rod tip manipulations.

Despite those apparent shortcomings, few lures have been as consistently effective on all species of bass as the plastic worm and the jig-and-pig.

Part of that effectiveness stems from the fact that these are relatively compact baits that usually are inhaled completely by the bass. While treble-hook-laden lures may leave a hook or two dangling outside the fish's mouth where it can foul on cover and pull the bait free, not so with these. The one stout hook takes a solid bite and many experts feel it is much easier to land a hooked bass on a worm or jig than with other lures.

Since these baits are commonly rigged to be weedless, they can be fished in places that other lures cannot. They have no peer when it comes to penetrating thick grass, fallen tree tops, the dimly lit reaches beneath boat docks and other thick cover locales that often hold bass.

Their inherent versatility lends them to a variety of fishing applications. Given the wide range of sizes and weights available, they can be fished as effectively in six inches of muddy water as in sixty feet of gin-clear water. Whether the angler is crawling one through a thick Florida grassbed in search of largemouths, swimming it down a sloping pea gravel bank for smallmouths or bouncing it off submerged channel edges for spotted bass, there will be few times and places where the plastic worm or jig-and-pig is not one of the deadliest baits you can tie on.

Unfortunately, the drawback to these baits is that they are not one of the more simple lures to use. Unlike other lures that often can be taken directly from the package, tied onto the line and catch fish, the worm or jig must be rigged properly by the angler before it becomes effective. And, in use, these lures require a more highly developed sense of "feel" than do other baits. Bass seldom smash a worm or jig hard enough to assist in the hooking process. Most often the take is registered as a subtle "tap" and the angler must respond quickly and correctly, if the fish is to be hooked.

Mastering these deadly baits, however, is not as difficult as some anglers may think. It simply takes practice, a bit of concentration and the right equipment and rigging. The place to start is in selecting the rod and reel used to fish these baits.

Picking The Right Rig: Worms and jigs can be fished with equal effectiveness on either casting or spinning equipment and many experts will use both. Spinning equipment often is chosen in clear water situations where lighter lines are an asset and in situations where short, highly accurate "skip" casts are required to place a lure in hard to reach areas. Casting gear often gets the nod when fishing heavy

Worms and jigs are overwhelming choice of anglers for the flipping technique and have won big money in many major tournaments. (Below) Heavy hook on jig at left identifies it as flipping jig for heavy cover. The lighter hook is for casting and makes setting the hook easier at an extended distance. Both Stanley jigs have nylon bristle weed guards.

cover, since it allows easier use of lines in the 14-pound and up range.

With either type of outfit, the rod chosen must be sensitive and capable of transmitting even the slightest vibrations with a crisp authority. Fishing worms and jigs is a game of feel and the better you can feel your bait, the better you'll do.

Graphite or boron is the best choice for rod material. Fiberglass rods do not have the sensitivity to deliver a crisp "feel" for the bait. A medium or medium/heavy action will aid in obtaining a solid set with the one large hook common to these baits, as well as providing the muscle needed to move a bass away from heavy cover quickly.

Models in the 5½-foot range are the best choice for short-cast situations, while open-water anglers will favor the six-or seven-foot rods. The 7½- to eight-foot rods are used when flipping the worm or jig.

Line size should be dependent upon the cover conditions. Open-water conditions can be handled well with

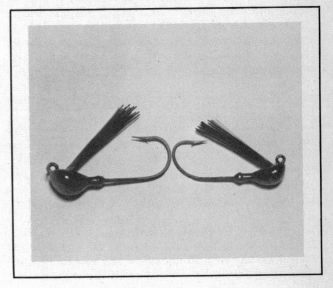

Plastic worms and jigs have reputation for producing big bass. This one was taken on Tennessee's Lake Chickamauga in 1986 BASS Master Classic. Of four largest bass weighed in by press observers, three were caught on plastic worms.

10- to 12-pound line, while heavy-cover anglers often spool up with line in the 17-pound and up range. For most fishing, 12- or 14-pound is a good all-around choice.

Fluorescent lines can aid in detecting strikes, since they are easier for the angler to see. Some hits will register as nothing more than a few quick twitches on the line. However, some anglers feel fluorescent lines can decrease the number of strikes they will get in clear water situations, so only use them in muddy or stained water.

Selecting A Worm: Plastic worms are available in an almost infinite variety of sizes, colors and configurations. but, when you sort through them all, you'll see there are only three basic types of plastic worms: straight tails, like the Fliptail and Mann's Jelly Worm; swimming tails, like the Gillraker and Ditto Verifier; and "action" tails like the Gator Tail and Ding-A-Ling. Each of these types, regardless of brand, will perform a bit differently than the others and often may be a better choice for a particular task.

Straight-tail worms normally possess more tail flotation than the other types. They stand up higher in the water when they are at rest. This can make them an excellent choice when the worm must be fished slowly or if bottom debris might hamper the bass's ability to see the bait.

They are a popular choice among the pros when fishing slowly around boat docks, fallen timber and submerged grassbeds, because many feel the higher tail flotation helps make them more visible to the bass.

Action-tail worms generate an almost violent tail shimmy as the bait sinks. This has made them popular in muddy or stained water where their increased vibrations can help the bass home in on the bait. They are also a good bet, especially during the warmer months when bass are more active, for use as a fall bait...where the angler expects the strike to come as the bait falls through the water. They can be deadly when cast next to a stump, hopped down an underwater ledge or flipped into heavy cover.

The swimming-tail worms offer a little of the characteristics of the two previously mentioned styles, which makes them a strong choice as a general-purpose worm. They can be effective under virtually all worm-fishing situations.

For general use, expert anglers usually select plastic worms in the six- to seven-inch range. These are small enough not to intimidate the younger bass, while still offering a decent mouthful for the larger fish. In areas where smallmouth or spotted bass predominate, four- to five-inch

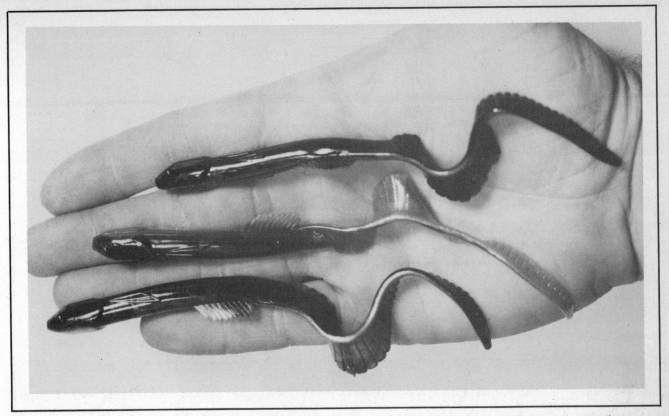

Swimming tailed worms such as these are versatile and have become popular with bass anglers for all-around use.

worms usually are preferred, while Southern largemouth anglers frequently will shift to eight- and nine-inch models, if seeking trophy-sized fish.

Environmental conditions also can play a role in selecting the most effective worm. Professional anglers have found, as a general guideline, that clear water conditions often are best handled with four- to five-inch worms that possess a minimum of tail action, while anglers probing stained or muddy waters frequently fare better with larger baits with a more pronounced shimmy.

Rigging Them Up: Plastic worms can be rigged for fishing in a variety of ways and some pretty off-beat techniques have been tried by innovative anglers. But when it's all said and done, three basic rigs have proven themselves able to handle virtually all worm-fishing chores.

The first, and the "grandaddy of them all" is the Texas rig. In this rigging, a conical shaped sinker called a bullet or worm weight is slipped onto the line ahead of the hook which holds the worm. This creates a compact lure that is as weedless as a bait can be and still hook fish. It is the rigging preferred for flipping, fishing in weedy cover or when casting around objects like stumps, laydown logs and boat docks.

To assemble this rig, slip the sinker onto the line and tie on your hook. Plastic worm hooks are available in a variety of styles, some of which feature compound bends in the shank that are intended to turn and position the hook in the fish's mouth for a better hook set. All of them work and which one an angler chooses is a matter of personal preference. Most of the pros, though, rely on a straight-shanked "Sproat"-style hook.

The proper way to insert the hook into the worm in order to render it weedless is shown in Figure 1. There are, however two things an angler should keep in mind when using this rigging:

1. After the worm is rigged, insert a piece of toothpick through the head of the worm and through the eye of the hook. This keeps the worm from sliding down the shank of the hook in heavy cover and aids in getting a positive hookset as well. The excess toothpick is snipped off with clippers.

2. When using a swimming-tailed worm, the hook should be reinserted into the worm body on the side of the worm opposite that to which the tail curves. Use the mould seam or parting line as your placement guide. This placement allows the tail of the worm to extend fully and achieves better flotation.

Some anglers also prefer to "peg" the sinker to the head of the worm by inserting a piece of toothpick in the line eye hole and breaking off the excess. This keeps the worm and sinker together and is an excellent idea when flipping or fishing in heavy cover. The toothpick can pinch the line, though, so the real pros slide the sinker up the line a foot after they peg it and clip off the line below it, then tie on the hook. This removes any line that may have been damaged when inserting the toothpick.

The proper hook size can give the worm a more lifelike action and aid in hook setting; many professional anglers use the following guidelines: four- and five-inch worms, 1/0 or 2/0 hook; six- and seven-inchers, 2/0 to 3/0; eight- and nine-inch models rate a 4/0 or 5/0. Thick-bodied plastic worms require one or two hook sizes up from comparable-

FIGURE 1

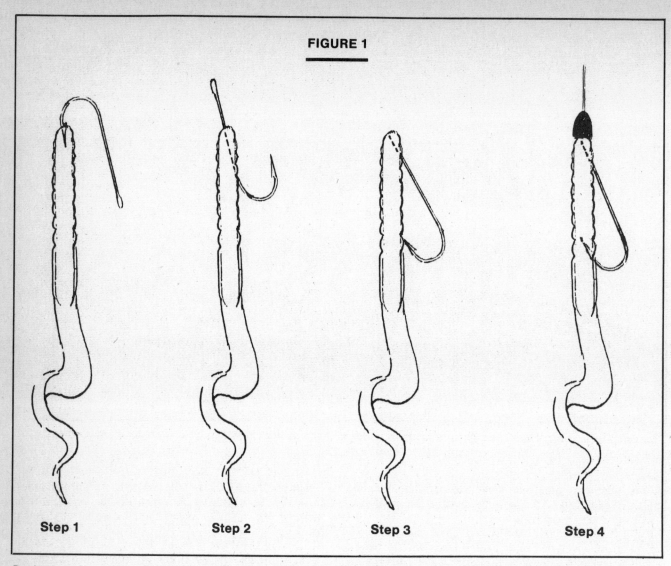

| Step 1 | Step 2 | Step 3 | Step 4 |

Basic steps in making a weedless plastic worm rig are: Step 1, insert point of the hook into head of the worm. Step 2, bring the hook point down into the head and out the side of the worm about 1/4 inch down from the head. Step 3, pull the shank of the hook downward until the eye enters the head. Step 4, insert the point of the hook back into the body of the worm. These steps should be done with the slip sinker in place on the line and the hook already tied on as shown.

length slender-body worms. Lighter lines require a lighter-wire hook, while heavier lines and flipping are best served with stout forged hooks in sizes 3/0 to 5/0.

The size of the sinker chosen will control the worm's fall rate and thus the speed at which it can be retrieved. These sinkers are available in sizes ranging from 1/32 ounce, up to one full ounce. For water depths less than five feet, the 1/16 or ⅛ are good bets. From five to ten feet, 3/16 or ¼ ounce are often chosen, while the ¼- or 5/16-ounce sizes will work well down to depths of twenty feet. Under windy conditions, many experts increase their sinker size to help defeat wind bow in the line and maintain contact with their worm.

Sinkers in the ⅜-ounce and up range often are employed when fishing deeper than twenty feet, when flipping in heavy cover where the weight of the sinker must drive the bait through the cover and down to the bass or when rigging the worm in the second popular method: the Carolina style.

The only real difference between the Texas rigging and the Carolina style is that the sinker is moved away from the worm in the latter.

With the sinker moved anywhere from six inches to five feet up the line from the worm, the action of the bait is changed completely. It floats higher and moves in a smooth, lazy swimming motion with each twitch of the rod. This rigging has proved highly effective in moving water, like tidal rivers, or in many open water situations, such as crawlng a worm down a sloping submerged point.

In this rigging, the worm can be attached to the hook in the same weedless manner as the Texas rig or it can be threaded onto the hook with the hook point left exposed. The latter is preferable, if bottom cover conditions allow you to fish an exposed hook point without hanging up.

Moving the weight up the line can be accomplished by sliding a pegged sinker up the line to the desired position, clamping a couple of split shot onto the line at the desired point; or by slipping a sinker onto the line, tying a swivel below it and attaching another section of monofilament below that to serve as a leader and hold the hook and worm.

Plastic worms and jigs are top bets for fishing around man-made structures like docks and piers. Being weedless, they seldom hang up and can be worked in a small area long enough to entice non-active bass to take them, author says.

All of them will work, although the last technique is preferred when sinkers over ¼-ounce are used, since it tends to keep them in the proper position.

With either the Texas rig or the Carolina rig, an alternative method of achieving a weedless rigging is to use one of the commercially available wire weed guard hooks, like the Eagle Claw #449WR. Here the worm is threaded onto the hook and the wire clipped over the point to protect it. This is not as weedless as reinserting the hook point into the worm's body, but it is a bit easier to get the hook set, since the hook doesn't have to penetrate the worm before it gets to the bass. Some light-tackle anglers prefer the wire weed guard hook.

The third rigging method is simply to thread the plastic worm onto a lead-head jig and leave the hook point exposed. This is a popular technique on many deep, rocky reservoirs where little cover exists to hang up the lure. Jig heads ranging from 1/16 to ¼ ounce, with a light wire 1/0 to 3/0 hook, are commonly used in conjunction with a four- or five-inch slender-bodied worm on light spinning tackle. When hopped, crawled or swum slowly down rocky points and gravel banks, it's a deadly technique for all species of bass.

In view of the versatility of the various plastic worm rigs, the lowly jig-and-pig would seem to play a distant second fiddle. But that's not always true. Although worms and jigs often can be fished in the same manner, the pros have learned that jigs often entice larger bass and may be the best choice for smallmouths and spotted bass. Jigs also seem to be more productive than the plastic worms during colder weather. Thus, the serious angler will want to carry both baits.

Picking Your Jigs: Jigs are a bit simpler to master than worms, simply because they offer less variations. Basically, there are only two different types: casting jigs and flipping jigs and the only real difference between them is the hook style.

Flipping jigs are intended to be used within twenty-five feet of the angler on stout line. Since their task is to wrestle bass from heavy cover under these conditions, they are made with heavy, wide-bite forged hooks that will take a strong hookset and drive through to the bone.

Casting jigs are intended to be fished at greater distances, on lighter lines and under conditions where the Bonzai! hookset of the flipper cannot be used. As a result, they are made with lighter wire hooks that will penetrate easily with only moderate hook-setting force.

Regardless of the jig type, the angle at which the hook lies in relation to the jig's head is important. Some makes have the hook point bending back toward the head, which effectively closes the gap and can cause an angler to miss fish.

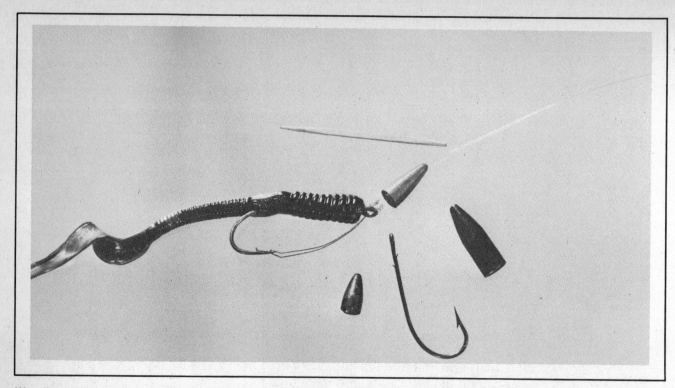

Weedless rigs can be assembled in several ways. The wire weedguard hook in this worm is easy for setting the hook and is a good choice for light tackle. Rate of fall for the worm is governed, of course, by the size of sinker used.

A quick test to see if the hook point angle is the correct one is to place the jig in the palm of your hand with the point facing the palm, then close your hand slowly around the jig. If the point of the hook pricks your palm, the angle is correct. If not, bend the hook point out with pliers — or buy a proper jig. Among those I have used and like are the Stanley Jig line and the Weapon Jig made by pro bass fisherman Gary Klein.

Another factor to look for on a quality jig is the type of weedguard it uses. These may be made of heavy monofilament line, Y-shaped pieces of plastic or nylon fibers. The overwhelming choice of professional anglers is the nylon fiber weedguard. It is more weedless than the others and provides enough give to get a good hook set.

As with the plastic worm, the weight of the jig determines its speed of fall and how fast it can be fished. But that factor can be altered quite a bit by the type and size of the trailer used on the jig. These baits are almost never fished without slipping a pork frog, plastic crawfish, plastic worm or pork strip onto the jig hook.

Since trailers come in a variety of sizes and types, each imparting its own characteristics to the jig's fall speed, an effective selection of jig heads doesn't have to be large.

Most anglers can get by with only three different sizes. A 3/16- or ¼-ounce head is used for a slow falling bait and can be deadly in colder weather, when the bass are not as active and prefer slower moving morsels, or for shallow water. A ⅜- or ½-ounce head often is preferred in water deeper than ten feet or during the summer months, while a 9/16- or ⅝-ounce head gets the nod if the jig is being punched through heavy cover or working depths greater than fifteen feet.

Jigs are most effective when fished with a trailer and two

distinct types exist: bulk trailers, like the Uncle Josh Pork Frogs or plastic crawfish like the Ditto Fireclaw; and action trailers, like the pork strips and Ripple Rinds or any action- or swimming-tailed plastic worm.

Bulk trailers often are used in shallow water where the jig's fall rate needs to be controlled. Action trailers produce more tail action and are preferred when the jig is fished in water deeper than ten feet, or when the jig is used in a "swimming-type" retrieve.

When choosing a bulk-type trailer, the larger the trailer the slower the bait will fall, since the trailer imparts water resistance and, in effect, acts as a parachute.

When choosing an action-type trailer, the heavier the jig head, the more pronounced the "action" of the trailer will be, since the faster the bait falls, the more violently the tail will vibrate.

Putting Them To Use: In actual use, plastic worms and jigs can often be fished in similar manners. Under some distinct conditions, one may be preferable to the other, but that's a factor the angler will have to determine on a daily basis.

In general, however, a few observations can be made:

1. The jig-and-pig, utilizing a pork trailer, is sometimes more effective than the worm in winter fishing conditions.

2. The jig-and-pig is frequently a better bet in waters where crawfish form the predominant forage, while the worm often proves more effective in waters where shiner minnows, shad or other fish make up the bulk of the bass's diet.

3. In waters where "soft" cover such as soft weeds predominate, worms are frequently a better bet than jigs. But in places where rock or wood is the most

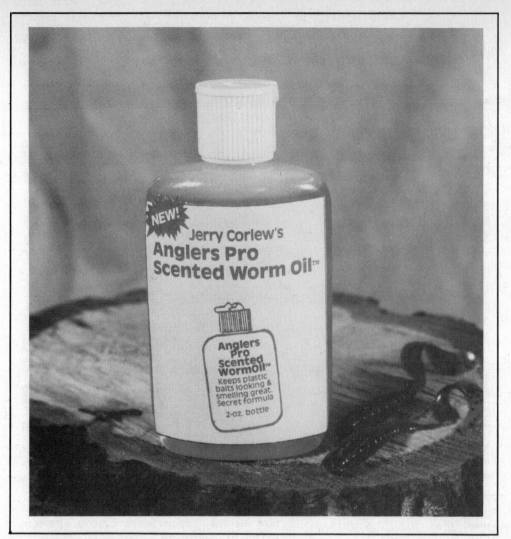

Variety of add-on scents is available for use on plastic worms. The author feels they are beneficial under most conditions.

prevalent cover, jigs can be a better bet.

4. Larger baits of either type can be more effective in the South, while Northern anglers — especially those in pursuit of smallmouths and spotted bass — frequently will do better with smaller baits.

Tips And Tactics: The inherent versatility of these baits makes them good choices for a wide variety of angling situations and the following tips should start an angler on the road to success.

As an object lure: A lure plummeting past a bass's nose often can trigger that bass to strike it, even if the fish has no intention of feeding. It's a "reactive strike" — much like dangling a string in front of a cat — an inherent predatory instinct.

When analyzing a piece of potential bass-holding cover, plan your casts to drop the worm straight down into each spot a bass is likely to be lying. As the bait hits the water, engage the reel handle, point the rod toward the target — and be ready to strike. Most hits will be telegraphed by nothing more than the line "twitching" or moving off to the side as the lure falls. If no strike results on the fall, let the bait hit the bottom, lie there for a second, then give it a slight twitch. Often a bass will be attracted to the falling lure and be watching it for the next sign of movement. Lightly weighted worms or a jig with a bulk trailer are top choices for this.

As a crawl bait: Large areas of potential fish-holding cover can be probed with a worm or jig. As the bait hits bottom after the cast, bring the rod tip to the 9:30 position facing the target, then "jiggle" the rod back up to the 11:00 position. Once there, drop the rod back to 9:30, while taking up the slack with the reel.

Use only the rod to move the bait, not the reel, which will interfere with your feel for the lure. Most hits will be nothing more than a slight tap as the jig or worm dances its way across the bottom.

When you feel what might be a hit, stop the rod and watch the line. If it moves or twitches, drop the rod tip toward the fish, take a few turns of the reel handle to remove slack and set the hook in a sharp upward snap.

Dropping down a break: Cast the bait into the shallow portion of a sharply sloping shoreline such as rock bluffs, gravel banks or sloping point and ease the lure toward you with the rod, until you feel it lose contact with the bottom. Let it fall and wait until it strikes bottom again before repeating. This isn't much different than using the bait as a fall lure and the hits will be similar. Once you've determined the approximate depth at which the bass are holding, you can concentrate your effort at that depth.

Deadsticking: Inactive bass often study a worm or jig for a long time before picking it up. In this situation, casting the bait to where you think the bass will be, just letting it lie

This worm rig has the point of the hook tucked into the plastic so that it becomes relatively weedless and will not hang up. Carolina worm rig (below) uses plastic bead beneath the sinker to protect the knot from being frayed in action.

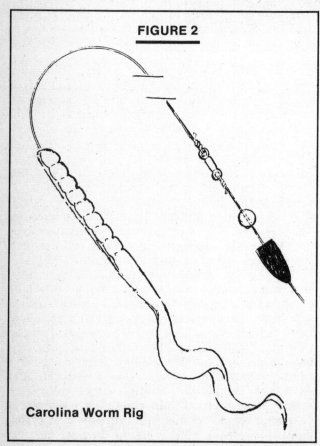

FIGURE 2

Carolina Worm Rig

on the bottom sometimes can prove effective. The worm or jig should not be moved, but it won't be motionless. Even the smallest water currents or just the water movement generated by a bass swimming around the bait will cause the worm to undulate and the jig's skirt to "breathe." Often that's what it takes to entice non-active bass. This is a deadly technique around laydown logs, boat docks or other obvious fish-holding cover.

One last point that needs to be discussed is what color to use. Sadly, while there are a lot of opinions, there are few hard answers in this area. Color can make a big difference in an angler's success with these baits, but just what colors will be most effective can vary from lake to lake or season to season. Some lakes show a distinct color preference and this often can be discovered by simply asking around the marina. In other cases, you'll have to experiment. Here are a few thoughts from professional anglers on getting started:

"When fishing a jig-and-pig," says tournament pro Lonnie Stanley, who also makes Stanley Jigs, "I've never been to a lake yet where a crawfish color — orange, brown or pink — wouldn't catch fish. Bream colors like blue, red, purple or black are also effective."

Stanley prefers to combine several of these colors in one jig and trailer, using multi-color jigs. He seldom fishes a one-color jig and usually uses a different colored trailer on the jig.

In plastic worms, water clarity is frequently the deter-

Attempting to fish in such dense cover as this is one of the challenges of seeking bass. With worms and jigs properly rigged, having a hang-up in the growth is less likely. But that pull on the line doesn't always mean you have a bass!

mining factor in which color one should start with.

In muddy water, where you cannot see your lure ten inches under the surface, the universal favorite among professional fishermen is a black worm with a fluorescent chartreuse tail.

In stained water, where your lure is visible down to about two feet, consider June Bug (black grape with chartreuse flake in it), black and blue combinations, black and red or black and brown.

In clear water, where the bait is visible down to six feet or deeper, pros favor clear worms with red flake, wine with silver flake, plain translucent purple, blue or red or a two-color worm of black and silver.

Matching the hatch also can be an effective color-selection tactic. If, for example, crawfish are a major forage item, try combinations of orange and brown. If shad min-

nows are on the menu, blue or a black and silver should prove effective. In the spring, when young water snakes hatch out, try combinations of green and brown.

It's also a good idea to use one of the various fish scent products on your worms and jigs. There are many — and I have had good success with Fish Formula, Mann's FS-454 and Berkley Strike. I don't really know whether they induce more bass to bite, but I'm convinced that those bass that do hit will hold the bait longer. That allows me to hook more of my strikes and it makes these products worthwhile, as far as I'm concerned.

While plastic worms and jigs may seem to be a complicated lure to fish, they're not as difficult as some anglers may believe. With the proper equipment, the right rigging and a little practice, they'll take bass anywhere...and from any type of water.

CHAPTER 10

ALL ABOUT CRANKBAITS

Few Lures Are As Easy To Use As These Versatile Baits

Above: Ken Cook displays the proper rod position for the retrieval of a crankbait. Low position helps bait reach deeper depths. (Left) Shaw Grigsby inspects a nice bass that busted a countdown crankbait cast along the weedline.

O F ALL the lures an angler can put into his tackle box, crankbaits are among the easiest to use. They're easy enough, in fact, that one professional bass fisherman observed, "You throw them out, reel them in and, if there's a fish on it, you take it off the hook."

Despite their ease of operation, though, crankbaits have established a sterling reputation when it comes to catching big bass and it's no wonder: It was crankbait that George Perry used in June 1932 to land the world record largemouth bass. Over fifty-five years later, his twenty-two-pound, four-ounce fish still stands as the largest ever recorded. In 1955, David Hayes sent a crankbait deep into the waters of Dale Hollow Reservoir and dredged up an eleven-pound, fifteen-ounce smallmouth bass. It still stands as the world record for that species.

Crankbaits also comprise one of the most versatile lures an angler can use. Want to quickly cover a rocky point? Crankbaits are ideal for this. How about a submerged grass flat? Crankbaits work fine for this, too. Submerged treetops? No problem with one of the long-billed models. And the same holds true for deep ledges, bluffs, flooded timber, boat docks, stump flats, submerged channel edges, weedlines; in short, just about anywhere a bass might care to hang out.

Getting the most out of these lures, however, does require a bit of thought and careful selection of the baits, themselves. There is, you see, no such thing as an all-around crankbait. They're available in a wide variety of styles, running depths and actions. They can be had in wood or plastic and each material will impart its own characteristics to the lure's performance.

There also are two distinctly different types of crankbaits: floater/divers that float at rest and dive to a certain depth when retrieved, and countdown models that sink when the retrieve is stopped and tend to remain close to whatever depth they've reached when the retrieve is started.

In view of this, expert anglers seldom select a few random examples for their use. Instead, they carefully choose a "crankbait system" that allows them to have the right action and running depth lures to handle the bass fishing conditions they encounter most frequently.

Here's how to start building an effective crankbait system of your own:

Floater/Divers: The most commonly used crankbait, this features a buoyant body that floats at rest and a front mounted lip that makes them dive when retrieved. Plastic models feature air chambers within the body to provide buoyancy, while wooden models achieve that through the natural buoyancy of the wood.

Lures in this group can be divided into four different depth/zone categories: shallow runners that dive to about four feet; medium runners that will hit seven or eight feet; deep runners that will reach ten to fifteen feet; and ultra-deep divers that will probe the twenty- to thirty-foot depths.

The most obvious factor determining how deep a lure will dive is the lip. Short-lipped lures will not dive as deep as will long-billed baits. Nor will small baits dive as deep as the larger models. The angle at which the lip joins the body also plays a role in how deep the bait can go. The deepest running lures feature a lip that joins the body at as close to the same angle of the body as possible. Lips that exit the

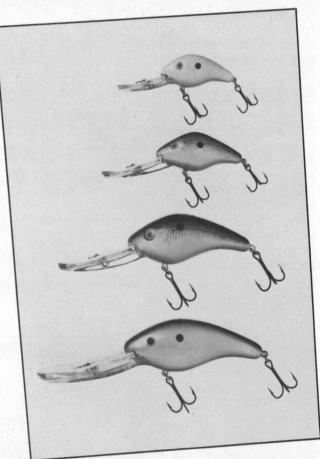

Mann's family of deep divers shows relative differences in size. From top are Deep 10, Deep 15, Deep 20 and new Boar Hog, that will reach thirty feet without any problem.

Left: Pro angler John Torian plays crankbait-hooked bass with rod tip held low so fish won't jump, eject the bait. (Below) Some experts add strip of fluorescent paint to belly of crankbait, replace factory hooks with widemouth treble models.

body at forty-five degrees or other angles moving away from the body will not reach great depths.

Most manufacturers will print the lure's approximate running depth on the package the bait comes in. Sometimes these stated running depths are a bit optimistic, but generally they're accurate enough for comparision purposes.

While each crankbait will have its running depth "built-in" by the manufacturer, anglers can alter it somewhat through their choice of line size. Smaller diameter lines — 8- to 12-pound test — offer less water resistance and can increase the bait's running depth by up to twenty percent. Anglers can gain still more running depth by sticking their rod tip down into the water while the bait is being retrieved. This decreases the line-to-lure angle and lets the bait dig deeper.

Equipping yourself with a selection of baits that allows you to handle different depth ranges effectively is important with floater/diver crankbaits, because if there is one real secret to their success, it can be summed this way:

"To me, crankbaits are not being fished effectively unless they are digging into the bottom or ricocheting off cover," says three-time world champion Rick Clunn. "Actively feeding bass may take a 'free-swimming' crankbait — one that is not hitting something — but most of the time you need to make the lure hit something in order to give it a sudden and erratic change of direction. That is the key to triggering non-feeding bass into hitting a crankbait."

An angler fishing a stump flat in three or four feet of water could use a deep diving bait to stay in contact with the bottom, but that would result in a slow retrieve as the lure would be digging into the bottom constantly. If a faster retrieve was called for, a crankbait in the shallow or medium-running category would be more appropriate.

Sometimes, anglers may want to shift to shallow-running baits simply because they are smaller and the size of the lure often plays a role in its success.

"I try to match my lure to the size of the forage the bass are eating," states former BASS Master Classic winner, Paul Elias. "In the late spring and early summer, most of the forage fish are smaller and I'll often use smaller baits. The water is usually a bit colder then, as well, and the bass may not be active enough to take a big bait. In late summer and fall, though, I usually use a large bait, because the bait fish have grown and the bass are used to eating larger forage."

In addition to selecting various sizes and depth ranges, anglers also should have baits in both wood and plastic. Each has its own characteristics that often can make one model more effective than the other.

For example, plastic-bodied crankbaits usually can be cast farther than wooden ones and are less bouyant. Longer casts can be important when fishing deeper than ten feet or so, because most crankbaits will reach their deepest depth about two-thirds of the way back to the boat. If you want to bang a crankbait into a submerged log in ten feet of water, you'll have to cast well beyond it for the crankbait to reach that depth by the time it reaches the target. Since plastic baits are less bouyant and don't float up as quickly when you stop reeling them, they tend to suspend at that depth and remain in the strike zone longer. This is an advantage when fishing submerged cover and one reason why plastic crankbaits often are favored for deeper water.

At times, it may be advantageous for the bait to rise quickly when the retrieve is stopped. This is especially true when fishing a crankbait over soft, clinging cover like submerged grassbeds that will foul the bait, if it gets too far into

Lightly hooked bass often are landed by hand, while those that are hooked solidly are flipped into boat with rod. Many pros play fish carefully to see how it is hooked.

the cover. Here an angler can crank a wooden crankbait down until he first feels it contact the cover, then kill the retrieve to let it quickly float free. A stop-and-go retrieve like this often can draw fish out of the depths of the grassbed to nail your lure.

Different materials also give the lures different actions and sometimes the bass prefer one over the other. Wooden lures, for example, usually have a wider wobbling action that gives off more vibrations. They often can be more effective in muddy or off-colored water where the increased vibrations can help a bass zero in on the bait. Plastic lures usually have a tighter wobbling action that has proven more effective in clear water.

These are generalities though, and the only way to really determine a crankbait's action is to put it into the water and test it. There are exceptions to the rule, one of the most notable being the Rapala Shad Rap. This is a wooden lure, but has tight wobbling action.

For years, many anglers believed that the faster they retrieved a floater/diver crankbait, the deeper it would run.

This has proven to be untrue and anglers now are discovering it's fine to crank a lure quickly down to its depth, but once there, the retrieve should be slowed to help keep it there longer.

Another important aspect to fishing these lures effectively is to constantly vary the retrieve, until you figure out what the bass want. Sometimes a slow stop-and-go retrieve does the job, while other times might call for more erratic speed changes. Professional anglers rarely retrieve a crankbait at a steady, unvarying pace.

Sometimes crankbaits will not track in a straight line. This could be due to the lure being damaged by cover or bass, but sometimes the bait is just "out of tune," as it comes from the factory, and will run to either the right or the left.

This will cause the lure to run more shallow, but it's not hard to correct. Hold the bait in your hand with the line tie eye pointing toward you. Then, using a pair of needle nosed pliers, bend the eye gently in the direction you want the bait to run. Most off-track lures can be corrected in this manner.

However, sometimes a bait that runs to one side can be a definite asset! This is true when fishing steep rock bluffs. A lure that will run constantly toward the bluff can be made to bounce off it and sometimes trigger a strike from a bass that might ignore a "tuned" bait. The same holds true for boat docks: A bait can be made to run under the dock, where many bass usually lie. Some expert anglers deliberately maltune a crankbait to go places a properly running lure won't. The procedure is exactly the same as when turning a bait to run straight; just bend the line tie eye slightly in the direction you want the bait to run.

Countdown Crankbaits: If assembling an effective selection of floater/divers sounds a bit complicated, the reverse is true with the countdown models. While there are a few minor, but important differences among the various models, they all share some common characteristics. All are compact lures that cast easily and for great distances. They all sink at a rate of six inches to one foot per second when not being retrieved, they all feature a tight wobbling action and they tend to stay at the same depth during the retrieve that they had reached before the retrieve started.

Because the angler has far more control over the depth and speed at which these lures will run, they often can be the answer to some frustrating fishing situations.

One of their most common uses is in pursuing surface-schooling bass. They are ideal for this, since they can be cast a long way, retrieved near the surface where the bass are feeding and their size is a close match for the shad the bass are feeding on.

Because they can be retrieved at shallow depths, they are also a top choice for fishing over the top of submerged grass, hydrilla or milfoil. In this situation, one of the smaller baits like the 6500 series Bayou Boogie can be "buzzed" over the top of the submerged grass in water as shallow as eight or nine inches! This can be a deadly tactic early and late in the day, when fish are actively foraging near the surface. Diving baits cannot do this.

Countdown crankbaits also can be retrieved at a much higher rate of speed than can the diving baits; quite often, speed will generate a strike.

A popular technique — and one that, surprisingly, works just as well in the winter as during warmer weather — is

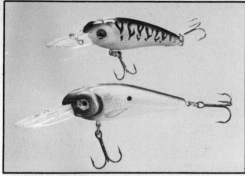

These Whopper Stopper Shadraks run with a tight wiggling action. Upper bait can reach six feet; lower model sinks to 10.

Some anglers use crankbaits to locate fish in open water. At less than 20 feet, this type strains water faster than other lures.

"burning" a countdown crankbait. For this, the bait is cast beyond a potential piece of fish-holding cover such as a stump, dock piling or log and retrieved as fast as it can be cranked without being made to roll up on its side.

An extremely high-speed bait zipping by a bass's nose gives the fish little time to make up its mind whether to strike or not. Its inherent predatory instincts often take over and it nails the lure.

I once was fishing a team tournament on a Florida lake during the early spring months, when my partner and I located some bass feeding over the top of some small, sub-merged patches of hydrilla. The *only* way we could get them to hit was to burn a Sugar Shad crankbait over the grass as fast as we could turn the reel handles. Other baits and slower retrieves went untouched. But speed cranking a countdown crankbait resulted in bass of 7½ and 6¾ pounds, as well as several other large fish being hooked and shaking free. The area we were fishing was crowded with boats and, apparently, the bass were spooky. If they had time to inspect a lure they rejected it, but one whizzing by their noses so fast that they couldn't get a good look at it was successful.

I've run into that situation many times since and have made it a practice to try burning a Sugar Shad through an area before giving up on it and moving elsewhere.

This also has proven to be an excellent tactic in cold weather, when the bass may not be actively seeking food. Even though they may not be actively feeding, a high-speed countdown crankbait burning by their nose can often trigger a reactive strike. I have used this technique to catch bass in Florida under weather conditions that were absolutely dreadful; thirty-degree air temperature, twenty-mile-per-hour wind and a bright, post-cold-front sky. Under these conditions I wouldn't have given the proverbial plugged nickel for my chances of catching bass with other techniques, including live bait. But speedcranking a Sugar Shad or Bayou Boogie caught fish.

On other occasions, the same basic stop-and-go retrieve used with the diving plugs will work well. So too, will banging the bait off a cover object. In fact, many professional

Shallow running crankbaits are deadly when retrieved slowly through cover, pausing to let the lure float to the surface. Bass will strike the bait as it is cranked under surface after such a pause in retrieve.

bass fishermen will tell you that, when they are fishing a small brush pile or other fish-holding object, they know it's time to find another spot, if they can bang a countdown crankbait into it a few times and not get hit.

"If you slam a Rat-L-Trap into a brush pile and don't get bit," says pro angler Johnnie Borden," It's because there aren't any bass there."

Another effective technique with these lures is to "walk" them down steeply sloping banks. After the cast, the bait is allowed to sink to the bottom, the slack line taken up and the rod pumped sharply upward to "jump" the bait off the bottom and toward the angler. When the bait sinks to the bottom again, the procedure is repeated.

This can be a deadly method for taking largemouths, smallmouths and spotted bass from steeply sloping points, submerged channel edges, underwater islands and other deep structure.

In short, countdown crankbaits often can accomplish tasks that the more commonly used diving baits cannot. And, they'll catch their share of big bass, as well. In fact, one of the largest bass taken in recent years, a nineteen-pound, three-ounce brute fell victim to a countdown Rapala in the hands of California angler, Arden Hanline. His tactic was to cast the lure out, let it sink to the bottom, then work it back over the cover in a series of short twitches. Although the technique is a bit unusual, Hanline had used it to catch a number of eight- to ten-pound bass from Southern California lakes, indicating it certainly was no fluke!

Anglers intent upon realizing the maximum potential from the countdown crankbaits can do it with a simple selection. Essentially, you'll want some one-quarter- or one-third-ounce models for use in shallow water. These baits don't sink as fast as the larger sizes and can be retrieved close to the surface. This is a big advantage when fishing over the top of submerged vegetation. Favored lures here would be the 6500 series Bayou Boogie or the one-quarter-ounce Rat-L-Trap.

When longer casts or deeper retrieves are called for, shift to a larger bait like the three-quarter-ounce Sugar Shad, Rippin' Rattler or Rat-L-Trap. An adequate selection doesn't have to be large.

Countdown crankbaits are effective when retrieved quickly over shallow grass beds and other structures. (Below) Each of these lures has different running characteristics. From left are Rippin' Rattler, Bayou Boogie 6500, Sugar Shad.

Neither does a productive selection of colors. Whether you're using the floater/divers or the countdown models, you'll be well served if your chosen colors match the natural forage on which the bass are feeding. Chrome with a blue or black back or gray shad are popular choices on waters where shad form the predominant forage. Crawfish patterns (brown/orange/red) often are a top choice in rocky reservoirs. Gold finishes are effective during the winter months in the South, when shiners comprise a significant portion of the bass's diet. You also may want to include some green/yellow "perch" patterns in your selection, as well. Many expert anglers add a strip of fluorescent orange to the belly of their lures with one of the popular lure paints, like Catchin' Colors. They feel this particular color can help in triggering strikes.

One last color that always should be carried is chartreuse firetiger — a chartreuse body with black strips and an orange belly. This is a highly visible color and is deadly in stained or muddy water.

In general, fluorescent-based colors frequently can be most effective in stained water, while reflective chromes and shad finishes can be a better bet in clear water.

Getting a bass to take a crankbait isn't difficult, but given the lure's small treble hooks and heavy body weight that the bass can throw, playing a bass properly becomes important with these lures.

Many professional anglers have discovered that "softer," more flexible rod tips give them a built-in shock absorber that helps prevent the bass from ripping the small hooks free. While graphite or boron usually get the nod in the majority of fishing situations, fiberglass — or composite rods that feature a glass tip section married to a graphite butt section — is the preferred choice when fishing any crankbait.

When fishing deep diving baits, where casting distance is critical in achieving the lure's depth, seven- to 7½-foot rods are favored. With shallow diving baits, or countdown models, 5½- to six-foot rods serve well.

"The position of your rod when you're retrieving the bait can also be important," says professional angler Ken Cook. He used crankbaits to win the $50,000 U.S. Bass Anglers Dream Tournament on Tennessee's Lake Chickamauga in May 1987. "The tip should be held down near the surface of the water and not pointed at the lure. A crankbait is a reflex action lure that the bass inhales. You really shouldn't even feel the bass strike when you're retrieving a crankbait quickly. The bait will just get 'heavy' and the fish is there. The bass will actually hook itself and, when you feel the fish on, you just keep reeling. If you give a big hook set or try to horse the fish in, you can pull the bait out of its mouth and lose the fish."

Most anglers will set their drag fairly loose, so even a two- or three-pound bass can pull line. When this is combined with a rod tip that flexes enough to act as a shock absorber, plus the low rod position, most bass will hook themselves and not be able to exert enough pressure to pull off the hooks. This technique will increase the number of bass an angler can land on crankbaits by a considerable margin.

Serious anglers will keep their hook honed to a razor edge and often replace heavier factory treble hooks with lighter-wire models that offer easier penetration in a bass. The VMC widemouth treble hooks are commonly used for this.

Setting up an effective crankbait system is a relatively simple affair and the techniques for their use are easily mastered.

CHAPTER 11

TAKE THEM ON TOP

Modern Surface Lures Add A New Dimension To Bass Action!

Left: More than respectable bass can be caught with lures that work the water's surface. (Above) Florida pro Cliff McKendree prefers long casts in shallow water to keep his bait in close contact with the cover in which he fishes. This professional angler contends that most fishermen don't give the bass enough time to make up their minds on bait.

Topwater baits can be effective during any month of the year, if proper noise/action model is chosen. Anglers who put surface plugs away in winter miss much action. (Below) Pop-R, at top, and Throbber are examples of the chugger lures.

THERE ARE few thrills in the angling world to compare with watching a potbellied bass explode through the surface in an attempt to dismantle a topwater plug. It's even more exciting if it happens to be your lure he's after.

Bass and topwater lures go together like politicians and promises. In fact, it's doubtful if any other species of gamefish is associated so closely with one particular fishing technique. Surface lures were among the first crude artificial baits employed in the pursuit of bass and they're every bit as effective today as they were over one hundred years ago.

Some professional bass fisherman even feel they are the best possible choice any time the bass are in shallow water.

"A topwater lure," says Jacksonville, Florida, bass pro Cliff McKendree, "is the lure I'll usually start with any time I feel the bass are within seven feet or so of the surface, because it's actually two lures in one. If the bass are in a feeding mood, it's a great food imitator that can represent either a terrestrial animal or an injured minnow. If they're not feeding — and that happens much of the time — it becomes a superb reaction bait that can aggravate the bass to the point where they must attack the lure."

McKendree, who has won over $100,000 in Florida tournaments over the last three years, is considered one of the best topwater anglers in a state that fairly bristles with them. And like many professional anglers, he has learned that the bass's inherent predatory instincts often can make it a sucker for a floating lure.

"It doesn't really matter whether the bass are roaming

Not all of the big bass are on the bottom of the lake as is evidenced by this heavyweight. Techniques work year-around.

around looking for food or buried up tight under a log. If you can get a topwater lure to that fish, you can keep it on top of the bass, making a commotion, until you literally make that bass come after the bait. You can't do that with other types of baits.''

While early floating lures were seldom more than crudely tied bits of feather or handcarved chunks of wood, today's angler will find a broad and varied assortment of surface plugs from which to choose. They can be had in wood, hard plastic and even soft plastic. They will gurgle, chug, swish, twitch or dance from side to side. In fact, it is doubtful that any other lure type has as many different variations to choose from and, under some conditions, bass may show a distinct preference for one particular type.

Anglers intending to become proficient with topwater baits should recognize the different types and their uses.

Professional anglers like Californian Rick Tauber often favor topwater baits in clear water, as they can draw in distant bass.

Minnow Lures: These slender-bodied offerings are best characterized by the classic Rapala Floating Minnow. Today they are available in wood (Rapala and other makes) or plastic (Whopper Stopper Hellcat, Cordell Redfin and others). They float at rest and dive to twelve to eighteen inches when retrieved steadily. They make excellent shallow-running crankbaits, but their appeal to expert bass anglers is as a surface lure.

These lures most often are worked in a series of short twitches that cause the bait to dance lightly on the surface without moving far from its original landing point. This soft, subtle action can draw bass from a considerable distance and they are one of the most effective baits for clear water situations.

The wooden models can be a bit awkward to cast on baitcasting equipment and most experts favor spinning gear with them. They also have discovered that the bait exhibits a livelier action when the line is tied to it with a loop-type knot or when a small split ring is attached to the line tie eye and the line tied to it.

Fore and Aft Propeller Baits: Available in wood or plastic, these baits have a propeller mounted in the front and rear that will kick up a considerable fuss when twitched with authority.

Popular models of this type include the Cordell Boy Howdy, Devil's Horse and Griffen Bass Baffler. These lures are deadly when heavy cover might prevent a bass from locating the lure visually and they can "call" bass from quite a ways off.

While most of these models move forward in a straight

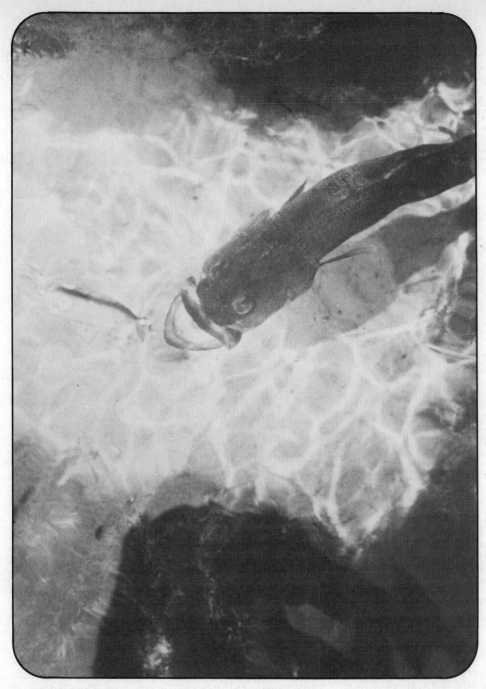

In clear water, bass can be cautious in an approach to a topwater lure. An angler should use long casts and work the lure slowly to give the fish the time to decide to hit the lure.

line when twitched, others tend to dart to one side. This can pose a control problem in and around heavy cover, where these lures are most effective. This is normally caused by both propellers turning in the same direction, which torques the bait to one side and can foul the line on the hooks. Solve this by grasping one of the propellers and turning the blades in the opposite direction. By reversing the blade pitch on one blade, the propellers turn in opposite directions and the bait will retrieve straight.

Rear Propeller Baits: These bits feature one propeller mounted in the rear. This creates a commotion, but also gives the bait a distinctly different set of moves than the twin prop baits. The weight of the rear propeller often causes them to take the tail-down posture at rest. Depending upon the skill of the angler, they can be retrieved straight or made to exhibit a side-to-side darting action, at a variety of different noise levels. This is one of the most versatile topwater lures and the best example of this type is the Whopper Stopper Hellraiser. I consider this lure one of the finest topwater baits ever made.

When retrieved in a series of short, sharp twitches, it is an almost perfect imitation of a shad skipping on the surface and can be awesomely effective any time shad minnows form the predominant forage.

Chuggers: These lures feature a deeply dished nose that creates a distinct "blooping" sound when twitched. They're often referred to as poppers and were one of the earliest topwater designs to become successful. They don't cover a lot of water, but they do work heck out of one spot.

These baits had fallen into disuse among professional

The physical characteristics of the bass make it a most effective predator when attacking from below. Topwater lures have been shown to be highly effective under a wide range of conditions. They can be used all year in right situation.

anglers until a few Texas competitors began achieving excellent results on the Rebel Pop-R. These pros were shaving the lower lip to reduce the sound levels and were retrieving the bait in a quick series of twitches that made it "bloop" its way across the surface in a rapid and erratic manner. This is not the traditional way to employ a chugger bait, but it won a lot of money.

This shows that, when you're dealing with a critter as notoriously unpredictable as the bass, the best lure in an angler's tackle box might well be an open mind. While many bass-catching techniques are presented as the "best way to do it," it should be remembered that each is only the "best way" we know of at the moment. Bass fishermen are an innovative lot; even if they can't always figure out how to build a better mousetrap, they often come up with new ways to use an existing one.

Stick Baits: Typified by the venerable Zara Spook, these baits got their name because they have all the action of a stick, until a skilled angler brings them to life with his rod tip. They are not the easiest surface lure to use, but when the big cigar-shaped plugs start zig-zagging their way across the surface, they have an uncanny ability to bring outsized bass charging up from surprisingly deep water.

These baits are worked with the rod tip pointing down toward the water's surface, being moved in a continuous series of sharp jerks while the reel constantly takes up the slack line generated. When done properly — which requires practice and the use of a fairly stiff rod — the plug will

"walk" forward in an exaggerated side-to-side dance. These baits have proven deadly on deep, clear impoundments, especially during the warmer months of the year, when bass are active enough to really charge a lure.

Soft Plastic Lures: This class of lure is a fairly recent development and was created to fill a specific need that the other types of surface lures could not: presenting a topwater bait in dense, sometimes surface-matted vagetation.

This type of cover often can hold large numbers of bass, but is usually far too thick to fish with an exposed hook lure. The Burke's Flex plugs are one example of this lure type, along with the various plastic frogs. They're made of soft plastic and the hooks are protected by wire forms that bend out of the way when a bass takes the bait.

Another type is that "floating" plastic worm or lizard. Examples of these are the Fliptail Floating Lizard — one of my favorites for spring bass'n in Florida — and the Zeta Bait Float-A-Hook worm. The term "floating" is a bit confusing here, because almost any plastic worm will float. But they won't do it with anything bigger than a light wire hook and they're not always heavy enough to cast on tackle stout enough to wrestle a fish out of the thick cover they are most effective in. The floating worm and lizard solve this problem by using special high-bouyancy plastics that allow the bait to float with a stout 3/0 or 4/0 worm hook inserted in it.

When rigged in the same manner as a Texas-rigged plastic worm, they are just as weedless and are heavy enough to

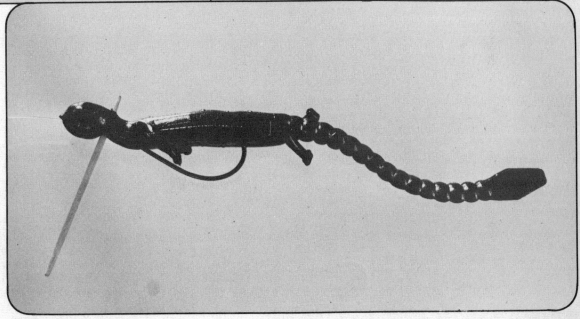

Stick baits such as this Dog Walker have reputation for producing big bass. They are especially effective in clear water of deep man-made lakes. (Below) Fliptail floating lizard is excellent choice to fish heavy cover. Toothpick is placed through hook eye after insertion in the lizard. Wood is clipped off flush with the sides of the bait to fish.

be cast on medium-weight baitcasting gear.

When rigging the worm or lizard, it is advisable to "peg" the head of the lure to the eye of the hook with a toothpick. Once the lure is rigged Texas-style on the hook, insert a toothpick through the bait's head and the eye of the hook. Clip off the excess. This helps prevent the lure from sliding down the shank of the hook, improving both its weedless properties and hook-setting ability.

The most important thing anglers need remember when using any of the plastic topwater baits is to delay the hook set until the bass actually has the bait and has turned downward with it. Striking too soon will result in a missed fish. I generally drop my rod tip toward the fish as soon as I see the strike, then wait a second or so until I see the line move. Then I set the hook as I would with a plastic worm; high and hard!

Rods used to fish topwater plugs are as varied as the lures themselves. Often, a certain rod action will prove most effective with a specific lure. For example, the Zara Spook requires a fairly stiff rod to achieve the proper action on the lure, as well as to cast its five-eighths-ounce weight. A 5½-foot medium-heavy casting rod with 14- to 20-pound line makes the job easier. On the other hand, that rod would not allow an angler to even cast a four-inch balsawood Rapala. This lure requires lighter gear and many experts use six-foot spinning rods spooled with 10-pound line.

As a general rule, lures featuring small #6 treble hooks are best fished on rods with a lighter action. This helps prevent pulling the small hooks free from the bass. Heavier baits, using #4 or #2 trebles, require a stiffer rod to get the larger hooks properly set in the bass. So too, will the soft plastic baits.

Some excellent topwater baits come from the factory equipped with hooks that are, quite literally, junk. Soft and dull, they are straightened easily by a decent fish. Why

Left: Boy Howdy (top) and Scrambler are good example of double propeller baits. Noisy surface lures will draw bass from a distance. (Below) Hellraiser comes in two sizes. It is the author's favorite plug to use in topwater fishing.

some manufacturers feel they can equip their $4 lure with a set of two-cent hooks is something that escapes me.

But serious anglers have learned to live with it and generally spend a few moments with each new lure to sharpen the hooks or replace the hopeless ones. The VMC Widemouth treble hooks and the Mustad Double Strong trebles are popular replacement choices. Many anglers keep these in their tackle boxes while on the water so they can replace any hooks instantly that might be damaged in use.

Once properly equipped, success with topwater lures is often the result of selecting the best noise/action model for the conditions at hand. On some days, bass may cheerfully assault any floating lure. On others, they may take only one type. This can depend on surface conditions, seasonal conditions or on a particular "sound signature" of the bait.

"My basic starting philosophy," explains Cliff McKendree, "is to begin by matching the noise and action of my lure to the mood of the fish. The colder the water, the more sluggish the bass will be and the slower and quieter a lure I would use."

During the winter and pre-spawn period, McKendree often begins with a minnow lure like the Rapala, twitching it slowly on top. Sometimes, he will even pull it down under the surface, then let it float back up.

Coldwater bass often prefer a "subtle presentation." As the water warms in the spring or if he finds his winter fish taking his Rapala vigorously, he may shift to a single rear propeller bait.

"This is a good compromise," McKendree explains," between a real noisy bait and a quiet Rapala or the plastic Rogue, which I also favor. It's a good transitional bait and I use it a lot in the spring."

On days when the bass simply swirl under his topwater plugs, McKendree has found dropping back to a quiet bait and slowing his retrieve can help turn curious fish into striking fish. If the bass are blasting the bait with authority, however, shifting to a faster, noisier bait allows him to cover the water more quickly, call bass from greater distances and ultimately show his lure to more fish.

As spring turns into summer and waters continue to warm, the bass become more active. McKendree goes right along with them by switching to larger, noisier baits, like the twin propellor models and the stick baits.

"The real key to topwater success," McKendree feels, "is to have a definite place to start, but not to be locked into it. If you start with a noisy lure and the bass just roll at it, don't be afraid to change baits and retrieves and, more importantly, the sound of the bait. Let the bass tell you what they want, then do your best to give it to them."

McKendree's topwater tackle box almost takes two men to carry. Within it lies one of the most varied selections of floating plugs you're likely to see. He wants to be able to "give the bass what they want." and his experience has shown that frequently can take some experimenting.

"I think the sound of the lure — not just the sound that type of lure makes but the actual sound made by that particular lure itself — can play a big role in whether or not a fish will hit it. I've proven this to myself many times while fishing at night: two men fishing the same lure, on the same water, from the same boat, only one of them getting hits. The only real variable was the sound of the individual baits and I've seen it make a difference."

When McKendree finds a particular plug among his collection that seems to produce better than average results,

Surface baits can appeal to large bass such as this ten-pounder taken during a major Florida tournament on a plug.

he guards it jealously. When it comes to selecting colors, he takes a very simple approach.

"I like the basic natural colors and flashes found on the forage the bass are eating," he states. "Shad and many small baitfish reflect a silver light and, if you hold up a shiner, you'll see a gold reflection. The bass is used to see-ing these colors on an injured forage fish and that's the one that's going to get blasted first. I always fish a shad, chrome or gold finish, usually with some sparkle flake on it, to help reflect that strike triggering light."

On a Texas bass-fishing trip several years ago, the most productive topwater color was a green perch finish. That

Minnow lures like Whopper Stopper Hellcat (top) and the Rapala floating minnow are quiet surface baits that are highly effective in clear water. Correct rigging can provide more lively action.

was explained by my host who informed me that we were fishing in an area where bream were spawning and the bass were feeding on them. Matching the hatch with topwater lures can be a highly effective way to select your colors.

Picking the best lure and color for the conditions at hand is an important part of success with topwater lures. But, according to McKendree, the biggest single reason anglers fail to realize the full potential of topwater lures has nothing to do with the model tied onto the end of their line. He's convinced that many anglers simply don't get the bait to the fish or keep it in front of them long enough to trigger the strike.

"A topwater bait," he speculates, "will make a fisherman an accurate caster, at least, if he wants to catch any fish. If you're not in close contact with the cover object you're fishing, you will miss many fish, especially the inactive ones that won't move more than a foot or so to take your bait. This is probably the most important aspect of fishing a topwater plug effectively. Get it tight to the cover, then don't be in a hurry to reel it in. Let it stay there and work for you."

Staying close to the cover, whether it be a fallen log, edge of a weedline or some other bass holding object, is almost

an obsession with McKendree. Frequently, he will position the boat so he can cast parallel to the object in order to keep his bait in contact with it for the maximum period of time. Making longer casts is another tactic.

"I like making long casts in shallow water," he explains, "because it gives the bass more time to make up his mind about the bait. If you're making a lot of short casts, some of the fish will follow the bait, but turn off when they see the boat. With a longer cast, the bass has more time to make a mistake — and a lot of them will."

While McKendree is giving the bass enough time to make a mistake, he makes certain he's not charged with an error.

"Another real key to topwater fishing," he points out, "is to keep your eyes glued to the lure while it's in the water. You need to concentrate on what's happening around the lure. Watch for swirls, boils and the wakes made by bass swimming up to take a look at the bait. These signs will give you clues regarding what changes you may have to make in your lure or retrieve. The bass will tell you what they want, but only if you're listening to them.

"When a bass does blow up on your lure, you've got to keep your eyes on it to make certain the fish actually has it

Few moments in bass fishing offer more of a thrill than to watch a big bass attempt to dismantle the topwater lure.

and didn't just swat at it. A lot of people take their lure away from the bass by striking at the noise or the boil made by the fish, when the fish doesn't have the bait.

"A lot of times, these fish will come back and get the lure if it's still there. But, if you strike too soon and take it away from him, you can kiss that bass goodbye."

Effective topwater bass fishing sometimes can be a slow and painstaking affair. Done correctly it does have a way of getting exciting in a hurry.

"My best topwater bass," McKendree grins, "was 11¼ pounds. It hit right in the middle of the day and blew water everywhere! To me, that's bass fishing and I'll always remember that one."

Topwater bass fishing can do that to you.

CHAPTER 12

Preferred forage size for the average bass is 2 to 4 inches. The Gitzit bait falls within that size range, while it exhibits a slender baitfish profile.

Author (foreground) gets a lesson in how to use Gitzit from its inventor, Bobby Garland, on a Tennessee river.

STRUCTURE LURES & FINESSE BAITS

...Or How To Choose A Lure
To Handle The Tough Times

Left: Selection of jig heads of different sizes allows an angler to fish any water depth or cover condition. As photo shows, they can be rigged exposed or weedless. (Below) Weedless Shakin' worm rig undulates as it falls in water; often tempts bass that ignore the conventional lures and retrieves.

IN THE vast majority of bass fishing situations encountered throughout much of the country, an angler is well equipped with a selection of the baits detailed in the previous four chapters. But, there are times when conventional tactics will prove ineffective.

"Tough times bass'n" can occur when bass move into water depths greater than fifteen feet, or so. Few lures can be presented properly and controlled at this depth. Clear water can cause problems as well, often rendering large lures ineffective. To combat this, a special group of lures has been developed that sometimes turn the tables on finicky bass. Depending upon where you live in bass country, they may be needed seldom — but when you do need them, you truly need them!

Slab Spoons: Also referred to as "structure spoons" or "jigging spoons," these compact baits can take bass effectively from depths of over eighty feet! Their most common use is a vertical jigging presentation that hops the bait along the bottom, underneath the boat. This vertical presentation is the most effective way to fish water deeper than fifteen feet, since the bait is lowered to the depth the fish are using and kept there. No time is wasted on the casting of the lure or in retrieve time needed to allow it to sink to the desired depth.

In use, the bait is lowered over the side and allowed to fall on a free line to the desired depth. The reel then is engaged and the rod pumped upward to make the spoon leap toward the surface about five or six feet. The rod then is lowered back toward the water's surface to allow the spoon to flutter downward. As the rod is being lowered, the angler should adjust its speed to put a slight amount of slack into the line. This "controlled slack" lets the spoon fall with a freer action than simply lowering it down on a tight line.

Repeated pumping motions will cause the spoon to dance and flutter at whatever depth the angler has chosen. In appearance, this resembles an injured shad and can draw strikes from even non-feeding bass.

These lures are available in a variety of sizes with the most commonly used being one-half-, three-quarter- and one-ounce weights. They are popular baits among anglers pursuing all three species of bass in highland manmade reservoirs; they are especially effective during the winter and summer months when bass school up on deepwater structures.

Chrome or gold finishes are the most popular colors, but some anglers have been successful by experimenting with small splashes of fluorescent paint on the spoon. Adding a dash of red or orange can often add to the effectiveness of the spoon.

Bobby Garland probes the shady recesses below a series of docks with his Gitzit. In clear water conditions, smaller lures, lighter lines often can make the difference between success, failure in this particular type of bass fishing.

When selecting a slab spoon, anglers should make certain that it has a split ring attached to the line tie hole and the line should be tied to this ring. Also, hooks should be thin wire treble hooks (size four is the most popular) and they should be razor sharp. Most strikes will be light: a subtle tick or just a twitch of the line as the lure flutters downward. Anglers must react quickly to snap the rod upward before the bass ejects the spoon. Sharp, thin-wire hooks will penetrate much more easily than heavy forged hooks and will increase the number of hook-ups for the angler.

Rods used for vertical jigging should be the most sensitive available. Graphite or boron models in a medium action are preferred and many expert anglers opt for lines in the eight- to twelve-pound range. Spinning or casting models work equally well. Spoons also can be cast to surface schooling bass and retrieved quickly near the surface to imitate a fleeing shad and they can sometimes be effective when cast over a deep structure and retrieved in a vigorous pumping motion. But there are better baits for those two tasks.

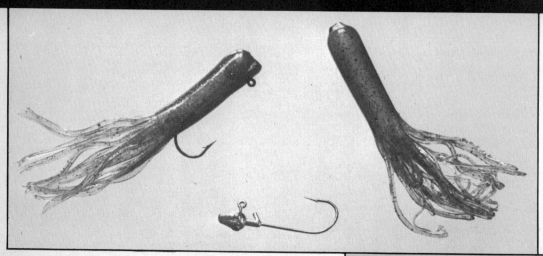

Above: Gitzit at left is rigged properly. Hook exits lure body forward of body-tail juncture. This prevents tail wrapping around hook to cause line twist. (Right) Craw George (left) and Whopper Spinner can be jigged or cast.

Lead Tail Spinners: Characterized by the famous Little George or the Whopper Spin, these lures are, in effect, lead countdown crankbaits with a tail-mounted spinner. They can be used for vertical jigging in the same manner as the slab spoons and are deadly when pumped across the bottom. But they are often most effective when cast and retrieved in contact with deep structure. They function in much the same manner as a countdown crankbait, but their heavy, compact form allows them to achieve far greater depths.

One drawback to these baits is that their weight — and the one small treble hook with which they are equipped — makes them relatively easy for the bass to throw. One way to combat this is to cut the hook off the lure and thread the line through the upper line tie eye, around the side of the bait, then through the lower line tie eye, where a #6 or #4 widemouth treble hook then is tied on. This lets the body of the bait slide up the line as a fish is played and removes the weight and leverage that bass need to throw the bait.

Jig and Grub: Long used by saltwater anglers in pursuit of trout and redfish, these diminutive plastic-bodied baits can be deadly on all species of bass as well. The most commonly used size among freshwater anglers is a two-inch grub body on a one-quarter-ounce head. Most experts prefer to fish these baits on 5½- to six-foot spinning rods spooled with six- to ten-pound line.

In use, they are cast over the structure, allowed to sink to the bottom, then retrieved in a series of short, sharp twitches of the rod that hops the bait across the bottom. They can be deadly any time of the year, with the retrieve being slowed in the winter months and speeded up in warm weather. They are among the most useful bass lures for anglers fishing in clear, unobstructed waters.

The grub bodies also can be had in curly-tailed models. These can be effective when fished in a conventional manner or when retrieved slowly and steadily over deeper

cover. These are excellent baits for probing submerged channel edges, deep points and sharply dropping banks.

Color can make a big difference with these lures and the most popular are: smoke, with or without silver flake; clear with silver flake; pearl white; light green; amber; and translucent chartreuse, with a bit of silver flake.

Tube Lures: Characterized by the Bobby Garland Gitzit, these odd-looking little baits comprise one of the most popular and effective lures an angler can fish in any clear water situation.

Originally made popular by anglers fishing the clear, deep waters of the Western United States, they have spread slowly across the country and are now in common use by anglers pursuing largemouths in Florida, smallmouths in New Hampshire or spotted bass in Kentucky. Although they resemble the jig-and-grub in outward appearance, they are far more versatile.

"The Gitzit's role falls somewhere between that of a plastic worm and a jig," says its inventor, Bobby Garland, who has won several major tournaments with the lure. "It makes a different 'noise' than either of them and the small tails on the bait vibrate differently to produce it."

Gitzits are available in two basic sizes: the three-inch body and the five-inch body. They are rigged for fishing by inserting the jig head into the body of the hollow lure, which results in a well streamlined bait.

Adjusting the weight and fall speed of the lure is done similarly to that of a plastic worm: the heavier the jig head,

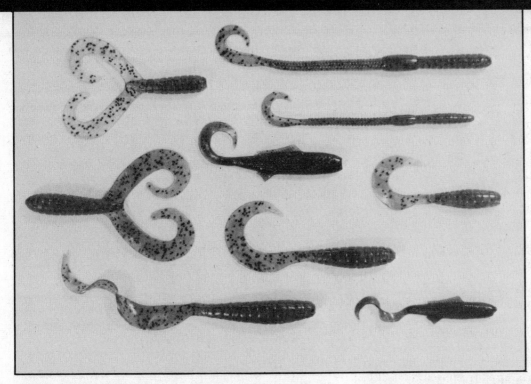

Variety of soft plastic baits can be used with Shakin' Dart head. The selection by Angler's Pro Specialties shows various combinations angler can choose from.

the faster the bait falls. Since the Gitzit, for some reason, is taken most often by the bass as it falls, it can be important to be able to select different fall rates.

"I would recommend that anglers carry a selection of three- and five-inch bodies and jig heads in 1/16, ⅛ and ¼ ounce," says Garland. "If you regularly fish in deep water, where the bass may be forty feet down, you'll want a few ⅜- or ½-ounce heads as well."

In water less than five feet deep, Garland often uses the 1/16-ounce head with the three-inch body. If the water is a bit stained or if the bass seem to be quite active, he'll shift to the five-inch body and might go up to the one-eighth-ounce head. "The five-inch body seems to catch bigger bass," he feels.

For water up to ten feet, or so, the three-inch body and the one-eighth-ounce jig head get the nod. Water deeper than that would call for a heavier head.

Garland can also adjust the falling action of the bait depending upon where he brings the hook eye out of the lures body.

"When you rig a Gitzit," he suggests, "moisten the jig head with a little saliva to help it slide freely into the body and be careful not to push any of the little legs or tails into the body with the jig head. When you have the jig head pushed into the body, grasp the rear of the body — where the tails join the body — between your thumb and forefinger and stretch it out so the hook point can be brought out of the body forward of the tail section. If the hook point is at the junction of tail and body, it can cause line twist. Always bring it out forward of the tail.

"After that, just press down on the line tie eye and it will pop through the body. It is important that the line tie eye

and the hook be centered in the body in a straight line with each other or you will get line twist."

To slow the fall rate and give the lure a spiraling action as it falls, bring the line tie eye out of the body about one-quarter inch rearward of the head end. For a straighter drop or, when fishing in soft cover that may cause the bait to collect weeds, bring the line tie eye out as close to the head end as you can.

Garland is convinced that the Gitzit begins to lose its effectiveness when fished on lines heavier than twelve-pound test. For the vast majority of his fishing, he opts for a 5½- or six-foot spinning rod spooled with eight-pound line, but will switch to ten-pound if he is fishing in cover.

While Garland makes the Gitzits in a wide variety of colors, he feels most anglers can start out with just five.

"Chartreuse with black flake is a good color when the fishing is tough. Fluorescent colors, like chartreuse, are 'attack' colors," he explains, "and they can trigger a strike from a bass. That's one reason a lot of pros add a bit of fluorescent paint to the belly of their crankbait. A lot of times, when I can't get bit on anything else, I can get a hit on this color.

"Electric blue or electric grape," he continues, "are good summertime colors. It doesn't look like anything a bass would eat, but it's bright and easy to see and it can sometimes trigger some kind of attack impulse from the bass."

Other colors in Garland's starter list include: either clear or smoke, with a silver glitter; salt and pepper brown (amber with black flake); and smoke/red flake with a touch of chartreuse in the body. Each of these imitates a basic forage item (minnow, crawfish and bluegill).

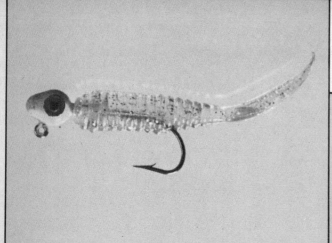

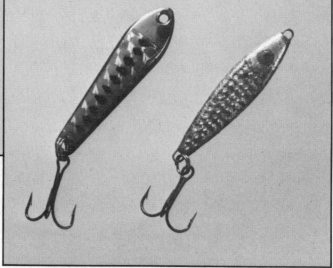

Left: Mann's Stingray Grub is favored by saltwater anglers, but is effective in open-water bass fishing, too. (Below) Schurmy Shad (left) and Mann O'Lure show the minnow-like compact shape of slab spoons, good for deep-water bass.

The Gitzit is one of the most versatile lures in an angler's tackle box and here is an example of how they may be used.

Bulldozing: "This type of retrieve works real well on clean bottoms without a lot of rock or brush," Garland explains, "I let the bait sink to the bottom, then just barely pull it along by raising my rod tip and reeling in the slack as I drop the rod for the next pull. This makes the bait kind of dig into the bottom and causes the tail to flip around."

Swimming: "In mossbeds or grass with a lot of pockets, I cast the bait over the stuff and crank it toward a pocket, keeping the rod tip high. When it gets to the pocket, I stop the retrieve and let the bait fall into the hole. Most of your hits will come as the bait falls, but sometimes one will blow up out of the moss and nail it as you're bringing it across."

The Gitzit also is deadly when a slower version of the swimming retrieve is used to swim the bait over the top of submerged hydrilla or milfoil. Adjust the retrieve speed until the bait is felt to just tick the top of the weeds.

Object Lure: The bass's tendency to strike a Gitzit as it falls, plus the lure's light weight and soft water entry, make it an excellent choice for casting to a specific spot where a bass might be holding.

In this technique, Garland often leans toward the target and drops his rod tip to put a bit of slack in the line to let the lure fall straight down. Many hits will be telegraphed by a few twitches on the line or the line moving sideways as the bass swims off with the bait. Because of the lure's hollow, soft body, bass seem to hold this bait for a long period of time.

The Gitzit also is effective when fished with the same short jigging motion used with a jig-and-grub. And, it is one of the best baits to use when a lure has to be "skipped" into hard to reach places. The compact shape of the bait lends itself well to being skipped across the surface.

"A lot of times," Garland says, "I'll skip a Gitzit to a target even when I have enough room to make a conventional cast. When a Gitzit skips up next to a long stump or boat dock, it looks a lot like a small shad skipping over the surface in panic. Then, it just sinks as if it were injured. A lot of people don't know it, but that can be a tremendous strike-triggering technique for a fish holding on that object. It makes them hit the bait."

Suspended bass: One of the most difficult of all conditions occurs when bass are suspended in open water, away from structure. But the Gitzit can work well here, too.

"I locate the fish on a graph," Garland explains, "and cast the Gitzit over them, allowing the lure to sink through the school with a little slack in the line. The real key is to find the right drop speed the lure should have. I remember one time on Lake Powell, when I graphed a school of good-sized fish suspended off a submerged channel bend. I tried them first with a three-inch bait on a 1/16-ounce head and that didn't work. Then I tried the same bait on a ¼-ounce head, and that didn't work either. Then I tried the ⅛-ounce head and got a hit the first cast. For the next twenty minutes I sat there and got bit almost every time I dropped that bait through the school. I just had to find the right fall speed to trigger the fish to hit."

As versatile as the Gitzit is, there is one other group of subtle baits that is rapidly gaining popularity, especially among California anglers and those fishing deep rock-bound reservoirs.

Sissy Baits: I didn't coin that name. The credit for that belongs to bass'n great Rick Clunn. But it does, with tongue in cheek, adequately describe a group of diminutive plastic worms and grubs that can be awesomely effective in deep, clear water lakes.

When teamed with a special exposed hook lead jig head,

called a Dart Head, or when rigged Carolina-style and crawled slowly over the bottom, this forms an effective pair of techniques for dealing with finicky bass.

The first technique is referred to as "shakin'" and it is explained by Jerry Corlew, president of Angler's Pro Specialties, the leading manufacturer of these special baits.

"The shakin' technique is especially effective during tough conditions. You can finesse fish into biting that are otherwise shut off. Using a Shake'N Dart head — which can be had in a weedless or exposed hook version — and one of several soft plastic baits, like our Shakin' Grub, Shakin' Worm, Shakin' Tails or others, you can impart the same natural, subtle motion you'll see, if you drop a night crawler into an aquarium. It undulates softly as it falls and is just too easy a meal for the bass to pass up."

Corlew advises anglers using this technique to select a 5½-foot graphite or boron medium or medium/heavy action rod spooled with six- or eight-pound test line. If fishing in cover like fallen trees or brush tops, twelve-pound can be used, but should be avoided if possible. "Use the lightest line you can get away with," Corlew says.

"The Shakin' technique gets its name from the action imparted to the rod tip by the angler as the bait sinks," he explains. "It's a shaking, quivering action that gives the bait its movement. There are several ways to use this technique and the easiest is in casting to visible cover. Once the lure is cast, the reel is engaged and the rod tip shaken as the bait sinks.

"For suspended fish, you allow the bait to sink freely with the bail open. This gives the bait a spiraling action as it falls and often triggers a strike. With either method, carefully watch your line as the lure falls, since most hits will be very soft and the only indication that a bass has the bait will be the line stopping before it reaches the bottom. You must close the bail and set the hook with a sharp upward wrist snap.

"Another popular method," Corlew notes, "is the vertical shake. First, you must find fish on your graph or LCR and determine their depth, or be fishing a deep structure where you're fairly sure there are bass. Then, lower the bait right down to the fish, close the bail and impart a shaking movement to the rod. This undulates the bait right in front of their noses and can be deadly for either suspended fish or bass in deep cover. With a weedless jig head, you can shake right in the middle of submerged trees, brush tops and other cover, without fear of hanging up. Another method for covering larger areas, like a deep point, is to lower the bait to the bottom and put the trolling motor on its slowest speed. Then just move around the area, while you shake the lure over the bottom."

"With either of the last two methods, the strike will probably be just a spongy pull...almost as if you're hung up on a little blade of grass. But, don't be hesitant to set the hook. These two techniques have caught many bass over ten pounds from California lakes.

"Another technique is called 'split-shotting.' It's noth-

Some anglers feel finesse baits take only small bass, but Bobby Garland has taken eight-pound bass on his Gitzit. Finesse baits have taken 12-pounders for other anglers.

ing more than light-line Carolina worm fishing. But with the small worms and grubs, plus a slow retrieve, it can be deadly on bass anywhere. Using the same rod and line used for shakin', a couple of split shot are clamped onto the line anywhere from six inches to three feet above the plastic bait. Four- and five-inch worms are used most often and they can be rigged with the hook point exposed or Texas-style, depending on the bottom cover. A slow retrieve makes the little plastic bait just inch its way across the bottom and it can draw some fine bass."

Light-line bass fishing has traditionally been considered the tool of choice for anglers facing extremely clear waters, especially those in search of smallmouth and spotted bass. But, as many tournament anglers have discovered, it can be a valuable technique to add to your repertoire regardless of where you fish, or which species you normally pursue. Under some conditions it can mean the difference between a noisy livewell or a day of casting practice.

CHAPTER 13

Deep, rock-bound reservoirs offer little in the way of shoreline cover. Particularly good areas are where flooded timber borders a submerged creek channel, the author contends.

THE YO-YO EFFECT

This Is The Key To Finding Bass In Our Man-Made Reservoirs

IF ONE should attempt to trace the current bass boom back to its infancy, he would find it firmly rooted in the "lake-building boom" occurring in the Forties and Fifties.

Prior to that the bass was a creature of placid ponds, sluggish rivers and meandering creeks. But, when millions of acres of new water were created by the need for hydro-electric power and flood control, it proved an ideal environment for all species of bass. Today, they have become the most popular places to pursue America's fish.

Man-made reservoirs can be classified into two major categories: highland and lowland.

The former is characterized by the abruptness of its depth changes: stark, rugged contours; and notable lack of

Once an angler determines which general area is holding bass, he must locate the specific types of cover they are using. This fat spotted bass held by bass pro Bobby Garland was snuggled under a dock in a small creek cove.

aquatic vegetation. The primary cover available for bass in these types of waters is wood and rock. The Arkansas/ Missouri impoundment of Bull Shoals is a classic example of a highland reservoir.

Lowland impoundments often are much more shallow in their maximum depths, frequently contain a variety of aquatic vegetation and usually are criss-crossed by a maze of twisting submerged creek channels. They have a far greater variety of cover types for bass to utilize. The Texas giant, Sam Rayburn, is a good example of this type of man-made reservoir.

Highland reservoirs usually offer a diverse mix of large-mouth, smallmouth and spotted bass. And, this type of environment can cause the bass to spend much of their time in deeper water, since the water clarity is often considerable.

When the three species of bass share the waters, they each seem to occupy a definite niche in the eco-system.

Largemouths usually opt for the shallower depths, small-mouths choose the mid-depths, while spotted bass prefer the deeper water. This is not carved in stone, however, and it's not uncommon to catch a largemouth on one cast and a spotted bass with the next to the same area. But anglers seeking a certain species will want to keep this depth preference in mind.

While smallmouths and spotted bass also may be present in lowland reservoirs, the largest percentage of bass will be largemouths.

Despite the differences in environment and population make-up, bass on man-made reservoirs share some common traits concerning how they utilize the water on a seasonal basis.

"Bass movements in man-made lakes," says Denny Brauer, "are a back-and-forth thing. In the winter, they're deep; in the spring, they move shallow; in the summer, they go back deep. In the fall, they go back shallow. It's a big yo-

Flooded timber is common on many man-made lakes and bass will use it as cover. Particularly good areas, the author has found, are where flooded timber borders a submerged creek channel. This angler seems to be in an ideal spot.

yo effect in response to the weather and temperature conditions."

Brauer is as well qualified to speak on the subject of man-made reservoirs as any angler around; maybe more so than most. A regular and highly respected competitor on the pro tour, his tournament winnings in 1987 easily exceeded $100,000. He also won the coveted Bass Angler Sportsman's Society Angler of the Year award as the best bass

fisherman in America. He's convinced that anglers pursuing bass on this type of water system need to follow that "yo-yo."

"Since the bass follow the seasons, you can't always expect to find fish in the same place you did the previous month. That's why it's important to understand this seasonal movement pattern.

If, for example, you found bass on a bluff bank in January,

*Careful study of a topo map can help an angler locate the productive fishing spots before he ever leaves home.
In his home in central Florida, professional angler Bernie Schultz does homework for upcoming tourney in New York.*

don't expect to find them there in March. But do understand why they're not there...where they will have gone ...and what route they probably took to get there. That's the real key to locating bass on man-made lakes of any type."

When faced with the task of locating bass on a man-made lake, the angler's first decision is *where* on the lake he wants to start.

"What I try to do," Brauer explains, "is to pick one section of the lake where I'm sure there are bass, and that has the type of structure they will be using during that season as well as 'positive' environmental factors, instead of negative ones. I don't feel that bass move around as much during their lives as some anglers think. So, my decision to fish the lower end of a lake, as opposed to the upper end, wouldn't be based upon the erroneous assumption that the bass may have moved to that section. It would be based upon the 'positive' factors I might find there.

"I wouldn't want to go into the upper end of, say, Sam Rayburn Lake in the winter months. It's not because there aren't bass there, but the water there will be cold, high and muddy. Those are negative factors for winter bass and the fish in that area won't be as active as fish in an area with positive factors. In the summer, though, the higher stained water would be a positive factor and that would be a logical place to go.

"Always try to start with as many positive factors in your favor and avoid the negative ones."

Winter Season: "The colder the water is, " Brauer explains, "the clearer the water you want to fish. Cold, muddy water is the worst possible condition you can have in the winter and that's why I would normally want to fish in the lower section, closer to the dam. This is where the water will usually be the clearest on the lake.

"Bass will be on deep structures during the winter and one of the most productive areas would be on the main lake, near the mouths of creeks. The key spots will be tapering points running to deep water, sheer bluff banks or the deeper, outside bends of submerged creek channels. If you have a major creek arm, then you have, in effect, a 'mini-lake' and you can move into it and locate the same type of structure. A good topo map is invaluable, because it can locate these areas for you before you ever leave home."

Another positive factor Brauer would seek is an area where these type of deep structures existed close to a known spawning area, like a small cove.

"If you know bass will be moving into an area to spawn when the water warms, there is a good chance bass are within a half mile of that cove right now. If you can find bluff banks, points and submerged creek channel bends in that immediate vicinity, they'll probably have bass on them."

During the winter months, Brauer advises anglers to avoid coves, the back ends of creeks and similar shallow cover. One thing he tries to find during winter is the deeper

There are videos made today, featuring the bass fishing experts that can help understand where fish hang out.

Pro angler Denny Brauer describes the seasonal movements in a man-made lake as a "yo-yo" effect.

California pro Rich Tauber feels California lakes are easy for locating the fish-holding structure, as there are no extensive creek arm coves for them.

structure that has schools of shad minnows in the immediate area.

"If you can find a big cluster of shad on your graph or LCR that is hovering over one of these winter structures, you'll usually find some bass on those structures," he notes.

While weather affects bass movements, they will not be prolonged or cover great distances during the winter months under even the best conditions. Should an angler find a school of bass holding on a tapering rock point at thirty feet, warm weather may move them up the point, while severe weather may cause them to drop to deeper water on that point. But, that thirty-foot depth will remain a returning point for the angler.

Winter anglers will find "finesse baits," structure spoons, jig-and-grubs and the jig-and-pigs, plus deep-diving crankbaits top choices for deep water bass. They're best fished on lighter lines and with a slow retrieve to match the bass's activity level.

Sometimes, though, even winter fish can get active.

"It's not common, but if you get a sudden rise in water levels combined with a four- or five-day warming trend, the bass can move right up on the banks for a feeding spree. It doesn't happen often, but it's great when it does."

Spring: "As long as the water temperature is below sixty degrees," says Brauer, "I'd still be looking for clearer water. But, I'd start moving shallower. My first areas to check would be the shallow sections of main lake points, as well as any small secondary points branching off of those. Bass will be starting to move from their wintering areas toward the shallow spawning areas and the word, *towards,* is important. They won't be in them yet and it can take several weeks for them to get to them."

This transitional process is gradual and, since the spring is one of the most unstable times of the year, the transition is equally unstable. A week-long warming trend may move bass almost to the spawning sites and an overnight cold front can drive them suddenly right back to the wintering grounds.

"Points and creek channels," says Brauer, "are logical migration routes that lead the bass from deep to shallow water. This is one reason why I feel it is important to understand the entire structural layout in a given area. If you know where the bass winter, where they spawn, what routes they'll take to get there, you can form a good idea of where the bass are going to be under most weather conditions."

In highland reservoirs, these pathways can often be the bank itself. It's common for a bluff bank of sheer rock to change into a more gently sloping "chuck rock" bank, then to an even gentler sloping pea gravel bank on which the bass actually will spawn.

In shallow lowland reservoirs, however, bass may show first on the channel ridges, move to the outer points, then to the outside edges of the grass lines. As the water continues

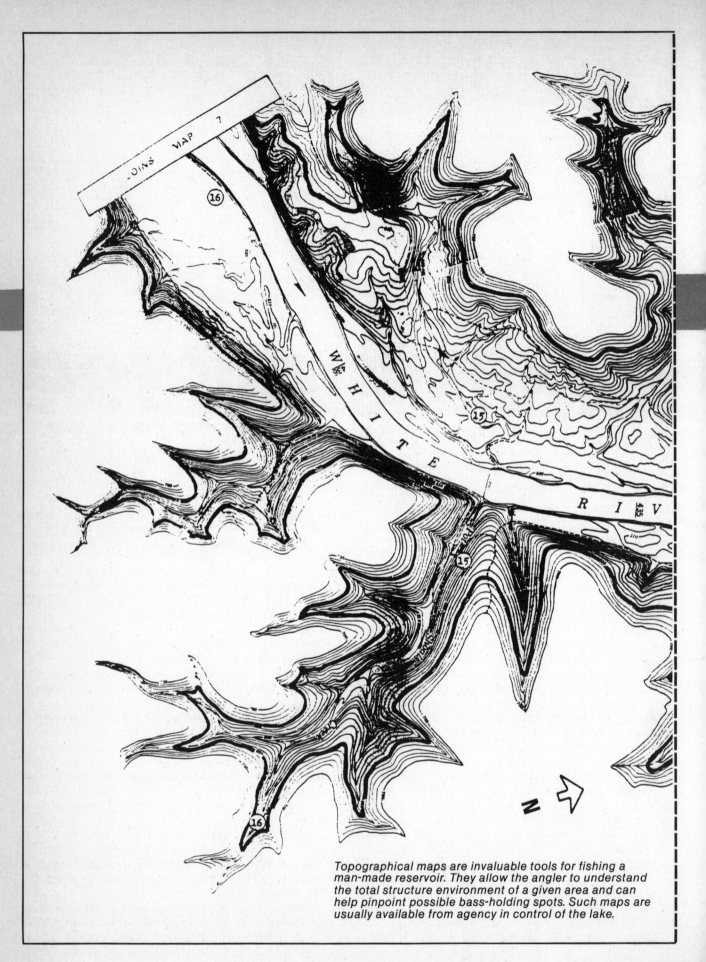

Topographical maps are invaluable tools for fishing a man-made reservoir. They allow the angler to understand the total structure environment of a given area and can help pinpoint possible bass-holding spots. Such maps are usually available from agency in control of the lake.

POINT
16

BIG BEND PARK

E6 (FUTURE)

JOINS MAP 9

"If people paid more attention to the weather patterns, they could almost forget the seasonal aspects at this time of year: Warm, stable water will send the bass shallow and put them in a positive mood. Cold, unstable water makes them pull back to deep water and become negative."

The Spawn: "The biggest postive factor during the actual spawning time — at least during the first spawn the lake will see — is quiet, protected water with the right bottom composition for the bass to spawn. On a highland reservoir, pea gravel is the spawning bottom. On lowland lakes, it is usually sand or some other hard-bottomed area.

"On lakes that are silted excessively, the spawning grounds might be areas with a lot of lay-down logs or cut-off stumps that the bass can fan off and bed on."

The location, on the lake, of these areas also can play a role in their use. As a general rule, the first spawn of the year usually will take place in those coves lying on the north, northwest or western side of the reservoir. These areas are most sheltered from the icy effects of the strong north and northwest winds that accompany spring cold fronts throughout most of the country. They also receive slightly longer exposure from the winter sun and thus tend to warm up slightly more rapidly than other areas of the lake. These factors do not draw more bass to these areas automatically, but simply allow the fish present to become active before those bass in other areas. Remember: The bass cannot control his environment, but merely respond to it.

"When I begin to see smaller buck bass milling around or fanning beds in an area," says Brauer, "it's a good bet the female fish are nearby. I would start looking for heavy cover in that area or, if the cover was sparse, drop back towards slightly deeper water until I found the first breakline out from the shallows. Any cover I found would be fished slowly and carefully, because the female fish often hold very tightly to it and may not be real active. Flipping a jig-and-pig can be deadly at this time of year."

So too can large-bladed spinnerbaits, topwater plugs, shallow-running crankbaits and plastic worms. Large baits sometimes can trigger a strike when smaller baits fail, due to the bass's protective nature at this time of year.

Cold fronts can stop this process at this time of year. What the bass will do often is determined by the existing cover. If a lot of heavy cover is present in the area, they frequently just burrow down into it; if cover is minimal, they have little choice but to drop back into deeper water. This is a season where the inquisitive angler can often score big.

"I would try to avoid creek arms and coves that had water flowing through them," says Brauer. "I want to find the most calm, most stable water I can find, as well as the warmest. Especially if it has the necessary deep winter habitat within the general area. This is a productive combination in the spring and it's worth spending even a whole day to find something like that."

Post-Spawn: If the actual pre-spawn and spawning periods of the spring season are relished by serious bass

to warm, they will move to the inside edge of the grass lines and the backs of coves where spawning takes place.

It's not uncommon for bass to "stack up" on a certain definable depth/cover situation during this transition.

"Rayburn is a good example of this," Brauer observes. "There are a lot of willow trees lying at depths of up to eight feet on the outside of the spawning areas. As the weather warms and the fish move shallow, they may pause at these for days. If the weather continues to warm, they'll move shallower still and you'll find them in the buck brush in about four feet of water. A cold front, though, might send them right back to the willows in eight feet.

BASS Master Classic champ Jack Chancellor jigs a spoon for spotted bass near a dam face. This can be productive, as bass often school up on deep structures like this.

anglers, the two-week period following the spawn is about as popular as a case of the flu!

"I dread the period right after the spawn," muses Brauer. "It's a frustrating time for the angler, especially if you're after larger fish.

"Post-spawn fish are a lot like a 'party animal' with a hangover. They don't feel like doing much of anything. In fact, in a lot of clear little bays and coves you can see good fish just laying around suspended. They're not alert or even relating to anything. They're just lying there out in the open. And they're definitely not feeding."

How do anglers handle this period? Simple, most of them try to avoid it!

"In a large lake," Brauer explains, "all the bass don't spawn at the same time. Some areas will be earlier or later than others. If you see evidence in the area you're fishing of recent spawning activity — and especially if you're not catching fish — go somewhere else."

For example, if your detective work has led you to one of the first spawns of the year in a quiet northwest cove, the possibility exists that the bass on the eastern side of the lake have not spawned. Or the bass in the upper river end may not have spawned. Prospecting these areas may put you onto bass that are in a pre-spawn mood and actively feeding.

It comes back to Brauer's basic tactic of putting positive factors together in determining what portion of the lake to fish. Why beat your brains out trying to catch "hung over post-spawn fish in one area, when the party may just be starting in a different section of the lake?

By tuning into the first spawning areas, an angler can continue to move to different spawning areas when the spawning activity is finished in the one he is fishing. By the time he makes the rounds, he can return to the first area and likely find the fish in their summer patterns. This is just smart bass fishing.

Summer: The summer months can be one of the most productive times of the year. Warming waters increase bass activity and there is a larger amount of forage available for them. But the positive factors affecting summer bass are quite a bit different than during the winter and spring.

"Environmental activity is desirable in the summer months," says Brauer. "Stained water, moving water, wind, clouds — all the things I don't want to see in the winter and spring — increase summer bass movement."

While Brauer shuns inflowing tributary creeks in other seasons, he relishes them in the summer.

"The upper ends of the reservoir can offer excellent fishing during the summer months and these usually will be shallow-holding fish, maybe three to six feet deep. These fish will be shallow, because the water isn't as clear as in the lower lake and there is more shoreline cover."

Brauer tends to move into upper creek arms at this time of year. By prospecting shallow shoreline cover, he enjoys the same fast-paced shallow water action he did in the reservoir's lower sections during the spring months.

If circumstances dictate that Brauer fish the clearer, lower end of the lake, he doesn't despair. He does, however, fish deeper.

"Although bass relate to the same basic types of deep structures in winter and summer, they prefer less sharply dropping structures during warm weather. A straight-dropping bluff bank and a fast-dropping point may hold a lot of bass in winter, but I've often found a bluff bank that has a series of distinct ledges or drop-offs at a forty-five-degree angle is better in summer. So too is a point with a longer, more gradual taper. The bass may use the same general depth ranges, but they definitely prefer more gradual changes in the structure during the summer."

The spring and fall of most years will see bass holding in the shallower waters of a majority of man-made lakes.

Bass also may move greater distances on a structure during warmer weather. Fish holding on a tapering point in the winter may not move shallower than the twenty-foot depth. But during summer months, they may move all the way up to the bank and blast a buzzbait in two feet of water.

Most often, bass will be on the most shallow portion of the structure during the early morning and evening hours. Cloud cover and wind, however, may hold them there throughout the day. Bright sunlight can send them back to the deeper water. Anglers must be aware of this daily movement trend in order to follow the fish.

One factor that can alter this is the presence of hydrilla or milfoil on the deeper structures. If this weed exists, the bass normally will not make a horizontal movement from deep water to the shoreline, but will stay in the hydrilla and make vertical movements. Good conditions will put them near the surface over the hydrilla, while bright light conditions send them down to the base of the plants. These two plants are covered in greater detail in Chapter 16.

Fall Months: The cooling waters of fall can spark some of the hottest bass fishing of the year. During this season, the bass once again return to the shallows and productive areas located in the spring often produce in the fall, as well. But not always.

"The positive factor in the spring is the bottom composi-

Author contends that locating bass on off-shore structures requires use of quality depth-finding equipment. Many an angler opts for both a graph and a second console unit, like the Fencolor LCR unit being used by this pro anlger.

tion. The bass are there to spawn and that's what they need. In the fall, the bass are there to feed and the positive factor is the presence of baitfish."

"During the fall," Brauer continues, "the baitfish will move shallow — right into the back ends of creeks and coves — and the bass will follow them. Some of the spots where you caught bass in the spring will be good and some won't. I like to look for the baitfish and let their presence help guide my choice of spots."

Sometimes bass may not make it all the way into the back ends of coves. In some highland reservoirs, they still feed along bluff banks, but they'll often be much closer to the surface than they were during the summer. One technique that has proved productive on highland reservoirs is "walking" large-bladed spinnerbaits right along the edge of sheer bluff banks, even though the water may be fifty feet deep!

A general guideline, though, is that the main lake areas that are productive in the summer and winter will begin to give way to creek arms and coves.

"When you are looking for bass on any type of water," Brauer concludes, "remember there really are no absolutes. About the best you can say is that, under such-and-such conditions, you would be able to find the greatest number of catchable bass under a certain set of conditions. You are

playing the percentages. But, don't rule anything out automatically. Some major tournaments have been won by anglers who left their rule books at home and did some experimenting when they got on the water."

One noticeable exception to the relationship between bass and creek arms occurs on lakes that lack creek arms!

"Many of the western lakes," explains a California bass pro and former U.S. Open winner, Rich Tauber, "do not have the extensive creek arm systems that the lakes from Texas eastward have, so bass can't relate to them.

"Western bass, especially those in the Southern California lakes, spend their time on main lake structures and whatever small coves exist. If you find bass on a tapering main lake point, it is a good bet it will hold some fish throughout the year. They do not change their environment as much with the seasons simply because the environment to do that isn't there. They will move shallower in response to positive weather conditions and drop a bit deeper when things turn negative. But, they won't be far from their home base and that's generally main lake points, rock banks and noticeable submerged cover like a rock cluster in fifteen to twenty-five feet of water.

"Since they don't have that much room to roam around, it does help simplify the task of finding fish-holding structure on these types of lakes."

CHAPTER 14

LOCATING BASS IN RIVERS

Left: Bernie Schultz admires a hefty river bass taken on a topwater plug. (Above) Anglers fishing rivers often fare better if they fish against the current rather than drifting with it. Bass expect forage to come with the current.

The Current Controls The Movement Of Bass — But There Are Other Factors, Too.

FOR THE angler who spends his days attempting to unravel the often wide-ranging movements of bass in a man-made reservoir, a bass'n trip to one of the nation's numerous rivers can be a refreshing change of pace.

"Given the choice of fishing a lake or a river," says Georgia pro angler Kim Carver, "I would choose the river. Most of these waters get very little pressure and the bass aren't nearly as lure-shy or educated as are those in a hard-fished lake."

Carver's river savvy not only resulted in his winning a major BASS tournament on Florida's St. Johns River, but helped earn him a berth in the prestigious BASS Masters Classic.

"Moving water not only makes bass more active, but helps concentrate the bass into easier-to-find areas," he contends. "It's usually easier to catch bass in a river, because the current is going to dictate many of the places they have to be. River bass just don't have as many possible combinations of depth and cover that they can use, so they're easier to find and catch."

While river bass may be a little more unsophisticated than their lake-bound counterparts, they're not necessarily the lightweights of the bass'n world. Far from it. In fact, one of the top trophy bass waters in the world is Florida's St. Johns River, which annually yields more bass over ten

pounds than some "hot" lakes will give up in a decade!

And, it's worth pointing out that George Perry's world record largemouth bass of twenty-two pounds, four ounces came from a shallow backwater slough off a south Georgia river.

Largemouth bass are not the only species to inhabit flowing water, however. Throughout much of the northeast and northwestern portions of the country, it is the smallmouth bass that becomes the quarry of river bassers. In the Ohio River Valley watershed, largemouth, smallmouth and spotted bass often inhabit the same streams.

In the Deep South, the largemouth predominates, but several sub-species of bass (Suwanne, Redeye and Shoal bass, all of whom bear a startling resemblance to the smallmouth bass) make their presence felt on some selected waters. There is indeed a bass'n smorgasbord awaiting anglers venturing upon moving waters.

One factor operating in the river angler's favor is that river bass, regardless of the type of river, seldom venture below the fifteen- to twenty-foot depth. This means river anglers are working essentially on shallow water fish.

Another positive factor is the bass's tendency to be a "homebody." Lengthy migrations are not common in a river environment — assuming that the water levels stay relatively stable — so the angler who locates bass along a particular bank during the winter months can be fairly cer-

River bass tend to be compact, chunky fish that will give the angler a solid tussle. A life of battling a current gives them a diet of muscle-building exercise.

tain the bass will be in the same general area throughout the year.

"The most important thing to remember about river bass," says Carver, "is the current. Nearly always they will face it, usually near some type of object that will help break the force of the current. These objects give the bass a place to hide and watch the world pass by."

For Carver, a trip to a new river or one he hasn't recently fished, usually starts with a downstream run.

"I like to ride the river first to pinpoint key bass holding areas. I'm primarily looking for eddies — slack water areas lying close to the main current — and current breaks; a fallen tree, a brush top, a stump or some other cover object the bass can hold on while staying out of the main current flow.

"The best current breaks are those that have water flowing through them — like a fallen tree top — because a bass can find a place out of the current and still be close enough to the main flow to dart out and grab a meal. This type of cover usually holds some fish that are actively feeding."

Another fish-holding condition that seldom goes unnoticed by the experienced "river rat" is an inflowing side creek. This is especially true if the river level is falling. Receding waters often force bass out of the shallow side creeks and stack them up at the junction with the main river. Additionally, the conflict between two intersecting currents often can set up an ideal feeding situation for bass. Any angler fishing a river who does not thoroughly explore the junction of two intersecting creeks is missing a big potential!

While such visible structure does indeed abound on many rivers and even on smaller creeks, Carver is also on the lookout for less obvious cover situations that frequently escape neophyte river bassers.

"One mistake a lot of fisherman make is to fish too fast," Carver points out. "They see a stump or fallen tree, fish it and go on quickly to the next one. A lot of times, there are submerged roots or undercut banks lying between the visible cover. This most often happens on the outside bends of the river where the current force is the strongest and can eat away the supporting bank.

"Some of the biggest river bass I've caught have come from such areas. Just because you can't see an object, doesn't mean there isn't something there that will hold a good bass. You have to look for it."

On any river, the current flow on the outside bends is usually the strongest and this often can stack up debris like fallen trees and other cover objects in the bends. The combination of high current and cover often proves irresistible to bass. One BASS Masters Classic on the Alabama River, near Montgomery, Alabama, was won by an angler who banged deep-diving crankbaits through fallen trees he had located on the outside bend of the river.

These trees were submerged in deep water and required a lot of effort to find, but Paul Elias contends the effort was well worth the $40,000 check it won for him!

Once Carver has surveyed the area, he swings his boat into the current and begins fishing the key spots he has found.

"It's important that you fish a river with the current," Carver advises. "Bring your lure down with the water flow instead of against it. Those bass will be facing the current and expect their food to be brought to them, not approach them from behind. That's not natural."

On smaller rivers, the majority of the bass you catch will be single, object-oriented fish. Seldom will a number of bass be ganged up on a single structure. This is not the case, though, on larger rivers.

Bass will gather in schools on larger rivers just as they will in natural or man-made lakes. Prime depth and cover combinations to seek out in this situation would be the mouth of an inflowing tributary or a group of fallen trees along a steep bank.

Another frequently overlooked spot is the mid-river bar. These "humps" or high spots can hold large numbers of fish. When actively feeding, they usually will move to the shallower sections on the upcurrent end of the bar, dropping back to the deeper down-current section when inactive. Obvious cover does not always have to exist on these bars to hold fish. Often the bass will simply relate to the changing contours of the bar.

This same situation also can exist in the inside bends of some larger rivers. Quite often a tapering point will extend from the shoreline of an inside bend to the main channel. An eddy or slower current area may exist on the shallow shoreline side that will serve as a resting point for inactive bass. When the dinner bell rings, they move to the faster water on the deeper end of the point to feed.

While bass do not make lengthy migrations in most rivers, they tend to alter their positions slightly with the seasons. During the winter months, the bass often hold tightly to cover and seek out those areas with the slowest currents. Bass are less active during the winter and prefer the more placid waters, but they want deep water close by.

Spring bass seek the same conditions as their lakebound brethren: the most calm and stable waters they can find that possess the proper bottom composition for spawning. Sloughs, backwaters and man-made canals are prime areas. In rivers that lack these features, look for spawning bass in the shallow waters on the inside bends of the river and in the eddy sections formed on the downstream side of them.

Summer bass usually prefer deeper sections of the river with a solid current flow and often move into shallow riffles, the upcurrent ends of long pools and mid-river bars during the morning and evening to feed. In effect, they are making the same deep-to-shallow migration that characterizes summer bass fishing in man-made reservoirs, although the actual distance traveled may be short.

Fall bass also display the same tendency to move into extremely shallow water that lake bass do and often are found foraging right along the banks.

In many rivers, the current runs in only one direction. This makes bass easier to find, since it is the current that controls their movements. In tidal rivers, however, the current will reverse each day as the tide takes over. This can cause some problems for anglers because, in effect, it means they have two totally different rivers to contend with: one on the outgoing tide, one on the incoming tide!

Tidal waters often are much larger than free-flowing rivers and the bass will have more in the way of offshore cover like bars and inside bend points to utilize.

Everything that has been said about rivers will apply to a considerable degree to tidal rivers. But there are some characteristics specifically inherent to this type of water that must be understood.

The most important is that the bass will move with the changing water levels caused by the tides. If that change is a large one — like New York's Hudson River, where four- and five-foot differences between tides are common — the distance the bass travel can be considerable. On the middle St. Johns River in Florida, the tidal fluctuation often is measured in inches and the bass move correspondingly lesser distances. But, move they will and their movements are somewhat predictable.

The incoming tide will flood shallow areas, moving baitfish and forage items with it. The bass will follow these. This tends to scatter the bass into shallow cover and can make it difficult to locate concentrations of them. On many

Shoreline cover can be productive in many smaller rivers. Bass use fallen trees and undercut banks to avoid the full force of the current and wait for a meal to appear.

rivers, the incoming tide also will be the slowest current flow, since it will be opposing the normal outward flow of the river.

The outgoing tide forces forage to move from the extreme shallows and will often "suck" injured forage fish from heavy cover where they may have been hiding from predators. Bass seem to instinctively know this and frequently stack up on the outside edges of shallow cover areas to feed.

Since the outgoing tide combines with the river's normal downstream current, it usually is the stronger of the two tides. During the summer and fall months, when moving water exerts a strong effect on bass activity, the outgoing tide often can be the one the bass will do most of their feeding on.

One area that should not be overlooked by a river angler is the intersection of a side creek to the main flow. A conflict of currents sets up an ideal feeding situation for bass, especially in tidal rivers on outgoing tide.

As a broad general rule, anglers should consider the incoming tide as a time to fish shallow cover slowly for less active fish; the outgoing tide is the time to fish the outer edges of that cover for actively feeding bass.

The seasonal depth and cover preferences for bass in tidal rivers are similar to those in free-flowing rivers with one major exception; fall bass do not always move to shallow water.

On some tidal rivers, they will. The Hudson River, for example, usually will see bass moving into the same shallow creek arms that they would use on a man-made lake. Florida's St. Johns, on the other hand, has big schools of bass stack up on offshore bars and that points to surface schools of shad. These fish will be hundreds of yards from the nearest shoreline and often can be spotted easily as they churn the surface to a froth!

While each tidal river in the country will have slight differences in how the bass relate to it, there are some almost universal depth and cover situations that anglers can count on; the most consistently productive being tidal creeks.

Large numbers of bass can stack up around the mouths of tide creeks on the falling tide much as they would in a river during dropping water levels. But moving up into the creeks also can pay off.

"My number one pattern on tidal rivers," says pro Hank Parker of Denver, North Carolina, "is to find a good-sized tide creek that has a deep cut or hole somewhere in the lower section near its mouth, with the rest of the creek

being fairly long and flat. When you find this, you have a situation that tends to concentrate the bass in that creek into one relatively small area."

Parker, a former BASS Masters Classic winner and Angler of the Year, will move up the creek and begin working his way back toward the mouth until his Humminbird

Florida pro Bernie Schultz looks for compression areas; places where large volumes of water are funneled into a smaller space. This provides excellent feeding for bass.

Some smallmouth streams are too small for many boats, but ideal for anglers making the drift in rafts or canoes. The same basic angling principles still apply, however, no matter what the size or depth of river being fished.

depthfinder shows him the first area of deeper water.

"That deep-water cut will be the central point for the bass in that area," he says. "From there, they'll move onto the shallow flats with the incoming tide and drop back toward that deeper hole with the falling tide. They'll usually stay within a few hundred yards of the area and you can find them by systematically fishing the area until you find the exact depth and cover they are using. Once you find the bass, you can stay with them through the tide stages: moving shallower as the tide rises, dropping deeper as it falls."

Another productive pattern, especially during the summer months, is to fish the main river grass beds. Most tidal rivers will have extensive grass beds, usually eelgrass, and the most productive will be those located close to the main river channel.

On the rising tide, bass will move well back into them and take up positions around any objects that can help break the force of the current. As the tide falls, the fish tend to move toward the outside edge where they will feed actively on baitfish brought to them by the falling water. One particular item to look for is where grass and other cover like rocks, fallen logs or old pilings come together. Multiple cover of this type tends to hold larger numbers of bass.

If there is one truly universal pattern to tidewater bass it is the species' affinity for old stands of wooden pilings. The reasons are both logical and simple.

During the country's earlier years, one of the easiest ways to move heavy goods inland was by river. On almost every tidal river deep enough to float a barge, loading platforms were constructed to allow the goods to be unloaded. The supporting pilings for these platforms ran from the shoreline outward to the first deep break to the main river channel, where the platform was constructed.

Consistently productive spots on a tidal river are old, abandoned stands of pilings, author has found. These were often constructed on edge of a deep-water channel.

On larger rivers, bass will gather on offshore bars to school on shad minnows. Anglers who can locate such a hidden hotspot can often boat a limit in short order.

With most of them no longer in use, the overhead decking long since has rotted away, in most cases, leaving only the pilings. They constitute a fish-holding structure that forms a continuous pathway from the deeper waters near the main channel to the shallowest portions of the shoreline. Bass love to use 'em!

Big bass can stack up on the deepwater end of these pilings at any time of the year, but most often do so in the summer and fall. Under conditions that promote bass activity, the fish may even move along their length to the shallow. But the deepwater end remains their "home."

Offshore bars — especially long tapering points coming off the inside bends of the river — can hold many bass. In a tidal river, though, the ones that will hold bass most consistently are those that have shell deposits on them.

Shell bars provide what probably is the least explored type of fish-holding cover on any tidal river. During summer, fall and winter, they can be most productive. Locating them, however, takes time and effort.

The best starting point is the appropriate chart of the river you're fishing. These navigation charts — available from the National Oceanic and Atmospheric Administration, Rockville, MD 20852 — are to the tidewater angler

what the topographical map is to the man-made reservoir fisherman. The map will show you the underwater contours, points and bars. The ones to be most concerned with are those lying in depths of four to twelve feet; tidewater bass are not often taken below that depth on most tidal rivers.

The maps will put you in the general area, but determining whether they have shell on them is best done by fishing the area thoroughly with a heavy Carolina worm rig using a one-ounce sinker. Shell deposits will feel "rough" while smooth sand will be telegraphed to the angler as just that: smooth.

The best feeding activity on these shell bars usually occurs just as the tide changes and on the strongest portion of the tide: the fastest water movement. On most tidal rivers, this will be the mid to final stages of the outgoing tide.

In locating bass in rivers, one universal pattern remains and it is every bit as effective on free-flowing streams, creeks, rivers, or tidewaters.

Actually, it is more of a concept, but it may be the most valuable bit of information a river angler can possess in his search for feeding bass, be they largemouth, spotted bass or smallmouth.

This facet could be called the "funnel concept." This is an area where a large amount of water — and the food it brings — is funneled into a much smaller area. Florida pro Bernie Schultz, a highly experienced river angler, prefers to refer to it as a "compression area."

These compression areas, he explains, "serve as prime feeding stations, but that doesn't always mean the fish present there are feeding fish. They may be there for comfort. The moving water may be cooler and more oxygenated. But once you identify them, these areas tend to hold the largest number of bass in that area.

"In effect, they become not only the best feeding areas in the vicinity, but a focal point for the bass as well."

These so-called compression areas can take on many forms. They may be as obvious as a situation that exists on the St. Johns River. There, seventy-eight-square-mile Lake George flows into a one-quarter-mile-wide section of the river on the lake's north end. Here a tremendous volume of water is compressed suddenly into a relatively small area. Not surprisingly, this is one of the best bass'n spots in that area of the river.

Or, it could be as subtle as the small shoal Schultz found during a major tournament on New York's St. Lawrence River.

"The time of the year dictated that the bass would be just finishing the spawn and begin moving back to deeper water," Schultz recalls. "I had found a small bay with evidence of recent spawning activity and, as I was looking for good holding areas at the deeper water near its mouth, I found this small rock shoal with my Fencolor LCR. The high spot on the shoal was about five feet and it dropped off quickly on either side.

"It wasn't a big area, but it was a classic compression situation; current movement over the shoal compressed baitfish into a smaller area. It was also the first deepwater holding point from the shallow spawning area and the bass were staging there on their way to deeper water.

"When the wind shifted to the same direction as the current flow, it accelerated the movement of water across

The author has discovered that rivers throughout the country can produce excellent angling for all three species.

the shoal and the bass moved up to the shallowest area to feed. When the current and wind slacked and the skies got bright during the midday, the bass didn't leave that shoal. They just dropped down deeper along the sides and stopped feeding. But, I was able to catch them on worms and jigs."

The St. Lawrence River is subject to tidal influence and thus to fluctuating current levels, but that did not cause the bass to vacate the area. This is common with compression areas on rivers. Bass often will remain near them, because they are prime feeding areas, moving right up into them when feeding conditions are right.

In effect, compression areas are any spot or situation where a large volume of water is forced into or over a smaller area, thereby compressing that water into a smaller area.

"The acceleration of water moving through a compression area," states Schultz, "creates a higher current level suddenly. This tends to disorient baitfish moving with the current and places the bass at a distinct advantage over the baitfish because of its speed and power."

It's one situation where ambush feeding is the most efficient tactic the bass can use and is common in virtually any moving water situation.

Obviously, a mid-river bar or shoal will create this situation, as will a large, deep pool flowing into a much narrower section of the river.

This also will occur where a straight stretch of river is reduced to a sharp bend or a series of S-shaped bends. Another common compression situation occurs on rocky rivers where underwater ledges jut out from a seemingly straight, deep bank.

Rising or falling water also can create compression areas. A small tide creek on an incoming tide may have baitfish and forage items pushed to the back, where the bass will have them trapped in a reduced area. As the tide falls and the water and baitfish are forced from the creek, any narrow section of the creek near its mouth also can become a compression area.

A sudden change in light levels can create a compression situation, even if there is no change in terrain that results in an accelerated current.

"Where there is a good flow of water that the baitfish are subject to," Schultz explains, "any area where the baitfish suddenly leave bright sunlight and enter a shaded area is a prime feeding spot. The sudden change from bright to dark disorients them, making them an easy mark for any bass holding in the shade."

This situation may take the form of an overhanging tree throwing a large patch of shade, a fallen log with a mat of floating vegetation lodged against it, a long dock or pier that juts into the main current flow or any other type of cover that throws solid shade on the surface.

Anglers who are alert to the presence of these compression areas will find the task of locating bass much easier on virtually any body of moving water, from the smallest creek right on up to a major tidal river.

Author probes a quiet side creek off Florida's Oklawaha River. Bass in such smaller waterways often are easier to locate, as current will dictate where bass will feed.

CHAPTER 15

BASS AND THE NATURAL LAKE

Left: Weedless lures often are the best choice on natural lakes, as fish relate to vegetation. Bass pro Cliff McKendree boats a bass taken on a spinnerbait. (Above) An angler hoping to score on natural-lake bass must learn to "read the weed" to determine the most likely spot for the fish to hold. These bass are "vegetation dependent."

THROUGHOUT MUCH of the country, man-made reservoirs form the largest water resource available to bass fishermen. However, east of the Mississippi River — and especially in the south-eastern portion of the country — natural lakes constitute a significant and productive part of the overall fishery. In fact, some of the finest trophy largemouth fishing in the world exists in the many shallow natural lakes of Florida.

The most common member of the bass clan encountered on these natural waters will be the largemouth, although smallmouths are present to some degree in the northeast-ern and upper midwestern regions. Spotted bass are not native to natural lakes and, while they may fare well in reservoirs, numerous attempts to transplant them to natural lakes generally have ended in failure.

Natural lakes may range in size from the 780-square-mile Lake Okeechobee, in south Florida, down to a few acres of bog pond in southern Maine. Regardless of the size or location, however, this type of water shares many common traits.

The vast majority of natural lakes are quite shallow in comparison to man-made reservoirs. While bass in a deep highland reservoir, like Bull Shoals, may be routinely taken at depths of over fifty feet, it is uncommon to catch a bass in a natural lake at depths exceeding twenty feet. In the South, many productive natural lakes may well have a maximum depth of less than fifteen feet!

Also, since natural lakes are ancient, when compared to man-made reservoirs, they often lack distinctive bottom contours. Centuries of sluggish water movement and silta-

Bass often retreat to the thickest vegetation during the brightest part of the day. For this reason, most of the truly experienced pros have found that they must learn flipping techniques. It's essential to success in this area.

tion have eroded and softened any noticeable bottom contours that may have been present. Offshore structure in the form of creek channel edges, ridges, submerged islands and such are scarce on these waters.

Most of our natural lakes are fed by springs and run-off, instead of inflowing creek arms. Without this creek arm structure, natural lake bass are forced to be main lake-related fish. Few natural lakes have any significant creek arms and those that do exist are often shallow and silted, preventing the bass from making any real use of them.

The single most distinguishing characteristic of natural lakes is the vegetation. On most of these waters, it is profuse and often quite varied. Each particular plant type will often occupy a specific depth range and grow in its own preferred bottom composition. Sometimes these different types of vegetation will mix, but more often, they will form distinctive break lines between each other. Anglers often can determine the relative depth and bottom composition simply by reading the vegetation. It provides a completely different environment from man-made reservoirs, and the bass respond accordingly.

"Natural lake bass can be a lot different than reservoir fish," states Florida pro angler Shaw Grigsby. "Anglers fishing natural lakes should keep in mind that there are four major differences between bass in lakes and bass in reservoirs.

"First, bass in natural lakes do not have as large a range of movements with the seasons as the reservoir fish do. If you do find some fish located in a specific spot, the chances are excellent that there will be some fish in that general

area throughout the year. While reservoir fish may run miles up a creek arm in the spring and return to the main lake in the summer, natural lake base can be relative homebodies.

"The second difference: There will be some catchable bass in depths shallower than four feet during any time of the year. This is true to an extent on any type of water, but very strongly so on natural lakes.

"The third difference to remember is that the depth/contour lines on natural lakes are quite subtle and not readily defined. Often they are expressed as nothing more than a change of vegetation type. Since the bass do not have clear-cut depth changes to relate to, they often relate to various types of vegetation and vegetation edges.

"In natural, shallow lakes, bass don't make the classic migration from deep water to feed in the shallows, then return to rest up. Instead, they make what is called a reverse migration. They move to the thinner outside edges of cover, or even open water, to feed, and return to the thickest portions of the vegetation when they are inactive. That's the fourth difference."

Grigsby, born and raised in Central Florida, has established an excellent reputation on natural lakes. It was his ability on this type of water that earned him the winner's check in the 1984 Red Man All American, second place in the 1986 Mega Bucks Tournament (both on Florida natural lakes) and helped him qualify for the prestigious BASS Master Classic and the U.S. Bass World Championships.

He is convinced that anglers intending to score well on

Bass may relate to only one type of vegetation. Anglers should observe where they caught a bass, as others may be there. (Below) Pro Shaw Grigsby has won over $250,000 by knowing how bass relate to nation's natural lakes.

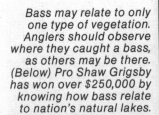

this type of water need to concentrate heavily on the type of vegetation the bass will use during the various seasons of the year. While bass may not make lengthy migrations, they often can show a decided preference for different types of cover as the seasons change.

"Bass in natural lakes require the same basic conditions during the spring as do the bass in man-made reservoirs," Grigsby explains. "They want a firm, hard bottom, usually sand, to bed on, shallow warming water and a sheltered environment. The most important factor concerning where bass will be during the spring months is the bottom composition and the type and amount of cover in and around that area.

"The first spawn of the year usually will be in the shal-

lowest waters that are suitable. These will warm up first, while bass later in the spring will be able to find the right water temperature in slightly deeper water. What I look for are areas in one to three feet of water that have a firm sand bottom and a good mix of vegetation in and around it. The best vegetation type you can find on many lakes are the small 'dollar pads.' These grow on a hard sand bottom in two to four feet of water and the bass like to spawn right in them. If you have a patch of these in an area that has other types of vegetation close by and some deeper vegetation in six to ten feet of water on the outside of the area, you probably have a place where the bass in that area will spawn."

On lakes that lack suitable amounts of dollar bonnets, Grigsby will often look for maidencane, bullrushes or eelgrass. All of these shallow water plants also are found on firm sand bottoms and will be used by spawning bass.

Some lakes may be so heavily silted, however, that bass cannot fan beds on its bottom. Although this may appear to prevent the bass from spawning, the bass are quite adaptable.

"On heavily silted lakes," Grigsby explains, "bass will find some type of hard object that they can fan clean and they will bed on that. Sometimes this is isolated cover, like fallen logs. But, most often it will be the roots of lily pads. On silted lakes, lily pad beds are the premier place to look for spring bass, because they are the only good spawning cover available."

Once Grigsby finds the proper spawning conditions, his search for bass narrows, depending upon the stage of the spawn.

"If the bass are in the pre-spawn stage — moving towards the shallows to spawn, but not actually there yet — I'll start from the actual spawning area and begin backing out towards deeper water. This pre-spawn stage often starts when the water reaches about fifty-five degrees and stays there for a few days.

"What I'll be looking for in pre-spawn," he explains,

Anglers can learn much from a quality video demonstrating how bass relate to cover. (Right) Cuts, boat lanes, open pockets in weedbeds can be the natural-lake bass' feeding areas.

"is thick, heavy vegetation on the outside of the actual spawning area. This may be lily pads, hydrilla, reeds or eelgrass and it usually will be in four to eight feet of water. This will be the first staging area that the bass use as they move to the bedding area; they'll hold here for days or even weeks, while they wait for the weather to stabilize and the water to warm enough to spawn. Most of these staging areas will be from one hundred to three hundred yards from the spawning grounds."

One additional type of area that can often draw large numbers of spring bass are man-made canals. These are quite common on some lakes and, when present, bass will use them if they have a depth of at least four feet. The best canals will be those with at least seven feet of water at the maximum depth and a thin fringe of vegetation of any type along the shoreline.

In the pre-spawn stage, the bass begin to gather around the canal mouth. At this time Grigsy looks for obvious fish-holding cover like boat docks, deep grass beds and even the drop-off at the mouth of the canal itself. As the water warms, the fish will move inside the canal, but they may not move to the banks to spawn immediately.

"Frequently," Grigsby notes, "the bass will stage in the middle of the canal for a few days until they orient themselves to the area. Plastic worms or crankbaits fished right out in the open water in the middle will take some of these fish. After that, casting plastic worms or spinnerbaits to the shoreline cover can be effective.

"Canals are overlooked areas on a lot of lakes," Grigsby feels, "but they can hold a lot of good bass during the spring. The only problem with canals is that the fish come and go quickly. You may do well in a canal one weekend and bomb out completely the next. Still, they're well worth exploring."

As the bass begin to spawn, Grigsby will follow the bass right up into the shallows, where topwater lures, plastic worms and spinnerbaits can provide exciting action. Once the bass finish spawning, however, Grigsby finds the dreaded post-spawn stage much easier to handle on natural lakes.

"Bass on southern natural lakes have a long spawning season. It may last four or five months of the year. For this reason, there really isn't a distinct post-spawn period. Northern lakes will have a much shorter spawning season, sometimes just a month. But bass season is normally closed on these waters until after the spawn, so it's not a factor.

"After the bass complete their spawning in the early stages," Grigsby notes, "you can move back out to the places that they staged in during the pre-spawn and find late-spawning fish there, as well as those post-spawn fish that are beginning to move towards the deeper weedlines for the summer.

"Bass don't leave the spawning areas quickly on natural lakes. There's a lot of food running around there, with the newly hatched fry and the panfish that normally come into the area to spawn after the bass are finished. That helps hold the bass, because they have to feed up and recover from the spawn. If you found bass spawning in one to three feet of water, then find them gone, you can often locate them again by just moving out to thicker cover in five to six feet of water. They will be moving towards deeper water, but they're going to take their time doing so while they feed up."

As noted earlier, some of these fish will remain in shallow cover throughout the year. Those bass that do continue to frequent the depths, however, aren't hard to find.

"The most consistent areas to find summer bass in are the deeper grass beds," Grigsby continues. "The best

Vegetation breaks — places where two or more types of vegetation come together — can be productive areas on a natural lake. These breaks can indicate a slight change of depth or bottom composition. Bass will relate to them.

plants to look for are those in five to ten feet of water that border on some of the deepest water in the immediate area.

"Also, those plants that produce large volumes of oxygen — like hydrilla, milfoil, and eelgrass, as well as maidencane — will hold the most fish. Oxygen production is important during the summer months on natural lakes, because being shallow, they can heat up quickly and warmer water does not hold as much oxygen as cooler water. The bass don't have much choice; they need oxygen and they need food. Both of these will be in best supply in the deeper weedbeds."

Bass holding in these deeper grass beds react much differently than deep fish in a man-made reservoir. Instead of migrating to the shallows to feed early and late in the day, then returning to their deeper homes during inactive periods, they do the reverse. They move to the thinner outside edges of the grass or even to open water to feed, then retreat to the thicker, cooler sections of the grass to lie up during midday.

"If you find a group of bass feeding along a grassline in the morning," Grigsby notes, "you can expect to have those bass move back inside the grass as the sun comes up. Often you can catch bass on fast-moving baits when they are outside, then just move back into the cover and flip the same fish in the middle of the day."

Like many expert anglers, Grigsby has found that the best summer grass beds will often be those that extend out to some of the deepest water in the immediate area. This immediate access to deep water is important to the bass in the summer and many grass beds located on shallow flats

Natural-lake bass often spawn in extremely shallow water. This makes an ideal target for the wading angler. This technique can be more effective than boat fishing in spring.

Regardless of the lake or the season, experts have found that there always will be catchable bass in a shallow natural lake. (Right) Flipping is a necessary skill for success in vertical presentation.

will see little use from the larger bass during the summer months.

While Grigsby favors the deeper cover for summer fishing, shallow water anglers also can fare well. Invariably there will be bass holding in heavy cover along the shorelines of most natural lakes, even during the hottest summer months. These will be scattered fish and seldom found in any significant schools or concentrations. They generally hold on objects that provide shade, cover and security. These may be fallen trees, brush tops, small patches of grass or reeds — and especially boat docks. It's no secret that bass and boat docks go together like politicians and promises and this is especially true on even the shallowest natural lakes.

Like those in man-made reservoirs, natural lake bass respond actively to conditions of "environmental activity." Normal feeding activity can be expected at dawn and dusk, but wind, cloud cover, water movement and other stirrings of the environment can promote activity any time they occur.

"As a general rule," says Grigsby, "the largest concentrations or schools of summer bass are going to be relating to the deeper vegetation. They'll move to thin edges to feed and retreat to the thicker areas to lie up. When they are in the thick stuff, they can often show some very distinctive patterns as to where they will hold.

"For example, if you have a large bed of maidencane that is broken up by occasional small patches of moss, lily pads or other plants, it often indicates a change in bottom composition or a slight change in depth...maybe as little as five or six inches. Bass in that area may be holding on these small patches or on the edge where they meet the predominant grass. Or they could all be concentrated on the points of the grass bed or along indentations. They can be very specific, instead of just scattering through the grass in general. Summer bass have a tendency to bunch up pretty tightly, and most of the adult bass in one three hundred-yard-square area could well be in only one small portion of it."

As summer gives way to fall, cooling waters will increase bass activity.

"This is one of my favorite times of the year to fish a natural lake," says Grigsby, "and one of the most produc-

tive. It's almost an anything-goes kind of situation, because not all the bass will be doing the same thing.

"Some bass will begin to move a little shallower, while other fish — especially the smaller bass — will actually move right out into open water and surface school on shad minnows. The bass will become more scattered than they were in the summer and they will be far more active. Instead of dawn and dusk activity, you'll be able to take bass throughout the day.

"You don't have the brief periods of activity during the day that characterize summer bass fishing. But you don't have the bass bunched up, either. Fall fish will tend to begin scattering. If many of the bass in one area were concentrated into a specific spot during the summer, you'll see those fish begin covering more ground. I like to start in the same places I found fish in the summer and just begin working my way shallower, until I establish some kind of workable pattern."

Grigsby favors fast-moving lures during his fall forays, with one of his favorites being the shad-imitating Rat-L-Trap.

"Bass are feeding actively on shad at this time of year and you can cover a lot of water with this bait."

If cover conditions are too thick for the Trap, he'll often shift to a Bumble Bee spinnerbait with a #5 willow leaf blade.

In *winter*, cold weather seldom moves bass far on most natural lakes. They really have no place to go. Grigsby finds locating them relatively uncomplicated, but getting them to bite can be.

"The deepest water you can find in the lake that has some form of vegetation cover will hold fish during the winter. So will the deepest outside edges of the emergent

Dollar bonnets like those in background are a favorite cover for bass during spring months. They grow on a firm sand bottom. In addition to offering bass dense cover in which to hide, they provide spawning area for the species.

vegetation. Actually, their summer homes aren't much different than their winter homes. They don't have that many depth and cover options."

Another situation that often will draw winter bass like a magnet, especially on shallow Florida lakes, is extremely thick cover located near some of the deepest water in the immediate area. This thick cover may be surface-matted hydrilla, floating hyacinths or just mats of "junk" growth. But it's worth seeking out, especially if it lies near six to ten feet of water.

"Winter bass fishing on natural lakes can be tough," Grigsby feels. "Just as these lakes warm quickly in the summer, they cool quickly in the winter and the bass become sluggish.

"A two- or three-day warming trend, though, can often spark a good feed from the fish. When this happens, the fish seldom move far from their wintering areas. They don't go shallow to feed like they might in a man-made reservoir. Instead, they just move closer to the surface and may take faster-moving baits. But, they'll do it right in their wintering area."

For anglers used to pursuing bass in deep, man-made reservoirs, shallow natural lakes can be a bit confusing on the first try. But once an angler learns to read the various types of vegetation that exist on these lakes and, more importantly, understands how the bass will relate to it on a seasonal basis, natural lakes can begin to offer some of the finest shallow-water bass'n around.

CHAPTER 16

Stout tackle and heavy line often are needed to wrestle bass through the thick plants and into the boat. Even a four-pound bass is strong in a few acres of hydrilla.

HYDRILLA: BOON IN DISGUISE?

Checkerboard effect of the rapidly emerging hydrilla provides open water areas for feeding, plus dense cover for retreat of the bass.

This Exotic Water Plant Will Change The Way You Fish For Bass

IT MAY seem a little strange to devote an entire chapter to one particular species of aquatic plant. But, hydrilla, — and its look-alike, milfoil — deserve it.

No single environmental factor has exerted as much influence on bass fishing during the last decade as that which has resulted from the rapid spread of hydrilla. In a lake that is heavily infested with the plant, the movements of the bass will alter radically enough to make the information contained in the previous three chapters almost useless. "Grass lakes," as they are commonly referred to by the pros, require a different set of tactics once hydrilla has taken hold in the waters.

Anglers who intend to be successful on these waters need an understanding of the plant, itself, and how bass relate to it.

Once confined to tropical countries in faraway regions of the world, hydrilla first gained a foothold in this country in the warm, shallow waters of Florida. Today it has spread as far west as California, and as far north as Delaware. In many Southern states the plant has virtually taken over entire lakes, forcing out native vegetation.

Some anglers have hailed hydrilla and milfoil as saviors for aging lakes. In some cases, this is true. Many other recreational water users, however, view the plant quite differently. Water managers, lakeside residents and pleasure boaters regard it as a noxious spoiler. That, too, can be an appropriate title for the exotic plant.

For biologists, it poses a complex problem, one we're going to have to learn to live with.

"We're going to have hydrilla forever," states Dan Thayer, a biological scientist with the Florida Department

Bass in heavily infested lakes remain offshore in deeper hydrilla beds through most of the year. Those anglers who pound the shoreline are usually wasting their time.

"Hydrilla will always have the edge on native plants when it comes to competing for space and nutrients within a system," Thayer explains. "It is a more efficient utilizer of nutrients, it can grow in a variety of bottom compositions and it can grow in waters too tannic or turbid for many native plants."

Hydrilla, it would seem, is one tough cookie.

"One of the limiting factors in the growth of submerged aquatic plants," Thayer says, "is that they get their nutrition from the water and the available nutrition in a system is limited. That nutrition is generally used up for the day within the first few hours of the morning, when many of the plants experience their growth for the day. Hydrilla begins growing at lower light levels than most plants and gets the first shot at available nutrition. In effect, it eats breakfast before the other plants even get up. In doing so, it takes that food away from native plants."

Hydrilla, an annual plant that does experience a peak and fall back, also begins its growing season before many native plants, thus getting a head start on establishing itself for the season. As a side effect, dense hydrilla tends to filter the water, allowing light to penetrate to greater depths. In effect, the plant clears its own path to take over the bottom of a lake.

During its peak growing season, it forms surface mats that shut out the light below, further decreasing the ability of native plants to grow in the vicinity.

"Hydrilla can literally take over a lake and crowd the native plants out," Thayer states.

Even during the cooler months, when hydrilla growth is at its minimum, the hardy plant assures itself of survival in the spring.

"At a water temperature of about fifty-five degrees," Thayer pointed out, "the plant begins to fall back. It will once again begin to grow at about sixty degrees, combined with the stronger light levels of spring. In the meantime, it produces underwater stems called rhizomes. These are tubers in the bottom soil that will sprout new plants in the spring. As many as five hundred of these have been noted per square foot. Another structure forms on the plants leaf axile. It looks like a little pine cone and it too is a survival mechanism that falls to the bottom as the plant dies off. These germinate new plants the following year."

Hydrilla can also rejuvenate itself through fragmentation. Even a two-inch piece of the plant can sprout and grow as soon as it comes into contact with a suitable bottom. It's a tough plant to kill.

"It's one of those plants that has spread around the world," Thayer explains. "We think its origin is Africa, where it is a problem. But it's also a problem in Asia, India, Australia and on many Pacific islands."

The problems associated with hydrilla are numerous. In irrigation and flood control canals, dense hydrilla levels can almost halt the flow of water. This same stilling of the water also contributes to increased mosquito breeding. And on many lakes and reservoirs, the plant can mat out so densely on the surface that even a 150-horsepower outboard engine cannot chop through it.

But hydrilla isn't always bad.

"On some bodies of water, it actually has helped the system. Any submerged plant will help the growth of food chain items and increases the area's overall fertility. The Potomac River is a good example. For years, they tried to

of Natural Resources. "It's here. It's spreading farther than we thought it would and it doesn't appear at this point that we can completely eradicate it."

Based at the University of Florida at Gainsesville, Thayer is one of the many researchers at that institution who has scientifically studied the plant during the last fifteen years.

Once known primarily to those in the aquarium industry — who can be credited or blamed for its introduction into this country — the plant first made appearances in the Miami and Crystal River areas of South Florida in about 1960. Within five years, it had spread far enough to be considered a real problem. Considering the plant's aggressive nature, that's not surprising.

Many professional anglers enjoy fishing the so-called grass lakes because of the number of bass always present.

get some type of submerged plant growing in it and couldn't. Then they accidentally got some hydrilla in there and it took off. Now they're catching shrimp there in areas where they never could before. It has helped that system. But if you have a varied population of native plants in a system already, I don't think hydrilla would be a good thing for that system.

"As a botanist, I feel a variety of native plants is preferable for the overall well-being of a system to a single primary plant. The problem with hydrilla is that it will go out of control and become that primary plant," Thayer concluded.

Many anglers might disagree that hydrilla — or its close cousin, milfoil, which affects waterways and bass in the same manner — is detrimental. Many times it makes lake access difficult, but it has a reputation for doing good things for the bass.

However, fisheries biologist Doug Colle, who has been studying the effects of hydrilla on fish populations at the University of Florida since 1974, isn't sure the plant actually does live up to its reputation for benefiting bass!

Both Colle and Thayer are enthusiastic bass fishermen and both will admit that a certain amount of hydrilla can be an asset when it comes to increasing the survival of the young bass of the year, because it provides protection from predators. They both also feel that thirty to forty percent surface acre coverage is the optimum figure for hydrilla. They view the problem of hydrilla in the sense that it's a lot like being pregnant: There's no such thing as being a little bit pregnant. You either are or you aren't. And when hydrilla inevitably "comes to term," the effect on the fish population can actually be detrimental, as Colle explained.

"Many lakes that experience an influx of hydrilla will also experience an increase in the total weight of the fish population, but that weight increase is attributable to the build-up of sub-harvestable bass — those under ten inches. There is a much greater survival rate among juvenile bass when hydrilla levels exceed seventy perecent, because the dense weed protects them from populations of small fish.

"But, that does not mean an increase in adult fish in future years. During a nine-year study on Orange Lake (one of the top trophy lakes in Central Florida), the hydrilla levels fluctuated from almost nothing to a high of ninety percent coverage. Our studies, during that time, failed to show a measurable increase or decrease in the numbers of harvestable bass, regardless of the hydrilla levels.

"What we did see," Colle recalls, "during periods of heavy hydrilla infestation, was a dramatic increase in the number of juvenile bass. But they were not recruited into the adult population at the rate one might suspect."

Colle also notes that, during periods of heavy hydrilla infestation, the juvenile bass experienced a first-year growth rate of 132 millimeters. During periods when hydrilla was less severe, though, those growth rates ran between 180 and 200 millimeters!

"It's become clear to us that heavy hydrilla retards the growth rate of young-of-year bass." The same stunting also was observed in bluegills, red ear sunfish and crappie. There were many more fish, but they were significantly smaller.

One factor that Colle and some of the his fellow researchers cited to explain the reduced growth rates is the fact that the hydrilla forms such a protective cover for forage that the bass cannot fully utilize it. As has been noted in previous chapters, bass cannot feed effectively in extremely thick cover.

"The forage bass in off-shore hydrilla beds is tremendous," Colle observed. "Run a net through it and you'd think, 'Good Lord! We can raise a bunch of fish on this.' But bass, especially adult basss, can't feed in that thick cover nearly as effectively as they can in a more open mix of vegetation. The food is there for them, but they have a hard time making use of it and that stunts their growth."

In addition to affecting their growth, the dense weed also alters the movement patterns of bass. This is why anglers plying their trade on "grass lakes" need to reconsider their basic bass'n tactics.

"We did some radio telemetry work on Pearl Lake, in Orlando, Florida (a fifty-four-acre lake completely matted over with hydrilla), to determine how bass moved and related to the weed. We ran our monitoring study for three months, then came in with herbicides to open up certain sections of the lake. We wanted to see if we could create open water situations that would draw the bass to them.

"What we found was that the normal home range of the bass was two to three times that noted in studies on non-infested lakes and that their movement patterns were completely random.

"As a bass fisherman," Colle continues, "I was interested in seeing how the bass related to the hydrilla. But by the end of the study, I couldn't identify a single factor — wind, sun, time of day, etc. — that has an influence on their movements. They did what they pleased and there didn't seem to be any reason for it."

The only consistent trait Colle observed was a total avoidance of the extreme shallows. Where bass might normally be expected to move to shallow areas to feed, then withdraw to deeper water or heavy cover during inactive periods, that was not the case. The bass remained in the deeper, offshore hydrilla beds throughout the year, the only exception being the spring spawn.

"When we came in with the herbicides and started opening up sections of the lake," Colle remembered, "we still didn't influence the bass's movements. The fish that were in the area before we sprayed it didn't leave; there was no avoidance behavior. But other fish didn't move in. It was almost as if we weren't there. The fish ignored our efforts."

A similar study in Orange Lake in 1977 achieved the same results. "In both cases we were not able to redistribute or alter the make-up of the bass population, regardless of how we altered the hydrilla."

Colle feels the wider, random movements of the bass could be attributed to their inability to feed effectively in the dense weeds and this caused them to roam farther to seek vulnerable prey. But he can't explain why opening sections of the lake — in effect, creating easier feeding grounds — failed to draw bass.

"Maybe we weren't able to alter enough of their environment to make a difference," he ventures.

Given the negative effects of hydrilla on a lake and its bass population, the success ratios of those who fish hydrilla and love it are surprising. But Colle has an answer for this:

"The fishing in a lake heavily infested with hydrilla can be excellent, despite what our studies have told us. But it is not something the hydrilla did to the bass that accounts for that.

Orange Lake bass was taken at noon on a bright day in August, flipping thick hydrilla mats in 10-foot water. Heavy hydrilla decreases the angling pressure on lake.

"The one thing we did notice during our nine years of study," he continued, "was that, during years of heavy infestation, there was as much as a ninety percent reduction in angling pressure. The people that were left were serious bass fishermen who knew how to fish hydrilla. When you decrease angling pressure that much, leaving only the serious fishermen, you will show a good catch rate. There are just a lot more bass left for the few who will fight the hydrilla to fish for them.

"The hydrilla did not biologically create a larger population of bass. We have not yet been able to document hydrilla's ability to increase the adult carrying capacity of any lake."

For these same reasons, however, Colle feels heavily infested lakes offer excellent chances for a trophy catch.

"It takes time for a bass to grow past seven pounds," he notes, "and sharply reduced angling pressure will give the bass a better chance to do that. This lack of pressure grows more trophy bass than anything the hydrilla might have done to the water body."

On any body of water infested with hydrilla or milfoil, the potential exists for outstanding fishing. But anglers need to "re-learn" some basics.

"Hydrilla," explains professional bass angler Harold Allen, "can change the way you have to fish a lake, because it changes the way the bass relate to it. Bass tend to stay in the deeper hydrilla beds for longer periods of time

Most fish found in hydrilla-infested lakes are healthy, robust specimens. Heavy growth of hydrilla often increases the forage base and can sometimes improve productivity of a lake, although bass have hard time feeding in cover.

and don't always make drastic depth changes in response to daily weather conditions, seasons or cold fronts. On many lakes, before they had hydrilla or milfoil, we could predictably catch bass in the shallows during the spring months, then follow them right out to their summer homes on the deeper structures.

"Now it's tougher to do that, because the bass do not always follow their pre-hydrilla movement patterns."

As noted earlier, studies have shown that bass in hydrilla infested lakes tend to stay offshore and roam around far more than their counterparts in lakes lacking the plant. Either of those factors can complicate the task of locating bass on strange waters. This is especially true for the angler who is used to banging away at visible shoreline structure like stumps, fallen logs and other fish-holding cover. On hydrilla lakes, that won't work very often.

Also complicating the task is the fact that bass will relate to hydrilla in a slightly different manner on a man-made lake than they will on a natural lake.

"In a man-made reservoir," Allen notes, "more times than not, growth of the hydrilla will follow the contour lines of the lake. In fact, if you've got a good topographical map, you can just about predict where the hydrilla will grow. Once it mats out on the surface, you can read the underwater contours of the lake just by reading the density of the hydrilla. Your shallow areas, ridges, humps and flats, will have the heaviest growth, while creek channels and deeper water will be more open.

"Even though the bass will remain in the offshore hydrilla beds, they still will follow and relate to the natural bottom contours of the lake."

In effect, the outside edge of a hydrilla bed now becomes a "shoreline;" cuts through the hydrilla beds become "highways;" a lone clump of hydrilla often points out a submerged island. All tend to hold bass, even though they may be hundred of yards from the nearest shoreline.

On natural lakes, however, especially on the soup-bowl shaped waters on the Southeast, readily definable bottom contours are virtually non-existent. For an object-oriented fish like the bass, the contours it follows will become the contours of the plant itself. In looking at a clump of matted hydrilla, consider it the same as the actual shoreline of the lake. Bass will use it just as they would the shoreline in a non-infested lake.

"One of the most difficult things about defining seasonal hydrilla patterns on a natural lake is that they tend to overlap," says Florida bass pro Bernie Schultz. "Bass don't relate as much to the seasons as they do to the growth level of the hydrilla itself. It's easy, on a man-made reservoir without much hydrilla, to say that bass will be at a certain depth during certain seasons. You can't do that on a natural lake with hydrilla. It's possible to establish a pattern...say fishing small 'coves' in major hydrilla beds...in the spring and have it hold up throughout the summer and early fall, as long as the hydrilla remains unaltered. The growth of the hydrilla can vary with the amount of control

From left: Charlie Reed, Larry Nixon and Harold Allen all are experts at locating bass in hydrilla and milfoil-laden waters. Reed won the 1986 BASS Master Classic by being able to determine where bass had moved after milfoil in which they were living was sprayed and removed for tourney. All know excess line can be fouled in weeds, a bass lost.

agents applied to it, the water levels or just yearly fluctuations.

"On a natural lake," Schultz adds, "anglers need to base their tactics more on the hydrilla growth levels and less on the season."

Despite the differences between man-made reservoirs and natural lakes, there are some times of the year when the behavior of the bass is remarkably similar on both. This is most true in the spring. As described in the preceding chapters on man-made and natural lakes, the requirements of the bass at this time of the year are fixed; they can't alter them. So, they still seek shallow, protected water in which to spawn.

"In the spring," explains Allen, "when the bass are moving up into the shallows to spawn, they'll move to the inside edge of the hydrilla beds near the bank. This is about as shallow as you'll see fish on a grass lake all year.

"These fish will get into the little clumps or islands of hydrilla and a fast-moving lure worked around them or over them can pay off. I like to have some water over the top of the hydrilla, anywhere from two inches to two feet. And I will definitely go looking for this type of cover situation near areas where bass will spawn. The surface water is what is going to warm up first and the bass will suspend near the surface right over the top of those hydrilla beds. A fast-moving bait ripped over them will get a hit."

Both Allen and Schultz rate spinnerbaits, topwater lures and vibrating crankbaits like the Rat-L-Trap and Sugar Shad as top choices for working across the top of submerged hydrilla during the spring months.

A spring cold front also causes a predictable response.

"If there wasn't any hydrilla," Allen has observed, "the bass following a cold front would normally do one of two things: They'd either fall back to the first breakline out from the bank where there is a good depth change or they'd bury down into whatever heavy cover — brush and such — was in the immediate area.

"But," Allen continues, "with the hydrilla, they just move to the grass edge nearest to where they were holding and bury into it. They don't move or feed. They just lie there."

Flipping the thickest, most heavily matted areas of hydrilla with a heavily weighted Texas worm rig often pays dividends following a spring cold front. Since the proximity of heavy hydrilla does not require the bass to make a lengthy post-front migration, anglers often can stay right with fish they found prior to the front by simply locating the thickest cover in the immediate area and concentrating on it.

Once the spawn is over and water temperatures rise, the bass begin to return to the deeper waters where they will spend the majority of the year in hydrilla-infested lakes. For Harold Allen, it's the signal to begin probing the deep outside edges of the grass.

"If I had to pick the best general depth for fishing summer hydrilla on a man-made lake," Allen says, "it would be between fourteen and twenty-two feet along the deeper edges of the grass. Open water over the top of the hydrilla isn't important now, because most of the surface activity is going to be limited to dawn and dusk. The rest of the time the bass will be relating to the bottom."

On natural lakes, however, Schultz has found that the summer months can bring on some of the best topwater action of the year, as well as being productive for anglers fishing shallow-running crankbaits.

"As the water warms after the spawn," he explains, "we'll begin to see a big increase in the growth of the open-water hydrilla. This is when I start to pay a lot of attention

Thick hydrilla growth can make it impossible for anglers to reach extreme shallows of many lakes, but bass often will move to outer edge of growth to take up residence and to feed near the edges.

to the density and growth stage of the plant. Bass will become more active and feed more, but they can't do that effectively in the thickest portions of the grass. They have to move to the thinner edges and contour lines where they can feed. In some cases, they will even use the natural contours of the grass to help them trap baitfish."

One such growth stage that Schultz often seeks is what he refers to as the "stranding" stage.

"Stranding is when the plant has not yet reached the surface and hasn't begun to form leaves on its stalks. It's just growing in strands and the water in these areas is usually a bit off-colored, because the plant hasn't reached the density necessary to filter it. The bass seem to use this off-colored water — and the strands themselves — as an ambush feeding situation. It seems they feed on larger baitfish like shiners and bream, at this time."

Large, noisy topwater plugs fished over this hydrilla growth stage can bring bass crashing to the surface. Rat-L-Traps and swimming worms, worked through the strands, often can take bass when they are not feeding.

"I get a lot of hits when I bang a crankbait into one of the stalks. When ripped free, it's almost a triggered strike."

As the hydrilla enters its matting stage, it will begin to form open bays and lagoons between the thicker clumps of grass. Both the bass and Schultz seek these out as well.

"Bass," says Schultz, "will use these open bays as feeding areas, often herding the baitfish into the very backs of them where they can trap them against a wall of hydrilla. In any area where there are only a few open bays in a solid mat of hydrilla, most of the feeding action in that general area could be concentrated in the backs of those few open bays."

By mid-summer, the continued growth of hydrilla on many natural lakes will swallow up the open bays, leaving a checkerboard mat of small open pockets and clear water along the deepest hydrilla edges. Some bass will remain in the thickest hydrilla, using what few small open pockets remain. Many more, though, will move to the outside edges, where the hydrilla forms a distinct wall or breakline.

This situation occurs on both man-made impoundments and natural lakes and the most effective technique for dealing with it is equally effective on both.

"By far the best way to fish deeper hydrilla edges," explains Harold Allen, "is to use a depth finder and a good pair of polarized glasses to find that outside edge or other contour lines, then keep your boat right on top of it."

Like many experts, Allen rates a bow-mounted flasher as the best tool for this task. At the present time, LCR technology does not allow them to "shoot through" hydrilla and give a true bottom reading. Graphs can, but they are far more expensive (paper and stylus) to operate. The old flasher does the job well and the influx of hydrilla may well be responsible for its survival in the face of modern technology.

Allen, like other "grass" experts, advises anglers to select a Texas-rigged plastic worm or a jig-and-pig heavy enough to punch through the thick grass and reach the bottom. Sometimes, this calls for weights of one-half ounce or more.

"Make little short pitch casts ahead of the boat," Allen suggests, "and when the bait gets down to the bottom, jig it up and down a few times before you pick it up to make another cast. You don't want to have a lot of line out when you are fishing deep hydrilla; it's just too easy for the bass to get that line all wrapped up in the thick grass and you'll lose him. That's the reason for the short casts ahead of the boat. If you have the boat sitting on top of the edge, your bait will be right in the strike zone."

Thick hydrilla tendrils may grow as deep as 25 feet. As plant reaches surface, it mats out, making access to waters difficult. (Below) Hydrilla, milfoil islands indicate a hump or ridge in deeper water. This is often where bass will take up residence.

When fishing in this manner, Allen also cautions anglers to be very alert.

"Many times a hit on a vertical presentation like this won't be a distinct 'thump.' You'll just pick up the worm or jig and it will feel heavy. Just because the bait feels hung up, don't start jerking it around trying to get it free, because sometimes it'll be a bass."

When in doubt, set the hook or just apply a slow, steady pressure to your lure with the rod. If the rod tugs back, set the hook!

As in any form of bass fishing, being alert to your surroundings also can be critical. During the summer months, one of the easiest ways to locate bass in deep, open-water hydrilla is simply to go look for them! Many, many days, I have gone on the water at dawn and just cruised around until I saw surface feeding activity; bass breaking or baitfish skipping.

Then, fishing topwater plugs or shallow running crankbaits, I had some superb action. When the fish quit, though, I didn't. Shifting to a flipping rod, I just began carefully probing the thickest mats of hydrilla in the immediate area and have often caught bass over eight pounds right in the middle of the day!

"If bass are up and feeding," Allen says, "in a certain area of hydrilla, many times there is something on the bottom that is holding them in that area. Remember that hydrilla bass do not move horizontally toward the shoreline to feed. They move vertically...from the base of the hydrilla, to the surface. Once they're done feeding, they'll often just go right back down to the bottom in the same area and you catch them all day long if you get a worm or a jig down to them.

"Sometimes," he continues "I've found bass up and chasing baitfish in the morning, but was unable to catch them then. However, coming back a few hours later, after the fish had stopped chasing bait and settled down to the base of the grass, I was able to catch them with the worm technique."

As with any other type of structure, bass can frequently relate to hydrilla in different ways under different conditions.

"Bright sunlight, severe weather changes or even heavy fishing pressure can move bass back into the thickest por-

tions of the grass," Allen points out. "Cloudy weather can bring them up to the scattered portions of the grass or the edges, where they're easier to catch. And don't forget wind and water movement. A lot of times, during the summer months, a good breeze will move bass to the windy hydrilla points and stack them up there. Like any kind of bass fishing, hydrilla fishing isn't cut and dried.

"Hydrilla can frustrate a lot of anglers, especially when it's thick and matted. There's just so much of it. The best thing an angler can do is to pick one small section of the lake he feels might have fish in it; maybe a small cove with a creek channel running through it and a couple of main lake points on the outside. Then, go into the area and work it thoroughly, instead of jumping all over by working the different 'types' of grass in the area — points, cuts, deep edges, thick mats — until you get a feel for how the fish are relating to the grass at that time. Once you get that done, you can usually go to other areas of the lake and catch bass the same way.

Getting a handle on hydrilla bass'n isn't difficult, if anglers will keep some of these basic facts in mind. Unfortunately, one factor that can upset even the most carefully laid plans is what happens when someone comes along and takes your hydrilla away.

Aquatic weed control is the "in thing" on many waters. Some agencies, like the Tennessee Valley Authority, have literally declared war on the plant. What's here today may not be here tomorrow, so anglers need to know a bit about control techniques and how to cope with them.

"The present thrust at hydrilla," states Dan Thayer, "is to manage it at levels beneficial to the fishery while still allowing other recreational and commercial uses of the waterway.

"As far as that is concerned, we possess the means to accomplish this. The only limiting factor is the cost of control. At the present time, we feel that the minimum figure for effective management, in terms of dollars, is about $800 per surface acre per year. We can not totally eradicate the plant, but we do have the means to control it.

Studies are currently under way at the University of Florida to determine the optimum mix between hydrilla

Outdoor editor/writer Mark Thiffault holds a good bass taken in the milfoil-infested waters of Tennessee's Lake Chickamauga. The same tactics are used for milfoil as when one is fishing hydrilla cover.

and native vegetation. The results of the study are not conclusive at this time, but both researchers and expert bass anglers are surprisingly close in their assessment of how much hydrilla a lake should have — and where it should be located.

"If I were going to design a dream lake," said pro angler Larry Nixon, currently the all-time leading money winner on the BASS Tournament Trail, "I would not want any hydrilla in water shallower than five feet. Leave that area for the native plants. I also wouldn't want it in water deeper than fifteen feet. Leave the mid-lake areas for the pleasure boaters and water skiers. Where I feel it would be most beneficial is in that five- to fifteen-foot range.

"Within that range it would provide cooler waters for the bass at the deeper levels in the summer months, while the shallower levels would provide the needed protection for young-of-the-year bass. A lake like this would be very unique and very productive."

Sculpting a dream lake is a frequent topic among the University of Florida researchers, who may well be the leading authorities on the subject of hydrilla.

"We talk about it a lot," says Doug Colle, "because many of us here are bass fishermen. If you could afford the cost of achieving an optimum level and placement of hydrilla to maximize your bass population, I would have it in a clump distribution to give you an increased edge effect. About thirty percent of the lake surface would be good, but not in a continuous mat. I'd want the clumps to function as small islands that you could easily fish, while still providing protection for the young bass and increasing the forage bass."

With that in mind, here are some of the control techniques available to biologists and how anglers can adapt to them when they are applied.

Drawdowns: Lowering the water levels to expose the bottom soil and kill all plant life can be a valuable tool for managing hydrilla on those impoundments that permit controlled water level manipulation. When done correctly, hydrilla can be controlled in the shallow areas of the lake without the need for herbicides. As a side benefit, drawdowns also can encourage the growth of some native plants, allowing them to reestablish themselves in the littoral zone.

"To make a drawdown work," Thayer explains, "it must be done in two stages. In the first stage, the water is lowered to kill the existing plant life. But it will leave you with tuber reserves or rhizomes, when the lake is refilled. You'll get a big growth of hydrilla from these. What must be done here is to again draw the lake down before that new growth has a chance to lay down its own rhizomes. You must make certain that you deplete the soil of them or the hydrilla will come back very quickly."

From a fisherman's point of view, drawdowns are beneficial in another way; by drastically lowering lake levels, the

Feeding bass often move to deepest outside edge of the hydrilla beds. The thick weeds hinder their efforts to trap the baitfish in the inner areas of heavier cover.

Open bays and lagoons in large hydrilla beds form ideal feeding situations for bass, since they can utilize the edge of the thick weeds to trap baitfish in small areas.

bass are concentrated into a much smaller volume of water. In a lake with a good population of bass, some of the finest bass'n an angler will ever have will come on a drawdown.

The best time to capitalize on this is when the drawdown has reached its mid-point. The bass may not react and move during the early stages, but by the time the lake reaches its half-way stage, the fish will have begun stacking up on the deeper main channel edges. Combine that with the increased flow of water, as the lake is lowered, and the fact that most drawdowns are held in the late summer and fall, when bass activity is increasing, and you're guaranteed some fast action.

Once the lake reaches its drawdown level, however, the bass will adjust to the new conditions and the boom will end.

Contact herbicides: Diquate and endothall are the two most commonly used chemical control agents. When sprayed onto hydrilla, they begin to knock the plant down immediately. So fast is their action that freshly sprayed areas may appear to have been cut mechanically!

These chemicals are seeing less use among modern waterway mangagers, however. Generally, they are restricted to spot treatment around launching ramps, marinas and for cutting boat trails.

This is the least desirable form of control from the fisherman's point of view, because of the large amount of dead, decaying vegetation entering the water in one small area at one time. This can deplete the oxygen in some cases and often will cause bass to leave the area.

This is precisely what happened to the 1986 BASS Master Classic winner, Charlie Reed, while he was pre-practicing for that tournament on Tennessee's Lake Chickamauga.

Reed had located a good school of bass in a milfoil bed near Ware's Branch. But, as he was actually fishing the area in his boat, a Tennessee Valley Authority spray boat came right at him depositing chemicals in the very spot he was fishing! Incidents such as this have given the TVA a reputation as one of the worst abusers of chemical control agents.

But how a veteran angler like Reed handled this situation can serve as a guideline for other anglers.

"Once that spray boat came through," Reed explains, "I knew that spot was going to be dead as far as the fishing went. But I also knew that there was a good bunch of bass there and they probably wouldn't move far to find a new home."

Reed began moving through the now denuded area, watching his graph and flasher. He was looking for a deeper water structure situation that would draw the bass now that their milfoil home had been destroyed. And he found it.

"I located this little creek channel that cut across the cove where I had found the fish. It varied between five and ten feet in depth and was really the only significant deepwater cover in that immediate area. When the spray boat killed the vegetation in the flats bordering the channel, I felt the bass would have no choice but to relocate there."

They did and Reed was the only one of the forty-one contestants able to manage a limit of bass on each of the three tournament days, winning the event.

Bass will often leave freshly sprayed areas, but they seldom move far, so long as there is some other form of suitable cover for them in that area. It can be well worth the time it takes to find it, since many bass may stack up on it.

SONAR: One of the newest weapons in the water manager's arsenal is a compound called SONAR, not to be confused with underwater listening devices. When applied early in the growing season, in pellet form, it sinks to the bottom and is absorbed through the newly emerging hydrilla tubers. Once the substance has been absorbed by the plant, it goes to work breaking down the pigments within the plant that are used to utilize sunlight in the plants' growth. In effect, it causes the plant to literally sunburn itself to death. Its effect upon native plants is minimal and, in many areas where it has been used, they are growing back quite well.

Because it works slowly and during the early season when there is the minimum amount of plant bio-mass in the water, it has shown no adverse effects on bass — or bass fishermen.

Left: Mechanical hydrilla harvesting proved too costly. (Above) Sonar will kill hydrilla as will some chemicals. Leaves turn white, as the plant dies.

This is by far the most effective control agent for the plant, and one that everybody can live comfortably with.

White Amur: In their attempt to control hydrilla and milfoil, a variety of biological control agents have been experimented with by biologists. One of the most potentially dangerous is the White Amur or grass carp.

"If you have thirty to thirty-five percent rooted vegetation in a water system," reports Texas Parks & Wildlife biologist Bob Bounds, "you have a healthy situation for the bass. And whatever is good for the bass keeps the other creatures in that system healthy, as well."

The ill-advised introduction of the White Amur into many of our nation's waterways threatens that healthy situation, however.

"There's no way to get around the fact," said Dan Thayer, "that lakes where the White Amur have been introduced will ultimately become completely weed-free."

Bob Bounds would certainly agree. He was a first-hand observer to the grass carp frenzy that literally stripped Texas's Lake Conroe of every single bit of aquatic vegetation.

The Lake Conroe experiment became one of the most emotional issues yet to arise among Texas bass anglers. And should serve to illustrate the fallacy of allowing public opinion and political pressure to interfere with the sound biological management of our lakes and reservoirs.

In order to understand this a bit better, it is necessary to know a little bit about the grass carp.

Native to the massive Amur River in China, the grass carp were first imported into this country for controlled research as to their benefits as a biological control agent for weeds. Many states had strict regulations concerning where these fish could be introduced. Others, though, did not, and reproducing populations have now been verified in the Mississippi River system.

The fish, which have been documented in Florida at weights of over forty-five pounds and ages exceeding thirteen years, grow rapidly during the first two to three years of life. Their consumption of aquatic weeds is at its maximum during this period. Once sexual maturity is reached, at the age of two or three, the carp will have reached a weight of about twenty pounds.

As a control agent for small pond or irrigation ditch environments, where gamefish management is not a concern, the carp have demonstrated their ability to keep the waters weed-free. However, no fisheries biologist I've ever spoken to recommends placing these fish in a large eco-system where gamefish management is one of the priorities.

When lakeside residents of Lake Conroe became fed up with hydrilla growth clogging their coves and bays, they asked the Texas State Legislature for help. Against sound biological advice, the lawmakers passed a law allowing Texas A&M University to experimentally stock grass carp in Lake Conroe, then one of the state's better bass lakes.

"It took those grass carp about eighteen months to clean out Lake Conroe," Bob Bounds remembers, "and they cleaned it out pretty good. They didn't just stop at the hydrilla, they took everything: the hyacinths, the rooted vegetation and they even stripped the willow tree roots along the shoreline, where they could get at them.

"I hate to see a large eco-system turned topsy-turvy without knowing exactly what you're getting into. It's the proverbial shot in the dark and that's just not the way biology should work."

What happened to Conroe?

"When they first cleared Conroe," Larry Nixon explains, "the fishing was great for a few years, because the bass had to go to whatever cover was left and it was easy to find. There was almost a bass on every stump. Once that little boom period ended, though, it became hard to catch a bass at Conroe."

Another user group has also suffered.

"A lot of people didn't know it," Bob Bounds points out, "but Conroe was one of the biggest feeding areas in Texas for redhead and canvasback ducks. When the carp cleaned out the vegetation, they eliminated those ducks from Conroe."

The spread of hydrilla and milfoil across the country is one of the legitimate concerns for both anglers and water managers, but it's not insurmountable.

Once anglers understand the techniques needed to fish it and water managers understand that common sense is the key to managing it, both water users and the environment itself should benefit from the plant.

CHAPTER 17

When looking for bass, pros have both anglers cast different baits to learn what the bass are doing on that day.

HOW TO LOCATE BASS

A Systematic Approach Pays Off In Putting It All Together

UNDERSTANDING THE types of depth and cover situations bass utilize on a seasonal basis is necessary if an angler is to be successful. But, it's no guarantee of success in itself.

Knowing, for example, that bass in man-made reservoirs show a marked preference for shallow creek arm coves in the fall serves only as a starting point in your search. It does not tell you in which creek cove arm the bass will be. Nor does it give you any clue as to whether the

fish will be holding in shallow shoreline vegetation, fallen trees lying in slightly deeper water or if the bass still are relating to deeper cover, such as the submerged creek channel.

In effect, an understanding of seasonal patterns serves only to put you in the bass's "home." Now, it's up to you to figure out which "room" the bass is using.

This is not always an easy task, because while bass may be utilizing a general, easily defined area, they can — and

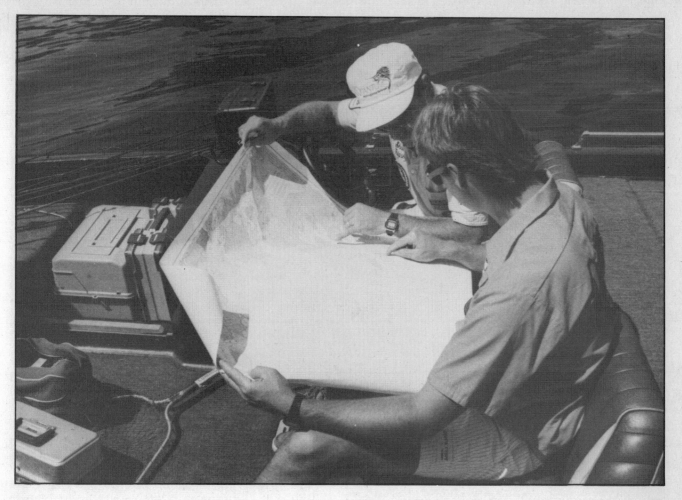

often do — shift their positions within that area in response to daily changes in weather, temperature or water conditions.

Locating the precise combinations of depth and cover the bass are using on a daily basis is basically a process of elimination. Professional anglers have found this to be a much easier process, if the angler adopts a systematic approach to his fishing.

"When I'm looking for bass," says Gary Klein, one of the top money winners on the pro tour, "I try to keep one basic thought in mind: Each day I'm on the water, I want to either eliminate something or establish something. This calls for organization and some discipline on the angler's part.

"Say, for example, that I'm going to be fishing a reservoir in October. I know that one of the prime seasonal patterns on that type of lake is creek arm coves. Before I even leave the house, I will have studied a topo map of that lake and marked out those creek arm coves that have good summer structure near their mouths or have good spawning cover inside them. These will be the ones most likely used, since they offer, within a relatively small area, all the conditions a bass needs on a year-round basis. Then I'll select a specific section of the lake that has several of these creek arms on it. That is where I will start.

"When I get on that lake," he continues, "I'm going to fish every one of those creek arms. I may move through them quickly, but I'll make certain I fish them with a variety of lures and check each type of cover in there. If you

The importance of a good topo map cannot be overestimated. The expert anglers refer to them often in their searches. (Below) Good electronics are an invaluable aid to serious bass fishermen. They provide understanding of depth and cover, plus submerged structure that might hold the bass.

Spring bass often are found in shallow areas with heavy vegetation. Seasonal movement patterns often indicate specific depths and cover situations for the angler. (Below) A successful angler systematically combs the water, until he locates a predictable pattern of bass behavior, then concentrates upon that specific pattern.

just whip through the area, throwing a spinnerbait at fallen trees, you may never know that bass are holding tightly in the trees and won't come out for a spinnerbait but would take a jig-and-pig flipped into the branches. I'll also be watching for baitfish activity and other signs of life."

Thoroughly working all the different combinations of depth and cover is important. Most professional anglers do it as a matter of habit when attemptng to locate bass. They'll carry anywhere from four to twelve rods, each rigged with a different type of lure, and as they approach a likely looking piece of cover, they may fish it with several different baits. A fallen tree might have a topwater lure tossed to its outer branches a few times. Then, the angler shifts rods and buzzes a spinnerbait through it. A plastic worm may make a few trips slowly through the branches before the angler moves right up to the tree and flips it with a jig. By the time the angler leaves that tree, he either has caught a bass or can be fairly certain there isn't a fish there.

"It may take a while," Klein admits, "but by the time I finish with those creek arms, I will either have established a fish-catching pattern or completley eliminated creek arms from further fishing. One way or another, I'm that much closer to finding bass. If I haven't caught a fish, I can now concentrate on points, channel edges or other types of cover and not have to worry about creek arms anymore.

"One mistake a lot of anglers make," Klein feels, "is that they don't discipline themselves to do this. They may start in a section of the lake that has five creek arms and fully intend to fish each one. But if they haven't caught a fish by the time they're halfway through the third arm, they get bored and go off looking for something else. Maybe they fish a point or two, then go fish a steep bank. If they don't catch any fish, they're in trouble, because they don't have an organized plan that will find them bass. They haven't established anything, because they caught no fish. But they

If an angler has an idea of the depth and cover conditions where he should find bass on the body of water he is fishing, it can pay off to drive around in search of those specific conditions. This is better than simply fishing random areas.

haven't totally eliminated anything either, because they didn't fish each creek arm. The fourth creek arm may be full of bass. Maybe it has more cover, a bit more current or it could just be that it has more baitfish. They won't know this, because they didn't fish it. All they've done is waste time and they're no closer to finding bass than when they started."

"Eliminating water" is a term used by serious anglers and does not describe a certain body funtion. It is simply the realization that only about ten percent of the water is going to hold any bass and sometimes the surest way to find that ten percent is to eliminate the other ninety percent. In the example quoted from Gary Klein, the concept can be visualized better by taking a topo map with those five creek arms on it and, after fishing them without success, simply black them out with a felt tip pen. Eliminate them from the lake and the lake suddenly gets a lot smaller!

The above approach sometimes can lead an angler to an area that has a good concentration of bass that may be using several different types of depth and cover combinatons within the area. Sometimes, though, the bass may be much more scattered. In this case, the same systematic approach can still lead an angler to a limit catch by showing him an "individual cover pattern."

With this type of pattern, an angler determines a specific set of depth and cover conditions that are holding bass, not just in one area, but often throughout the entire lake.

A bass cannot change its environment; it can only respond to it. Since the movements of the bass are simply a response to the environmental conditions existing at the time, it has been found that, if a certain number of bass are behaving in the same manner in one section of the lake, it is likely that at least some bass in other sections will be doing the same thing — if the same conditions exist. If that sounds a bit confusing, a recent trip I made to Tennessee's Chickamauga Lake might illustrate it more clearly.

Bass can be shallow, deep or in between. The successful angler knows it pays to check out a variety of depths and cover situations in his search for the big bass.

It was May, 1987, and, with fellow outdoor writer Jack Mitchell, I was in Chattanooga to cover a major U.S. Bass tournament. Having six hours to kill one day, Mitchell and I grabbed our tackle, borrowed a new Skeeter bass boat from the U.S. Bass staff, and headed out to do a little fishing.

It was the type of situation commonly faced by many anglers. Neither of us had been on the lake since the previous August, when we had spent three days riding as press observers in the BASS Master Classic. I had no idea where fish were hitting or what lures they would take. I did know that one common seasonal pattern on this lake would put bass on submerged milfoil beds, near channel edges, in five to eight feet of water. Unfortunately, I had neglected to obtain a topo map that would allow me to find that specific condition. And, with only six hours to fish, looking for bass on off-shore structures without a topo map would have been an inefficient way to use our limited time.

I did have a general lake map, purchased at the marina prior to our departure, that showed shoreline contours. I was also aware that, even though bass would be starting to move to deeper water, it was still fairly early in the summer and some bass could be expected to still be in the shallow sections of the lake near the shoreline. As I was looking at the map and wondering where to start, Mitchell pointed to a small point near the launching ramp and told me he'd seen two bass caught there in August.

A look at the map showed that the point dropped off to

deeper water, had a couple of small creek arm coves where bass would have spawned a month earlier near it and had a half-mile-long section of tree-lined bank on its north end. That was pretty varied selection of depth and cover in one small area and, since I now knew that bass had been caught there, it was as good a spot to start as any.

I rigged up three rods for myself, equipped respectively with a topwater plug, shallow-running crankbait and a spinnerbait and asked Mitchell to fish a plastic worm exclusively. As we moved down the shoreline, I would strain the water ahead with the three faster-moving baits, while Mitchell probed every piece of cover with the worm. This basic locating approach is far more effective than having two anglers throw similar lures.

Two hours later, we had covered the small area thoroughly and had three small bass to show for our efforts. I put my three rods away and took one rigged with a plastic worm. Firing up the boat, we began running up the lake, looking for a certain type of cover. In the next four hours, we probably spent an hour-and-a-half running and the rest of the time fishing. But we caught eleven bass in those two-and-a-half hours.

Why was our second-half performance so much better than our first? During our slow and methodical start, we had discovered a definite pattern to the bass. Each of the three small bass we caught during that time was taken by Mitchell on the plastic worm. Each of the fish had taken the worm as it was crawled slowly down the edge of a sub-

Jack Mitchell unhooks one of the bass taken during Lake Chickamauga trip. By being observant as to the conditions under which he and the author caught their bass, they were able to establish a productive pattern in record time.

Experienced anglers keep up to a dozen rods rigged with different lures in prospecting for bass. It saves time in changing baits and size of the rod.

merged log lying on a section of the main lake bank that was composed only of red clay.

Once we determined this, we went looking for that same set of conditions: lay-down logs on red clay main lake banks. When we found that exact set of conditions, we fished it thoroughly with plastic worms. We didn't catch fish at each stop, but we caught enough to prove the tactic far more effective than simply picking a spot and fishing everything.

What we did, essentially, was "eliminate or establish."

We caught no fish on points, in the creek coves or on any section of main lake bank that had rock or sand on it. We also caught no fish from vegetation, brush tops, rocks or small stick-ups. We eliminated all that from further fishing. We also could eliminate topwater lures, crankbaits and spinnerbaits. We'd had no hits on those either.

By being observant as to where and how we did catch fish, we were able to establish that at least some bass were behaving in the same manner. Once we identified those conditions, we were able to concentrate exclusively on

Florida pro Cliff McKendree probes the shaded areas beneath a boat dock in an effort to establish a pattern of behavior for bass. Anglers seeking this species, especially in strange waters, should leave no stone unturned in their searching.

them and not waste our time in fishing unproductive water.

While we covered about fifteen miles of shoreline that day, that same pattern held up wherever we found it. I later talked to a couple of the pros fishing in the tournament and found that some of them were fishing the same pattern as much as twenty-five miles from the launching site!

An individual cover pattern like this one often can be the quickest way to find fish, since less water can sometimes be covered. But the drawback is that it doesn't always hold up on repeating days. A bass caught from a particular piece of cover may not be replaced for several days, unless there

are a large number of bass in the area.

Had Mitchell and I returned to fish the same pieces of cover the following day, we probably wouldn't have done as well. In this situation, most professional anglers usually continue the pattern in other sections of the lake, instead of fishing the same pieces of cover over again.

Using this systematic approach to bass fishing is easy. The technique is fairly simple, as long as the angler has developed the necessary confidence to make it work. If there was a specific checklist for locating bass on strange waters it would probably read something like this.

1. Start in an area you are fairly certain contains

Shaw Grigsby checks a front-mounted depth finder in his search for bass. Author says it is important to know depth at which first couple of bass have been caught, as this can narrow the search.

bass. Many of these areas can be pin-pointed through map work before an angler ever sees the lake. Once an angler arrives at the lake, it's a smart move to start asking questions. Some fishermen may not tell you where they're catching fish, but you can often find out general areas, certain specific types of cover, what lures they might be taking and the depth at which they are being caught.

If this information falls within the seasonal pattern the bass should be using, it can be a big help. If it doesn't, it's no guarantee that it's wrong. Bass are not the most predictable of critters. And, since seasonal patterns can vary slightly on even the same types of water, getting some on-the-spot information can always be a help. The more positive factors you can put together before you hit the lake, the more successful you could be.

2. Once you reach your starting point, pause for a moment and take a look at exactly what type of depth and cover you have in the area. All too often, anglers

Above, left: A comprehensive lure selection allows angler to show the bass a variety of lures in strange waters. (Above) Gary Klein, one of the top pros on the contesting trail, uses systematic approach to fish strange waters.

start fishing before they start thinking! Look at the shoreline cover and break it down into its different types: fallen trees, rocks, brush, etc. Then, look at what cover might be available in some of the waters away from the shoreline. Bass might well be in a shallow cove...but, they may be holding on the deepest bends of the creek channel in that cove. Once an angler understands what conditions the bass have to utilize, he's in a better position to be sure he covers them all.

3. Don't get hung up on a particular lure or retrieve. If you slaughtered them yesterday on a white spinner-bait, it's an indication that it could be a good bait today. But, it's not a guarantee. Many anglers, returning to an area where they have caught bass, will fish it with the same lure. If no bass respond, they conclude the fish have "left." Often that's not the case.

The bass's activity level may have changed and you may have to alter your lure and retrieve to match it. Bass that took a topwater plug fished next to a fallen tree one day may be buried down in the tree the next and have to be coaxed with a worm or jig. Topwater lures and fast-moving subsurface baits often work well when bass are foraging actively for food. But, when they are inactive, slower baits and presentations often can take fish from the same area. Bass seldom make lengthy moves overnight.

4. Lastly, be alert enough to recognize when you have found a concentration of bass or an individual pattern. You'd be surprised how many anglers will fish down a half-mile section of bank without a hit,

catch three fish from one fifty-yard section, then keep right on moving down the bank!

Bass are normally gregarious; find a couple in one relatively small area and you can bet they've got some buddies with them. That fifty-yard section may have dozens of bass that could be caught if refished. You may have to change lures and show the bass something different. You may have to move deeper or shallower, but if you're looking for bass, it doesn't make sense to leave them once you find them. Not, at least, until you're sure you've exausted all the possibilities.

The same holds true when you catch a fish. Ask yourself exactly where the bass was. What was it doing there? If you catch another bass or two doing the same thing, you have found a definite pattern to the behavior of some bass. Not every bass in the lake may be doing the same thing. It is common for many patterns to be in use on any given day. The more of them you can find, the more bass you're likely to catch. All you have to do is be observant enough to recognize a pattern — and have the confidence to act on it.

The bass is truly the "thinking man's" fish and those who experience consistent success invariably have their minds in gear before they make that first cast.

CHAPTER 18

BASS VERSUS THE LONG ROD

There Are Moments When The Fly Rod Is The Most
Effective Way Of Taking This Species

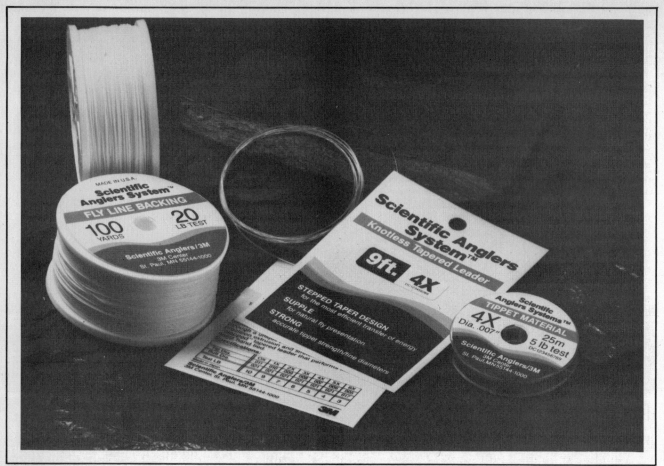

The commercially produced tapered leaders are adequate and much easier than making your own if fly fishing for bass is your thing. The author has found that a nine-foot leader with ten-pound tippet is best in heavy cover.

IT'S A PRETTY safe bet that the first bass ever taken on sporting tackle fell victim to a fly rod-toting angler. I say safe, because prior to the late 1800s, the fly rod was not only the principal type of sporting tackle in use, but usually the only type available.

That, as we all have seen, has changed drastically. Sophisticated casting, spinning and spin-cast reels, coupled

Minnow-imitating streamers like the Keel fly models are good choices for an angler seeking bass in a small river or stream. If fish hold tight, use sinking tip line.

with rods built of such Space Age materials as graphite and Boron, have pretty much taken over the bass fishing scene.

The long rod has been lost somewhere in this high-tech shuffle and it's popularity among bass fishermen has suffered considerably. One reason, no doubt, is that the fly rod is not nearly as efficient a fishing tool as others in water much deeper than six feet or so. There are, of course, a variety of sinking lines and weighted streamers and bucktails that allow anglers to probe relatively deep water, but it's a much slower process, resulting in considerably more time spent on each cast. Also, fly rods are not legal in most tournaments and much of the current bass'n techniques and tactics have their roots implanted firmly in competitive angling.

Among contemporary bass fishermen, fly rods are something of an anomaly.

None of this bothers dedicated fly fishermen, however. They suffer their affliction nobly; in their minds, aesthetic values take precedent over efficiency.

What many of them don't tell you is that — aesthetics aside — there are some situations where the fly rod is one of the most effective bass fishing tools available! An incident occurred about three weeks ago that shows just how effective this overlooked equipment can be.

Dusk was still a few hours away as I eased my elderly Ranger bass boat from its slip at Camp Henry on the north end of Florida's Lake George and headed for a small,

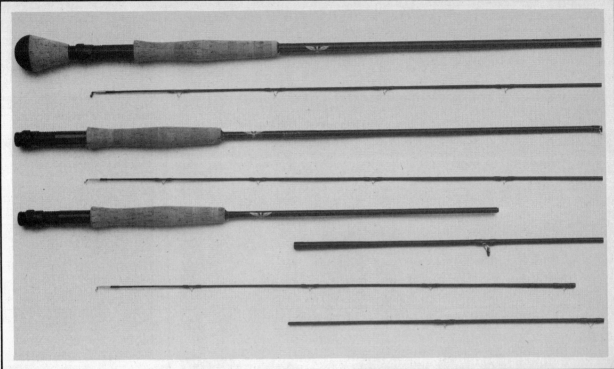

The modern graphite rods like these World Class models by Fenwick can be combined with a lightweight reel. They are easy to handle, yet strong enough for serious fishing. A nine-foot #9 is good for heavy-cover angling.

Bass bugs are available in different sizes that behave in differing fashions in the water. From left (clockwise) are a slider head for little surface disturbance; a deer hair bug for a softer presentation; noisy popper to call bass.

weedy section of the lake's east shore, about four miles from the camp. It was late spring and the spawn was winding down quickly, but there was still a considerable number of bass hanging around the extreme shallows. Like most bass in shallow, natural lakes, they would retreat to the thicker cover during the midday hours and venture forth to feed along the thinner edges early and late in the day. I knew one little patch of dollar bonnets that was holding a pretty good bunch of fish and the dinner bell was fixin' to ring.

Arriving at my bonnet patch, I was a bit dismayed to find two anglers in a big bass boat pounding it to a froth. Buzzbaits would gurgle across the thickly matted lilies, plastic worms would slither through the cracks and spinnerbaits zipped along the edges. It was a thorough assault, complete with a thrashing twenty-four-volt trolling motor that chewed through the shallow vegetation like a weed-eater gone berserk.

I stopped about a hundred yards away to watch and it soon became apparent that they hadn't had much luck and were moving along quickly in an effort to locate fish. I decided to wait them out and fifteen minutes later they were thrashing their way down the shoreline, beating another patch of bonnets into submission.

The sun was still a little high, so I slipped the trolling motor on low speed and took my time covering the hundred yards that separated me from my evening fishing spot. Along the way, I took the time to check the leader on my #9 weight Fenwick World Class fly rod, knot on a yellow and brown Keel Fly deer hair bug and make a quick inven-

tory of my battered old fly fishing vest to make sure I had the equipment I would need.

Reaching one end of the fifty-yard square stand of bonnets, I dropped a twenty-pound anchor over the side to hold the boat and slipped into the thigh-deep water.

For the next hour and a half I slowly waded around the bonnets, flicking the little deer hair bug into every pocket, cut and indentation I could comfortably reach. The soft-landing bug made barely a ripple as it touched down and the only sounds were the gentle swish of my Levi's parting the water and the subtle click of the reel as I stripped line from it.

By the time the setting sun indicated it was time to return to the boat, I had caught and released fourteen bass. The smallest was a pugnacious ten-incher that made up in enthusiasm what it lacked in size. The largest might have

The ease with which big bass can be taken with a fly rod is reflected in this photo of a Florida youngster's trophy.

gone six pounds and took the bug in a gentle slurp. All the bass came from that one small area that had been pounded heavily before I made my first cast.

In the decade I've been prowling Florida's shallows, I've seen the same thing happen with regularity each spring.

Bass can become surprisingly cautious when they venture into extremely shallow water. Often, the movement of a heavy bass boat, the sharp whine of an electric trolling motor or even the splash of a heavy lure can send them diving for cover. In this situation, a carefully wading angler actually enjoys a distinct advantage, especially if he's armed with a fly rod.

A deer hair bug can be dropped quietly into each and every pocket in the cover and, if no strike results, it can be picked up with one smooth backcast and dropped into

Modern fly fishing equipment is much improved over earlier outfits, but popularity among bass fishermen has decreased. (Below) A chunky bass can be a lot of fun on the fly rod.

another. There's no need to retrieve the bug over thick cover, as would be the case with conventional tackle. Not only does this keep the surface undisturbed, but it actually lets the long-rodder effectively fish more targets than the angler who has to wrestle his treble-hook-laden lure through the greenery after each cast.

I'm convinced that any time bass are present in vegetated waters that are shallow enough to wade comfortably — three feet or less — a wading angler equipped with a fly rod is employing one of the most efficient techniques for catching them. And it makes no difference where an angler happens to be. I've used the same techniques in shallow New England lakes, Midwestern farm ponds and in the shallow backwaters of some major impoundments and rivers.

Outfitting oneself for this exciting aspect of bass'n is simple. A minimum of equipment is necessary and even desirable.

I favor a nine-foot #9 weight rod, the Fenwick World Class models being my first choice. These graphite rods are light, yet powerful enough to drive a wind-resistant deer hair bug with authority. To keep things light, I rig it with one of the smaller model single-action reels from Fenwick or the Scientific Anglers 456 series. These are designed to hold lines in the 4- through 6-pound weight range, plus some backing. Mine holds my #9 Air Cel Bug Taper

Cork-bodied popper (top) and deer hair bug are productive baits for shallow water. Both are tied on the Keel hook.

With the array of long-rod fly fishing equipment available today, there are many possibilities for taking bass.

floating line and nothing else. But when you're fishing forty-foot casts in thick cover, eighty-two feet of line is more than enough. Any fish that takes that much line is gone anyway, so why lug around a larger reel than you need? The lighter weight afforded by this setup makes extended casting periods easier.

Dedicated fly fishermen often make up their own leaders from varying lengths of leader material of different diameters. It's not complicated, but I have found the commercially available tapered leaders from Berkley and Scientific Anglers just as effective. I use a nine-foot leader that tapers to ten- or twelve-pound test and, after repeated bug changes shorten its length, I just knot on a couple of feet of ten-pound monofilament with a blood knot and I'm back in business. One tapered leader can last a long time.

Selecting flies is equally easy. There are a tremendous number of patterns and styles on the market and many are tied in the required weedless versions. I use two types and for shallow water surface fishing I've yet to find myself needing others.

The first is a simple deer hair bug tied on a Keel hook. These hooks feature an up-riding hook point that is protect-

ed by bucktail strands on the fly. It is as weedless as you can make a fly, but it hooks fish easily. Aside from its ability to be thrown into literally any type of cover without hanging up, the upward hook point most often sticks the fish in the upper jaw or the gristle at the corner of the fish's mouth. This is a major advantage in shallow cover, since it has been my experience that a bass so hooked will come to the surface with only moderate pressure, while a bass hooked in the lower jaw has a tendency to bulldog downward. The ideal situation for playing a bass in heavy cover on a fly rod is to have the fish on the surface, where you can keep your line from fouling in the weeds. The Keel fly hook assists in this.

The deer hair bug is a soft-landing bait with a subtle action when twitched. It gets the nod for most of my fishing.

Sometimes, however, when bass are especially active a noisy approach can draw more strikes. At this time, I shift to a cork-bodied popper, also tied on a Keel hook. While the bug is often crawled through cover, the popper usually is tossed to an opening or edge and worked in place with a series of short jerks that produce a noisy "bloop."

Today's floating lines seldom require added dressing to float. A quick pass with a cloth saturated with fly line cleaner every few trips will keep it floating high. (Below) Fly lines can handle surprisingly large bass if the angler understands the techniques for proper fish fighting in heavy cover.

The deer hair bugs have proven effective in natural browns, yellows and greens and I keep a few bright yellow and red bugs for use late in the evening under dimmer light. They're easier to see, both for me and the bass.

Since I only use the popper when I feel the bass are very active, I choose visible combinations of black/green, red/yellow, and black/yellow.

One of the biggest problems with fighting a bass in this type of heavy cover is the cover, itself. If your line becomes entangled in the cover, you will change the angle of pull on the hook and often the bass will pull or twist off. Any pressure points on the line between you and the bass will negate the excellent fish-fighting qualities of the long rod. So the first thing an angler needs to do when a fish strikes is to get every bit of line off the surface of the water and do it on the hook set.

This is one reason I favor the nine-foot rod and try to restrict my casts to thirty-five feet, with forty as maximum. I also seldom retrieve the bug more than five feet. This keeps stripped line which can tangle in the vegetation to a minimum. By keeping the rod pointed toward the bug every moment it's in the water, a normal hook set will snap the line and leader off the surface most of the time. Combined with the upper jaw hold of the keel style hook, this brings most fish to the surface quickly.

Another advantage to working a relatively short line is that it minimizes the need for false casting. Bass instinctively look for predators from above. Ospreys, eagles, herons and such come from this direction and a shadow passing over a bass will often send it fleeing immediately. Excessive false casting can do the same thing. But, with a nine-foot rod, thirty-five feet of line and less than five feet

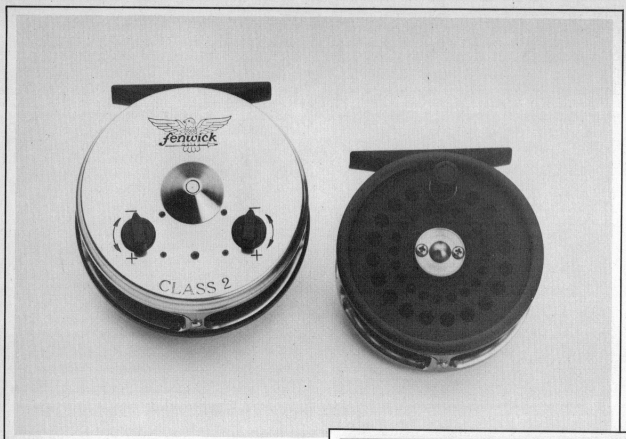

Backing is a needless item on a fly reel used for bass in heavy cover. Smaller reel (right) results in lighter, more easily handled outfit with no loss of fishing efficiency. (Right) Sinking lines can be used to probe deeper waters with wet flies and streamers, extending angler's abilities.

of stripped line at your feet, you can pick up the bug smoothly on the back cast and send it to the next target in one smooth motion.

Playing a bass, especially one of the larger specimens, at short range also requires some thought and sometimes some quick feet. After the bass is hooked, the ideal situation is for the angler to have the rod tip jammed high overhead, with the bass thrashing on the surface and hopefully making its way to open water where the rod can wear it down. If things aren't proceeding in this direction, you need to give him a helping hand.

When a hefty bass heads for thick cover, you sometimes can turn it toward open water by clamping a hand over the reel and back-pedaling a couple of feet. Trying to out-muscle a bass at the wrong time, however, can send it running for cover.

If the bass is heading where you want it to, just wander along behind it and let the rod do the work for the first few seconds. Big bass have a lot of power initially, but often lack stamina. If you make it through the first thirty seconds or so you're in good shape. Bass often are more cooperative than one might suppose; most hooked on the outside edge of cover will run toward deeper water.

Should the bass wrap up tightly in the cover, don't try to pry it loose with the rod! You'll break something and it won't always be the bass's hold on the cover. Instead, walk down to it, follow your leader to the fish and start slinging

weeds until you can see enough bass to grab. Most bass that burrow into thick cover will stop fighting and can be retrieved in this manner.

While wading is undoubtedly the most effective way to work the long rod in shallow heavy cover, some anglers prefer to keep their feet dry and opt for a boat. Since many boats have a considerable number of things that stripped line can snag on, savvy anglers often drape plastic sheeting or a monofilament cast net over the bow deck to cover them and prevent that stripped line from tangling.

Another situation where the long rod often can outscore

The author considers the long rod a deadly tool for bass in water that is shallow enough for wading. Noiseless approach of the angler and soft water entry of deer hair bug work well. Technique spooks far less bass than does boat-bound angler.

its modern contemporaries is when pursuing bass in a small to medium stream environment. In this type of water, the current will dictate where the bass must hold and an experienced stream angler can "read" these lies easily. Unfortunately, the bass may not move far from its lie to take a bait or lure, making accurate casting a must.

A fly rod-equipped angler enjoys an advantage here, since he can pepper these lies with a series of short, accurate casts. Landing the fly slightly upstream of the lie, he allows the current to sweep it past, then instead of having to retrieve the lure, he simply picks up the line and shoots his next cast. The principle is much the same as when working shallow, heavy cover: short, precise casts to a specific spot combined with the inherently soft water entry of a bug, streamer or bucktail.

In some cases, the same weight rod can be used, but in tight quarters, many anglers opt for an 8- or 8½-foot #7 or 8 weight rod. A weight-forward or bug taper line works well if bulky flies are your offering, but the traditional double taper line sometimes can be a better bet. The weight-forward lines require a certain amount of line past the rod tip to properly load the rod and, if twenty- to twenty-five-foot casts are the order of the day, you may not be able to get the required amount of line out.

Double-taper lines, on the other hand, suffer no such restrictions and also offer the angler the ability to more easily execute roll casts in extremely tight quarters.

Stream anglers also will want to carry an additional spool for their reel filled with a good sinking tip line. These allow sinking flies like streamers and bucktails to get a bit deeper and present baits to submerged cover.

Surface bugs can be decidedly effective in this situation, but sinking flies are often the best bet, since not all bass in a current situation will move very far to take a bait or lure.

I still favor the Keel-style hook for these baits. A good selection of streamers and bucktails would include the venerable Muddler Minnow, Royal Coachman Bucktail and many minnow-imitating patterns. Generally, streamers in the two-inch range and tied on a #1 or #2 hook are effective. Some natural patterns should be carried, as well as some vibrant combinations of mylar and marabou. Wet flies such as the Woolly Worm can also be highly productive.

Regardless of where you choose to fish the long rod, there are some accessories that can make you a bit more effective. Most important for the wading angler is a lightweight vest to tote things. I prefer those models with large upper pockets, since I seem to invariably get the lower ones wet.

Early-season anglers will welcome a good set of insulated waders and the chest type are often superior to the hip-type variety. I often find the best casting position I can take for a particular target is about one inch deeper than whatever hip waders I happen to be wearing.

Streamers and wet flies can be stored adequately in a sheepskin fly book, but bulky deer hair bugs suffer in such enclosed spaces. The small, hand-sized plastic boxes made by Fenwick, Plano and others are a good choice for bugs.

Many deer hair bugs eventually soak up water and start sinking. A pair of line clippers worn around the neck facilitates quick lure changes, but you can extend the bug's time in the water by dressing it with a bit of Webber's Silicon Fly Line paste.

To the modern high-tech angler, the fly rod may seem a bit out of date, but there are times when it can be the odds-on favorite.

CHAPTER 19

ON THE TRAIL OF A TROPHY

Bagging Big Bass Often Calls For Specialized Tactics

Fall months are excellent to bag a trophy bass. In more crisp weather, they go on prowl to build up fat. (Below) Stout tackle is required to wrestle big bass from heavy cover.

A happy customer and his guide display a 12-pound bass taken from Florida's St. Johns River on a live shiner. Author has found that this type of bait accounts for a majority of the trophy bass taken in Florida's waters.

THERE ARE few thrills in the angling sport that can compare to that of catching a trophy-sized bass.

For some anglers, it is a thrill seldom, if ever, experienced. For others, catching big bass is more a matter of course than an accidental encounter.

Are some anglers just inherently "luckier" than others? Not always! In fact, the chances are excellent that those anglers who manage to take large bass regularly are doing it in a deliberate and systematic manner that will guarantee a much higher chance for success than is the case for anglers who simply rely on "luck."

There is a difference between the true heavyweights of the bass'n clan and the average run-of-the-mill bass. That difference is often shown in habitat choices, forage preference and feeding habits. Anglers who understand these differences and develop an angling technique designed to capitalize on them will often be far "luckier" than other anglers.

The first step in adopting a systematic approach to big bass is to define the term in relation to where one fishes and what species of bass he pursues.

For example, an Ohio angler can be pleased rightfully with a five-pound largemouth, but it might take a bass of six or seven pounds to raise eyebrows in Tennessee. Moving South, an eight-pound largemouth qualifies for the wall, but in Florida, California and some parts of Texas, ten pounds is the mark of a real bass.

Anglers pursuing the spotted bass — which rarely exceeds six pounds — can consider a four-pound fish a legitimate trophy. However, the Alabama spotted bass sub-species has been documented at nine pounds. A four-pounder would be a "nice" fish, but it would take a five- or six-pound Alabama spot to be considered "big."

The same holds true for smallmouths. A four-pound Canadian smallmouth will raise eyebrows north of the border, but it would take a six-pounder to get attention on Tennessee's famous Dale Hollow Lake.

The reason for defining the term is simple: Once you know what a "big bass" is within the region you fish, you can begin locating the most likely places to find one.

Not all of the available bass water in a given region will be equally productive for big bass. This stems from the fact that not all lakes have the same levels of fertility; this can

Veteran fishing guides Jim Smith (left) and M.J. Lee rely on shiners for the vast majority of their guiding. The same systematic approach they use will work in nearly any shallow, vegetated lake, using this type of bait.

affect the growth rates of the bass in various waters. Fishing pressure also can play a role. It takes time for a bass to reach trophy size and the greater the fishing pressure, the more likely a fish will be caught before it has that chance.

When Ray Easley caught his twenty-one-pound three-ounce bass from Southern California's Lake Castitas in March 1980, local anglers flocked there in such great numbers that the bass population took a severe beating. The lake hasn't been the same since.

Knowing which lakes are likely to hold the best chances for a trophy bass in his area will allow the angler to concentrate his efforts on the most potentially productive waters. There are several ways to find this out.

One of the best sources of information will come from state fisheries department personnel. They often spend a considerable amount of time on the water doing creel surveys and population counts and frequently can point you in the right direction. Another source to watch is any local Big Bass contest. If the winning fish seem to come from a particular lake or river, it's a good bet that locale has a better-than-average lunker population.

Local outdoor writers, guides and bass club members

also can be informative sources. A look at state records, IGFA line class records, and the Freshwater Fishing Hall of Fame records may show which waters have a consistent level of big bass production. My friend, Matt Vincent, has taken the time to compile all of those into handy charts and you'll find them in this chapter.

Once several potential areas have been chosen, the angler then must figure out the best time to fish them.

Timing is important in the pursuit of trophy bass. This is not only to determine the best daily feeding periods, but the weather conditions and even seasonal conditions that can put big fish on the feed.

By the way of example, one of the best big bass patterns on my section of the St. Johns River during the early summer months is to fish a big buzzbait across eelgrass points during the last hour of the day. I often slip out for a few hours fishing in the evening and will take a half-a-dozen bass over eight pounds each year between the first of May and the Fourth of July.

But fish those same areas in the morning or mid-afternoon and you'll come away empty-handed. These are feeding areas and big fish do not move there to feed until dusk.

STATE-BY-STATE BASS RECORDS

	LARGEMOUTH		SMALLMOUTH		SPOTTED	
	POUNDS-OUNCES / LOCATION	NAME / YEAR	POUNDS-OUNCES / LOCATION	NAME / YEAR	POUNDS-OUNCES / LOCATION	NAME / YEAR
ALABAMA	14-11¼ / Coosa River	Allen Bryan / 1984	10-8 / Wheeler Dam	Owen F. Smith / 1950	8-15 / Lewis Smith Lake	Philip C. Terry Jr. / 1978
ARIZONA	14-2 / Roosevelt Lake	Ed Smith / 1956	6-14 / Roosevelt Lake	Joseph A. Cross / 1980		
ARKANSAS	16-4 / Lake Mallard	Aaron Madris / 1976	7-5 / Bull Shoals	Acie Dickerson / 1969	7-15 / Bull Shoals	Mike J. Heilich / 1983
CALIFORNIA	21-3.2 / Lake Casitas	Raymond Easley / 1980	9-1 / Clair Engle Lake	Tim Brady / 1976	9-1 / Lake Perris	Jeff Mathews / 1984
COLORADO	10-6¼ / Stalker Lake	Sharon Brunson / 1979	5-5 / Smith Reservoir	Russ Moran / 1979		
CONNECTICUT	12-14 / Mashapaug Lake	Frank Domurat / 1961	7-12 / Shenipsit Lake	J. Mankauskas Sr. / 1980		
DELAWARE	10-5 / Andrews Lake	Tony Kaczmarczyk / 1980	4-7 / Quarry pond	Richard Williams / 1983		
FLORIDA	20-2 / Big Fish Lake	Fritz Friebel / 1923			3-7 / Apalachicola River	Ronald Bundy / 1981
GEORGIA	22-4 / Montgomery Lake	George Perry / 1932	7-2 / Lake Chatuge	Jack Hall / 1973	7-12 / Lake Nottely	Robert Kincaid / 1972
HAWAII	8-0 / Kilauea, Kauai	Earl Vito / 1977	3-11 / Lake Wilson	Willie Song / 1982		
IDAHO	10-15 / Anderson Lake	Mrs. M.W. Taylor / Unknown	7-5.6 / Dworshak Reservoir	Don Schiefelbein / 1982		
ILLINOIS	13-1 / Stone quarry lake	Edward J. Walbel / 1976	6-7 / Strip mine	Mark Samp / 1985	6-12 / Strip pit	James M. Kyle / 1982
INDIANA	11-11 / Ferdinand Reservoir	Curt Reynolds / 1968	6-15 / Sugar Creek	Ray Emerick / 1985	5-1½ / Unknown lake	John William Pio / 1975
IOWA	10-12 / Lake Fisher	Patricia Zaerr / 1984	6-8 / Spirit Lake	Rick Pentland / 1979		
KANSAS	11-12 / Farm pond	Kenneth Bingham / 1977	4.73 / Milford Reservoir	Terry Stanton / 1983	4-7 / Marion County Lake	Clarence McCarter / 1977
KENTUCKY	13-10¼ / Woods Creek Lake	Dale Wilson / 1984	11-15 / Dale Hollow Lake	David L. Hayes / 1955		
LOUISIANA	12-0 / Farm pond	Harold C. Dunaway / 1975			4-14 / Tickfaw River	Vern C. Johnson Jr. / 1976
MAINE	11-10 / Moose Pond	Robert Kamp / 1968	8-0 / Thompson Lake	George Dyer / 1970		
MARYLAND	11-2 / Farm pond	Rodney L. Cockrell / 1983	8-4 / Liberty Reservoir	Gary Peters / 1974		
MASSACHUSETTS	15-8 / Sampson's Pond	Walter Bolonis / 1975	7-4 / Quaboag River	Michael Howe / 1984		
MICHIGAN	11-15 / Big Pine Island Lake / 11-15 / Bamfield Dam	Wm. J. Maloney / 1934 / Jack Rorex / 1959	9-4 / Long Lake	W.F. Shoemaker / 1906		
MINNESOTA	8-9.5 / Fountain Lake	Timothy Kirsch / 1986	8-0 / West Battle Lake	John A. Creighton / 1948		
MISSISSIPPI	13-8 / Farm pond	Lucious Gregory / 1974	7-5 / Pickwick Reservoir	Jesse G. Clifton / 1976	8-2 / Farm pond	S. Ross Grantham / 1975
MISSOURI	13-14 / Bull Shoals	Marvin Bushong / 1961	6-12 / Bull Shoals	Norman J. Klayman / 1983	7-8 / Table Rock	Gene Arnaud / 1966

	LARGEMOUTH			SMALLMOUTH			SPOTTED		
	POUNDS-OUNCES LOCATION	NAME YEAR		POUNDS-OUNCES LOCATION	NAME YEAR		POUNDS-OUNCES LOCATION	NAME YEAR	
MONTANA	8-2½ Milnor Lake	Juanita Fanning 1984		4-11½ Horseshoe Lake	Bob Higson 1975				
NEBRASKA	10-11 Sand pit	Paul Abegglen Sr. 1965		6-1½ Merritt Reservoir	Wally Allison 1978		3-11 Sand pit	Tom Pappas 1968	
NEVADA	11-0 Lake Mohave	H.P. Warner 1972		3-2 Dry Creek Reservoir	Bill Gibson 1984				
NEW HAMPSHIRE	10-8 Lake Potanipo	G. Bullpit 1967		7-14½ Goose Pond	Francis H. Lord 1970				
NEW JERSEY	10-14 Menantico Pond	Robert A. Eisele 1980		6-4 Delaware River	Earl H. Trumpore 1957				
NEW MEXICO	11-0 Ute Lake	Bud Marks 1975		6-8.75 Ute Lake	Carl L. Kelly 1972				
NEW YORK	10-12 Chadwick Lake	Matthew Rutkowski 1975		9-0 Friends Lake	George Tennyson 1925				
NORTH CAROLINA	14-15 Santeetlah Reservoir	Leonard Williams 1963		10-2 Hiwassee Reservoir	Archie Lampkin 1953		0-14½ Hiwassee Reservoir	Robert Dyer 1980	
NORTH DAKOTA	8-7½ Nelson Lake	Leon Rixen 1983		5-0 Sakakawea	M. Erhart 1982				
OHIO	13-2 Farm pond	Roy Landsberger 1976		7-8 Mad River	James Bayless 1941		5-4 Lake White	Roger Trainer 1976	
OKLAHOMA	12-1.6 Lake Lawtonka	James E. Porter 1983		5-11.25 Texoma Lake	Jack Pryor 1986		8-2 Pittsburg Co. pond	O.J. Stone 1958	
OREGON	10-15 Selmac Lake	Butch Stauffacher 1983		6-13 Brownlee Reservoir	Mark Weir 1978				
PENNSYLVANIA	11-3 Birch Run Reservoir	Donald Shade 1983		7-4 Youghiogheny River	Larry Ashbaugh 1983				
RHODE ISLAND	10-0 Abbott Run	Ray LeBlanc 1981		5-15 Wash pond	Butch Ferris 1977				
SOUTH CAROLINA	16-2 Lake Marion	Paul H. Flanagan 1949		5-4 Toxaway River	Carl D. Hood II 1971		3-7 Lake Hartwell	Danny Joy 1985	
SOUTH DAKOTA	8-14 Jackson Co. Stock Dam	Irene Buxcel 1986		5-2¼ Missouri River	Robert Roth 1986				
TENNESSEE	14-8 Sugar Creek	Louge Barnett 1954		11-15 Dale Hollow Reservoir	D.L. Hayes 1955		5-6 Center Hill	Erwin Cole 1986	
TEXAS	17-10.7 Lake Fork	Mark Stevenson 1986		6-8 LBJ Reservoir	Donald Edgar 1985		5-9 Lake O' The Pines	Turner Keith 1966	
UTAH	10-2 Lake Powell	Sam LaManna 1974		6-12 Lake Borham	Roger L. Tallerico 1983				
VERMONT	8-4 Lake Morey	Michael Poulin 1983		6-12 Lake Champlain	George Carlson 1978				
VIRGINIA	16-4 Lake Conners	Richard Tate 1985		7-7 New River	John Justice 1986		6-10 Flannagan Reservoir	Joe Jett Friend 1976	
WASHINGTON	11-9 Banks Lake	Not Identified 1977		8-12 Columbia River	Ray Wanacutt 1967				
WEST VIRGINIA	10.8 Sleepy Creek Lake	William Wilhelm 1979		9.75 South Branch	David Lindsay 1971		3.5 Bluestone Lake	A.K. Maynard 1978	
WISCONSIN	11-3 Lake Ripley	Robert Miklowski 1940		9-1 Indian Lake	Leon Stefoneck 1950				
WYOMING	7-2 Stove Lake	John Tetters 1942		4-12 Slater Ash Creek	D. Jon Nelson 1982				

Records researched and compiled by Matt Vincent from information provided by the Freshwater Fishing Hall of Fame, International Game Fish Association, and State Fish & Game Departments.

IGFA FRESHWATER LINE CLASS WORLD RECORDS

LINE CLASS	LARGEMOUTH		SMALLMOUTH		SPOTTED	
	POUNDS-OUNCES / LOCATION	NAME / DATE	POUNDS-OUNCES / LOCATION	NAME / DATE	POUNDS-OUNCES / LOCATION	NAME / DATE
All Tackle	22-4 Montgomery Lake, GA	George Perry 6-2-32	11-15 Dale Hollow Lake, KY	David L. Hayes 7-9-55	8-15 Lewis Smith Lake, AL	Philip C. Terry Jr. 3-18-78
2-Pound	11-0 Lake Casitas, CA	Frank T. Gasperov Jr. 5-25-82	5-13 James River, VA	Robert H. Blevins 3-20-85	6-5 Lake Perris, CA	Gilbert J. Rowe 3-17-85
4-Pound	14-4 Cachuma Lake, CA	Clint Johanson 5-8-85	6-13 Pickwick Lake, AL	Michael A. Curry 2-22-83	7-5 Lake Perris, CA	Gilbert J. Rowe 3-27-86
8-Pound	21-3 Lake Casitas, CA	Raymond Easley 3-4-80	10-8 Hendricks Creek, KY	Paul E. Beal 4-14-86	9-0 Lake Perris, CA	Jeffrey L. Mathews 2-5-84
12-Pound	18-8 Lake Isabella, CA	Chris Moore 1-6-85	8-8 Watts Bar Lake, TN	Lenny Cecil 4-6-84	8-0 Lake Lanier, GA	Patrick D. Bankston 5-20-85
16-Pound	17-4 Polk County, FL	McArthur Bill O'Berry 7-6-86	7-6 Tennessee River, AL	Charles L. Tibbs 3-5-86	8-15 Lewis Smith Lake, AL	Philip C. Terry Jr. 3-18-78
20-Pound	17-12 Lake Tohopekaliga, FL	John Q. Faircloth 7-11-86			8-10 Smith Lake, AL	Billy Henderson 2-25-72

1987 HALL OF FAME WORLD FRESHWATER FISH RECORDS

DIVISION I ROD/REEL

LINE CLASS	LARGEMOUTH		SMALLMOUTH		SPOTTED	
	POUNDS-OUNCES / LOCATION	NAME / DATE	POUNDS-OUNCES / LOCATION	NAME / DATE	POUNDS-OUNCES / LOCATION	NAME / DATE
All Tackle	22-4 Montgomery Lake, GA	George Perry 6-2-32	11-15 Dale Hollow Lake, KY	David L. Hayes 7-9-55	8-15 Lewis Smith Lake, AL	Philip C. Terry Jr. 3-18-78
2-Pound	6-11 Lake Henshaw, CA	Les Imler 6-1-85	7-6 Chickamauga Lake, TN	Kirk Jensen 3-29-85	4-13 Lake Perris, CA	Les Imler 8-12-83
4-Pound	15-9 Castaic Lake, CA	Richard King 9-21-85	7-4 Pickwick Lake, AL	Jim Rivers 1-15-87	5-8 Weiss Lake, AL	Benny E. Hull 10-4-84
6-Pound	16-0 Castaic Lake, CA	Chuck Strauss 7-8-83	7-15 Pickwick Lake, AL	Jim Rivers 3-19-86	5-8 Weiss Lake, AL	Benny E. Hull 9-9-82
8-Pound	21-3 Lake Casitas, CA	Raymond Easley 3-4-80	10-8 Dale Hollow Lake, TN	Paul Beal 4-14-86	7-15 Bull Shoals Lake, AR	Michael J. Heilich Jr. 3-26-83
10-Pound	16-9 Lake Isabella, CA	Stephen P. Merlo 10-1-83	7-7 Pickwick Lake, AL	Jim Rivers 4-24-86	8-0 Lake Lanier, GA	Patrick Daniel Banston 5-20-85
12-Pound	13-0 Lake Jackson, FL	W. Singleton 2-4-75	6-14 Lake Cumberland, KY	Bill Vanover 5-28-78	2-6 Green River Lake, KY	Gerald Gallagher 10-22-86
14-Pound	8-14 Clarks Hill Lake, GA	Ronald H. Ketterer 6-26-83	2-5 Patoka Lake, IN	Douglas R. Gallagher 6-15-84	1-12 Twin Creek, IN	Brian Smith 6-23-86
15-Pound	12-13 Midland Valley, SC	Jerry K. Wren 7-30-85	5-13 Lake Monona, WI	Michael Amrhein 5-3-86	OPEN	
16-Pound	9-9 Lake Hartwell, SC	Walter Prince 4-12-86	5-14 Lac LaCroix, Ont. Ca	Tony Fidanzo 6-15-83	8-15 Lewis Smith Lake, AL	Philip C. Terry Jr. 3-18-78
17-Pound	16-12 Chatuge Lake, GA	David R. Presley 3-27-76	5-7 Sebasti Cook River, ME	Wayne Morey Sr. 8-16-86	OPEN	
20-Pound	10-0 Columbia River, WA	Dan Collins 5-31-84	5-10 Medicine Lake, WI	Darrelle Verkuilen 9-27-86	8-10 Lewis Smith Lake, AL	Billy Henderson 2-25-72
25-Pound	10-5 St. Johns River, FL	Stanley H. Williams 8-5-84	OPEN		OPEN	
Unlimited	16-3 Ocala National Forest, FL	Henry C. Daniel Jr. 2-7-76	4-12 Lake of the Woods, Ont. Ca 8-19-84	Richard R. Zebleckis	OPEN	

While baitcasting gear is recommended in fishing live shiners, stout spinning gear can work in open water.

bodies of water, the bass are at their seasonal peak condition immediately prior to the spawn.

How much does their weight fluctuate? Well, after a decade as a trophy bass guide in Central Florida, I can tell you that if you catch a twenty-inch bass on the St. Johns River from late January through March, it will make the five-pound mark easily. Catch a twenty-inch fish from late July through the first week of September, though, and it will be lucky to make 4½ pounds!

The high water temperatures of the mid-summer months stress the fish, putting them at the downside of their seasonal condition. Once the waters begin to cool in the fall, they go on the mend and reach their peak seasonal condition prior to the spawn.

This is not mere coincidence. Mother Nature has planned things this way.

The spring spawn is one of the most stressful times of the year for bass. They require considerable amounts of energy and stamina to survive this period and much of that is supplied by the fat reserves they build up during the winter months. Fillet a bass during February and you will find extensive fat deposits that are absent during the summer months. Combine that with the two roe sacks carried by the females and it's not hard to see why pre-spawn bass will be robust and pot-gutted, while the same fish in mid-to-late summer are leaner and lighter.

How much weight a bass actually loses after the spawn is a subject of debate. I've often heard anglers on my home waters state that the nine-pound bass they caught in July would have been a twelve-pounder in February. That's probably an exaggeration, though.

The weight the bass will lose will be the fat deposits and the eggs. It's doubtful whether that comprises more than fifteen percent of the bass's body weight at peak condition. It may be as little as ten percent.

I once had the distasteful task of cleaning six bass, all about six pounds, that had died in a holding tank. The bass were caught from a bedding area on the St. Johns River in mid-February and were in peak condition prior to their demise. I carefully separated the roe sacks while cleaning the bass and weighed them. The average was six ounces of roe per bass. If we assume an equal weight of fat — probably on the high side — we would find the fish only three-fourths of a pound heavier at its peak condition. Many taxidermists have told me they never have seen a ten-pound bass carrying more than nine to eleven ounces of roe, so it would seem that, on a bass of average health, the pre-spawn weight increase is fairly proportional to its size.

It's doubtful that nine-pounders turn into twelve-pounders — at least not without consuming a couple of pounds of bait fish immediately prior to capture!

But, for the trophy bass hunter trying desperately to crack the magic ten-pound mark, an extra nine to fourteen ounces of weight is most welcome!

This is one reason why the pre-spawn period is the best time of the year to bag a trophy bass. The other is that the spawning period is virtually the only time of the year when just about every big bass in the lake, river or reservoir is actively and forcefully moving to shallow water where they are more accessible to anglers.

Put a bunch of fat, healthy bass in a depth and cover

A similar situation occurs during the spring spawn: Slip into a spawning area quietly at dawn and begin throwing a noisy topwater lure and you're likely to tangle with a very large and very irate bass. Come in later in the morning, though, and the bass probably will have moved back into heavy cover where they will be unreachable.

Daily weather conditions can affect the feeding of big bass, as well. The bigger the bass, the less comfortable it becomes in shallow water. Add bright, clear skies and you will have a highly spooky fish that will not remain there for long. Substitute a heavily overcast sky, a bit of wind, maybe even a light drizzle, and you'll find large fish remaining in the shallows longer.

A big factor in determining the peak time to hunt a trophy is the seasonal condition of the fish. Although one so-called bass-fishing "expert" has stated the best time to catch a trophy is in the summer months, after the spawn, guides, tournament anglers and other professionals will tell you that's hogwash!

Bass are much like whitetail deer in the sense that their body weight and general condition will fluctuate during the course of the year. They will gain and lose weight as forage availability and environmental conditions change. On most

This 19-pound 3-ounce bass taken by Arden Hanline from California's Lake Morena in February, 1987, is a result of his systematic approach to seeking big bass. A trophy attitude is the most important asset an angler can have.

situation that is easily fished and you've got a made-to-order situation for the trophy angler.

This is not to say that a trophy-sized bass cannot be landed in any season of the year. In fact, a quick look at the record charts accompanying this chapter shows that about half of the records were taken at other times. This is most often in the early summer immediately following the spawn, when many large bass are still relating to shallow water areas. It happens again in the fall, when cooler water levels begin to spark increased feeding from the bass.

But, there's no denying an angler's chances of catching heavier bass are best during the pre-spawn period.

Once the angler determines when and where he will fish, the next question is how. And that's important, because consistently bagging bigger bass often calls for a shift from conventional tactics.

Big bass are far more deliberate feeders than their smaller brethren. While a yearling bass may chase a lure to capture it, larger fish tend to be far more leisurely in their approaches. Since a bass instinctively knows it cannot gain substance from foraging, if it invests more energy to obtain the forage than it receives from it, large fish show a decided preference for large baits, in most situations.

Among trophy hunters, various "big bass tactics" have been developed and refined over the years. Nowhere is this more evident than in the tactics used by the trophy bass guides of Florida.

Armed with stout baitcasting rods, lines in the 25- to 30-pound test range, plus a handful of styrofoam floats, they routinely send six- to ten-inch golden shiners into places you wouldn't want to send a good rabbit dog. And the numbers of trophy largemouths they pull out each year boggles the mind.

In the Sunshine State, shiners are king when it comes to

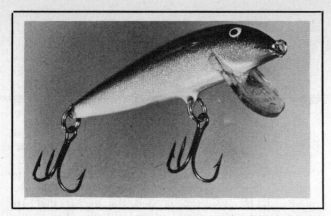

Countdown Rapala used by Hanline was modified by him to include yellow feathers on rear hook. (Right) Anglers after smallmouth, spotted bass find pork frog is good.

bagging trophy bass. Of the several hundred such fish my customers have taken during the decades I've guided there, I would venture that over two-thirds of those fish fell victim to a shiner.

The reason for the shiner's effectiveness is fairly simple: Big bass seldom chase baits like smaller fish and they spend much of their time in areas of cover far too thick to probe with artificial baits. A live shiner could be considered a self-propelled lure that will emit its own fish-enticing action while offering a solid mouthful for a big bass.

Depending on how the minnow is rigged and fished, it can be positioned in one spot to await a bass, sent into thick cover to seek one out or trolled over a wide area to find scattered bass. Once shiner and bass meet, the inevitable panic-reaction of the shiner is often more than enough to trigger into striking a bass that was simply curious.

There are a variety of ways to make a shiner work for you, but all start with the proper tackle. Conventional bass tackle is not a wise choice for this type of fishing.

Reels used for shiner fishing should be capable of holding one hundred yards of 25- to 30-pound monofilament line, but many modern baitcasting reels lack the spool capacity. Favorite choices become the older *Ambassador* casting reels, like the 5000, 5500 and especially the larger spooled 6500. These are filled with a premium brand line that exhibits good abrasion resistance such as *Maxima* or *Triline XT*. Your line will be in constant contact with cover and tougher lines are needed.

These thick, stiff lines would make casting conventional lures difficult, but work quite well for tossing a one-half-pound shiner twenty to fifty feet.

Two types of rods are favored among experienced guides: The first is a seven-foot saltwater popping rod. Glass composition is favored over graphite or boron because of its durability and strength. Sensitivity and finesse are not required. The second rod is a shorter model: five to 5½ feet. Again, glass is preferred and the most popular actions are those often named by manufacturers as Muskie models. They should be extremely stiff and strong.

Pistol-grip casting rods generally are avoided and most experts prefer a solid through-the-handle "trigger stick" model with an all-metal reel seat.

Terminal tackle is simple: a hook and sometimes a small float.

One of the better hooks for shiner fishing is the Mustad #37140 wide gap in 5/0 for shiners up to six or seven inches or 6/0 to 7/0 for larger baits. If you're fishing in wood cover, you can lose a lot of these, so most guides buy them in boxes of one hundred, which brings the cost down to six or seven cents apiece.

Floats should be kept on the small side; about the size of a plum. Larger floats commonly used by inexperienced shiner fishermen can weaken or even kill the shiner as it drags the float around. Larger floats also tend to hang up in heavy cover and can cause the bass to drop the bait. The Southland #3 string float is popular, as is any similar-sized styrofoam float. When used, these floats are threaded on the line and held in place at the desired distance above the bait with a small plug inserted in the line hole.

Collecting a good batch of bait is as important as the proper selection of tackle, because sluggish, inactive or dead shiners catch few bass. You need a strong, lively bait that will work an area thoroughly. Some shiners, depending upon how they were treated after their capture, can be in such poor shape that they will go "belly up"' on the first cast. This type of bait isn't worth wasting your money or time on.

The best are the "wild" shiners netted from the waters you'll be fishing and placed for twenty-four to forty-eight hours prior to use in a spring-fed holding tank treated with Catch & Release or Shiner Life. Both chemicals help toughen the shiner and prevent scale loss or parasites. This treatment "cures" the bait and actually makes it stronger.

If cured bait is unavailable, the next best thing is a freshly captured shiner. It will be acceptable if used within a day of capture. Commercially raised hatchery shiners should be considered a last resort. They lack the strength and stamina of the wild bait.

Some live bait is not worth having. Obvious signs of poor quality are fungus growth, open sores or an inability to maintain an upright swimming posture in the bait tank. More subtle signs include a dark brown color (healthy shiners will be a golden/bronze), missing scales or scales coming off on your hands when the bait is handled. If this is the only bait you can get, go play a round of golf, instead.

As a rule, there is at least one source of quality bait on

Long-standing records are falling, as anglers learn more about habits of larger bass. But big bass often require a different approach than do their smaller brethren.

any Florida lake that has facilities for selling bait and tackle. It's worth the time it takes to find it.

Most guides prefer shiners in the six- to eight-inch range, since these are big enough to tempt a real trophy, but not too small for the "little" five- and six-pounders to handle.

Many anglers find that catching their own shiners is easier and cheaper than purchasing them. On most Florida lakes, shiners cost $8 to $12 a dozen. Since a full day's bass fishing with shiners requires three to five dozen baits, a hefty tab can be run up in short order. During peak periods there can sometimes be a waiting line of anglers willing to pay $12 a dozen for these premium baits. Sometimes demand far exceeds supply.

Wild shiners are a school fish that prefer shallow, quiet weedbeds. They are found easily in areas of mixed vegetation in depths of four feet or less. Many productive areas can be found within site of the dock and they can be "sweetened" up to hold shiners consistently.

Once you've found the right type of weedbeds, locate openings in them about six feet in diameter and mark them by driving a wooden stake into the bottom on one side of the hole. Wrap a pound of soybean cake or the same amount of one of the gravy-making dog foods into a weighted piece of old panty hose and toss it into the middle of the hole. If there's a school of shiners in the vicinity, they'll be there in thirty minutes or less. Bait up several holes, about twenty-five yards apart.

A five-foot cast net usually will corral the shiners effectively, as will a light canepole, a pea-sized float and a #12 barbless hook. Appropriately, this is called a shiner hook and is sold in most Florida tackle shops. Many experts prefer the canepole system, since it doesn't damage the shiners as much as the net. A moist bread ball or a small pinch of canned biscuit dough makes an effective bait for canepole anglers.

Take good care of your shiners. Place them in the largest livewell in the boat and don't overcrowd them. Four dozen is about the maximum that will live in most bass boat livewells at one time. Add some Catch & Release and set your livewell aerator to run either constantly or every five minutes, if you have a timer system. Bait buckets that hang over the side are a poor, poor choice.

Armed with the proper bait and tackle, there are three basic ways to fish shiners, but one of the easiest ways to locate bass on unfamiliar waters is to troll or drift them.

For this the seven-foot rod is used, because it affords better striking power when the shiner is a long way from the boat. Slip a float onto the line four or five feet above the bait, add a small rubber-core slip-on sinker of one-quarter-ounce a foot or so above the hook, then hook the shiner upwards through the bottom jaw and out one of the upper nostril holes. Wing a rod out on either side of the boat, set the trolling motor on low speed and go fishing.

This can be an excellent way to cover large areas of submerged vegetation like eelgrass or hydrilla, as well as being a solid bet for prospecting weedlines. When fishing the edge of emergent cover, steer the boat close enough to the weedline to bring the inside shiner into close contact with it. This can draw bass waiting on the edge of the weedline. The outside shiner gives you a good shot at fish holding on unseen submerged cover like planted brush piles lying off the grass. Keep your baits about sixty to seventy feet off the stern of the boat.

It is important to keep an eye on your floats when trolling shiners. Many times they'll find fish for you, even if the bass don't hit them. Many times I've had shiners "go panicky" when passing through a particular area. This can indicate that bass are there, but not feeding. By remembering those spots and returning later in the day, I've taken some huge bass that wouldn't hit on the first pass. Shiners are a lot like bird dogs; if you watch them, they'll eventually tell you something good!

Trolling or just using the wind to drift you through an area is an excellent way to explore, but when obvious holding areas are found, it's wise to switch tactics.

Among the most consistent depth and cover situations for big Florida bass are places where floating vegetation such as hyacinth has drifted together to form a solid surface mat near deeper water. This could be on a submerged creek channel, the outside bend of a river or the plants might just have drifted into a stand of bullrushes or lily pads located near a drop off. Regardless, this should draw big bass.

Depending upon the water depth or the amount of cover under the mat, you can either cork a shiner along the outside edge, or run one up underneath the cover. Either can be deadly for bass.

When corking a bait — positioning the shiner under a float — the cork is not intended to signal a hit. Instead, it's used as a means of precisely positioning the shiner right on

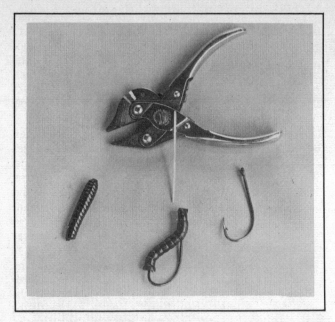

Some anglers fishing shiners in heavy cover make their own weedless hooks, using a piece of plastic worm as a weedguard (Right) Buzzbaits can produce outsized bass. This angler buzzed his bait over submerged grassbed.

the edge or a foot or so under the cover. With the float positioned about three feet above the shiner, the bait is flipped to the edge of the mat and the shiner allowed to dart underneath. Once there, the cork will lodge into the vegetation and effectively hold the shiner in that one small area. Once you get the shiner locked in, leave it alone! Any bass cruising the edge for a meal, or holding back underneath, will become aware of the shiner.

One drawback to corking a bait is that monofilament line will soak up water and sink, as explained fully in another chapter. This can foul the line in underwater debris and prevent the angler from getting a tight line to the bass after the bait has been taken. Solve this with a tin of Weber's Silicon Fly Line Paste.

Before you begin fishing and while the line is still dry, strip off about twenty yards of it into the bottom of the boat, then reel it back on the reel while passing it through a patch saturated with the paste. The line will float high and dry, allowing the fisherman to see and control it. This one step should allow a shiner fisherman to hook fifty percent more of his strikes.

If the water under the mat is deep or relatively open, it often can be more effective for the angler to "free-line" or run his shiner to the bass.

In this tactic, the short muskie rod is used, because with the shiner well back under the cover, the hook should be set downward and to the side to avoid pulling the bass up into the root system where it can foul. During the fight, the rod is also held down to pull the bass from under the cover, instead of up into it. The best bass any client of mine has yet to land — 14.4 pounds — was taken this way in Rodman Pool.

In the free-lining technique, strip all corks and weights off the line, leaving just the hook. While trolled and corked shiners should be hooked through the lips, free-lined shiners must be hooked on the underside, just to the rear of the anal

fin. Anywhere else and they will fight the pull of the line and may not run under the cover.

Position the boat fifteen to twenty feet off the edge of the floating cover and, using a gentle underhanded flip, toss the shiner right to the edge. If you can get the shiner's nose to just "kiss" the edge of the cover on the cast, the chances are good the bait will dart under. If the bait lands several feet off the edge, the shiner will often turn and run back to open water and that's not where you want him.

Especially if there is a big bass under the mat, the shiner may have to be recast a few times before it will go underneath.

Once the shiner has the right idea, strip off line from the reel and let the bait run back under about five to ten feet, then use gentle thumb pressure to hold him there. Detecting a hit with this method is easy: The shiner will transmit gentle tugs on the line, but once taken by a bass, there will be a strong, steady pull.

With all three of the techniques described above, the hook-setting procedure is essentially the same.

When a bass takes a shiner he has to be allowed to run with the bait in order to position it and scale it for swallowing. For this reason, the reel should be left in the free-spool position whenever a bait is in the water. One of the advantages of the older Ambassadors is that the spool tension adjustor is located on the left side and readily accessible.

Timing is important. Anglers must be on the water when the fish feed, even if it's midnight. Night bassing is a common tactic in clear lakes. (Right) A large net is a must. It's basic, but many big bass are lost for its lack.

This is tightened down slightly to the point where the shiner cannot strip line from the reel, but a bass can.

How long you allow a bass to take line from the reel is a matter of debate even among the guides. But a slow count to "one thousand five" is a good starting point. On some days, the bass may be more aggressive and get the shiner down sooner, while missing a couple of fish would indicate they need more time and the count should be increased.

When the decision is made to set the hook, the most efficient technique yet found is to use the "power hook set."

When a bass is moving with the bait, it may be heading back into the cover or out to open water. In either case, the line is likely to become entwined in the weeds, which will put a belly of slack into it. Trying to tighten the line slowly

to the fish may result in your feeling the line hung on the roots and, assuming that's the bass, setting the hook without removing the slack from the line. Or the bass may feel the pressure you're applying and drop the bait. Don't get into a "feeling" contest with a bass, because you'll lose most of them.

Instead, stand up, point the rod at the place where the line enters the water, engage the reel and crank down fast until you actually feel the fish. Then hammer him!

What you are doing here is using the speed of the reel and the momentum of the moving bass to penetrate the point of the hook into the fish. The hard hook set serves to drive it home and get the bass coming your way.

When using a float, the hook should be set in a normal

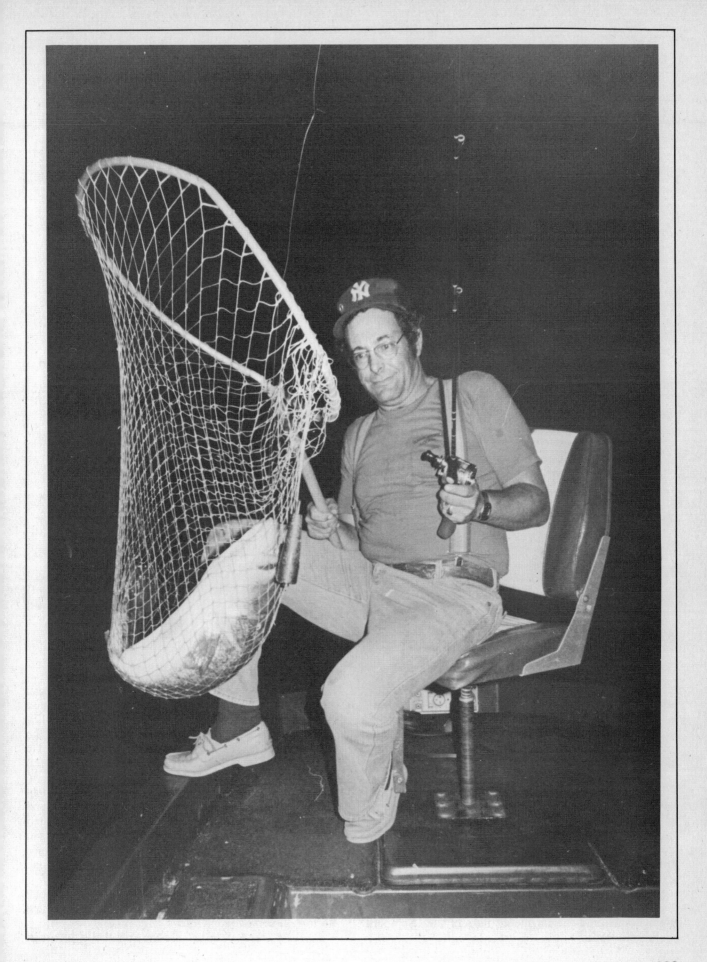

Arden Hanline, like most knowledgeable deepwater anglers, favors light spinning tackle. Clear, open waters are best handled with lighter lines on Fenwick outfit shown. Hanline took his 19-pound 3-ounce bass with this tackle.

upwards motion. When free-linning, though, it should be set down and to the side to bring the bass out from underneath the cover.

This systematic approach to shiner fishing is surprisingly simple and, as many satisfied clients can attest, decidely effective.

Although developed in the shallow, weedy waters of Florida, the system also has been effective in similar types of environment in other parts of the country. A number of my clients have taken it to other states and, using commercial shiners in the four- to six-inch range or even chub minnows in the same size range, they have taken large bass from their home waters. In any shallow, weedy lake it is an excellent technique for tangling with large bass.

When faced with deep, rock-bound lakes, savvy trophy hunters shift to crawfish when seeking bigger spotted bass, smallmouths and the largmouth bass of the Southern California lakes.

It was a crawfish that fooled Easley's twenty-one-pound three-ounce bass, which stands as the second largest bass ever officially recorded.

Crawfish can be fished in several manners, but in the deep, clear lakes where they are most effective, the tackle requirements are pretty much the same. Most experts favor six-foot medium-action spinning rods, with graphite a first choice. A quality open-faced spinning reel with an excellent drag is loaded with line in the four- to ten-pound range. Spotted bass and smallmouth anglers have found the lighter lines are needed to fool the real heavyweights in these clans, while largemouth anglers can get by with lines in the six- to ten-pound range, with eight-pound being one of the most popular choices.

A small rubber core sinker in the one-eighth- to one fourth-ounce range, plus, a light wire sproat hook in size #4 to 1/0, complete the rig.

The best crawfish to use are the soft shells, although

The majority of larger smallmouth and spotted bass are found at depths greater than 15 feet, along sloping banks, submerged edges of channels, other deep structures in man-made reservoirs.

these are not often available. If using regular crawfish, some successful anglers have found crushing their pinchers with a pair of pliers will add a scent trail to the water, making the bait more effective.

A variety of so-called crawfish rigs are on the market to secure the bait to the hook, but many anglers simply hook the crawfish in the second segment up from the tip of the tail, from the under side, out through the top.

One effective technique for fishing crawfish is to place the sinker 1½ feet above the bait and cast it out to deeper points and sleeping banks. Let the bait sink to the bottom and then retrieve it slowly back to the boat in a slow lift and fall, much like fishing a jig-and-pig. The movements should be slow and you don't want to move the bait more than about six inches per lift. This is an excellent way to cover large areas of deep structure.

Smaller areas like ledges, rock piles and such are often fished better with a vertical presentation.

Position yourself over the structure, using a bow-mounted depth finder and simply lower the bait straight down. Then, using the wind or your trolling motor, move slowly around the structure to present your bait to any fish holding there.

With either technique, the bail on the reel should be left open and the line held with a finger. The bass must be allowed to run several feet with the bait in order to get it positioned before the hook is set.

In some areas of the country, water dogs are a popular big bass bait and they can be fished in much the same manner as the crawfish.

While live bait is the most effective way to tangle with outsized bass, lures can prove quite effective. In fact, the world record smallmouth, largemouth and spotted bass all

Few thrills in angling compare to bringing one home for the wall. A systematic approach to the trophy hunt is more successful than luck.

were taken on a deep-diving crankbait, shallow-running crankbait and spinnerbait, respectively.

Any artificial lure will take a big bass on occasion. But anglers deliberately hunting trophies would be advised to concentrate on those baits that have displayed an affinity for attracting big bass on a regular basis. There are several to chose from.

One of the most versatile is the plastic worm. This is especially true in shallow, weedy lakes. Larger baits, with an action tail like the Ditto Gator Tail, can be one of the best choices. These can be cast, swum or flipped into heavy cover. While other anglers in the boat may be taking more small bass, the one who sticks with a proven trophy-getter like the Gator Tail often takes the largest. The largest bass I have ever taken on an artificial lure — 12½ pounds — took a big black Gator Tail crawled off a weed edge in early March.

Another proven performer in shallow water is the buzzbait. The big one-half-ounce model has always been my first choice and, if the cover allows it, a trailer hook is added.

This bait has been most effective during the warmer months of the year when fished around heavy cover near deep water, but in a water depth of less than six feet. Dim light, like dawn and dusk, or an overcast day seem to help position the bass closer to the surface and make them react more to noise and motion. It's not a lure I would throw under bright light, but under proper conditions, it is awesomely effective.

During the spring spawn, the larger females can be highly territorial and will protect it from intruders. Few intruders are more obnoxious than a big tandem willow leaf spinnerbait, which may be one reason it is an extremely effective big bass bait during the spawning period. These baits, with #6 to #8 blades, can provoke strikes from big bass when smaller baits are ignored.

The jig-and-pig is another proven performer, especially on man-made lakes with a lot of wood or brush. This is a standard "winter" bait in Texas and presently holds the Texas State record of seventeen pounds ten ounces. When crawled slowly through deeper wood structure, flipped

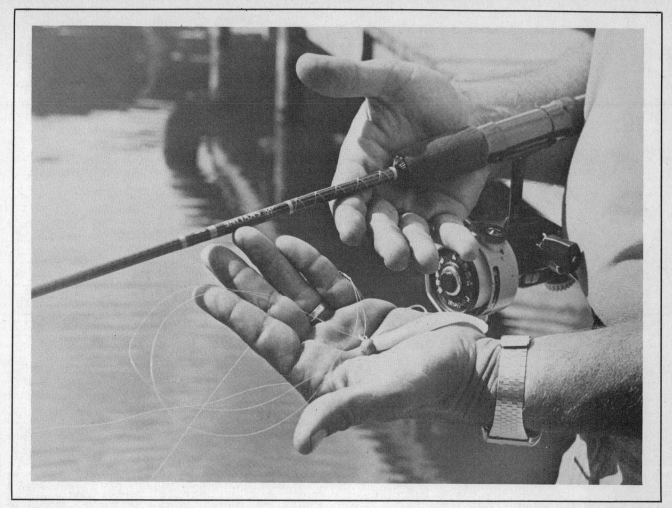

Spinning gear chosen by the angler to use in open, deep water should be top quality and have ultra-smooth drag. (Right) Anglers after big bass should choose the waters carefully. A demonstrated reputation is what to seek.

into brush piles or swum down steeply sloping banks, they're strong medicine for bigger bass.

Regardless of the bait or lure used, the most important asset a trophy hunter can have is a "trophy attitude." In much the same way a deer hunter will pass up opportunities to take four- and six-point bucks while he waits for a ten-pointer, so too must the big bass hunter.

Develop confidence in the techniques chosen and stick with them after four hours without a hit — or after four days without a hit. Resist the impulse to try a lake known for large numbers of smaller bass, instead of one with a reputation for heavyweights.

Plan your on-the-water forays to coincide with the best conditions for big bass to feed. In short, think big bass.

If catching a trophy bass was easy, everyone would do it. By the same token, don't be afraid to explore and experiment. As stated earlier, the best weapon in a bass fisherman's arsenal is an open mind.

For example, one of the largest bass taken in the last five years fell victim to one of the most unusual techniques I have ever heard of.

Arden Hanline, a Southern Californian, takes a small countdown model Rapala minnow and re-wraps the rear

hook with yellow-dyed feathers. In use, he allows the bait to sink to the bottom, then retrieves it to the boat almost like a plastic worm, using a series of short twitches. In February 1987, he landed a nineteen-pound three-ounce Lake Morena bass doing that! He has several other bass over ten pounds to his credit with his system, proving it's certainly not a fluke catch!

Which certainly illustrates the point that big bass often require odd-ball tactics.

CHAPTER 20

An ESPN camera crew covers finalists in the 1987 U.S. Bass Angler's Dream Tournament. With $50,000 in cash for the winner, such contests are becoming big media events.

THE TOURNAMENT TRAIL

There's A Big Boom In Competitive Bass Fishing And Some Pros Are Making Big Loot

Much of the equipment enjoyed today was developed out of tournament competition needs. This Ranger Bass Boat is safe, quick and sturdy on-the-water transportation. It features state-of-the-art design as well as accessories.

COMPETITION IS as American as apple pie. It doesn't make much difference whether it's a Wednesday night bowling league, a Saturday afternoon Skeet shoot or a few friendly side bets on the golf course, we as Americans inherently love to compete with one another.

Nor is this something we learn as adults. Our competitive nature is moulded well before we play our first Little League game and is reinforced continually throughout our high school and college years. We do love a contest and, if it can be held in a clean, healthy outdoor environment, so much the better.

It's not surprising that our competitive spirit has extended to our pursuit of America's fish: the bass. While some anglers may view the current proliferation of bass tournaments as a fairly recent phenomenon, they're only partly

The angler in the rear of the boat usually has the same chance of catching fish as the man controlling the bow. But the rules state that each fisherman will have equal opportunity to control the boat for half the fishing day.

In a well run tournament, weigh-in procedures assure the survival of the bass. The first step is to place the angler's catch in a water-filled bag while alive.

right. "Fishing contests" of one kind or another have been around since the turn of the century. In some cases, they were nothing more than big-fish contests, whereby the angler catching the largest member of a species was awarded some sort of prize. In later years, though, the first actual forms of organized competition surfaced in the form of "fishing derbies." Anglers would contribute a couple of bucks to a general pot and the one dragging in the biggest bunch of bass took home the money.

In most cases the rules for these derbies were rather loose and even more loosely adhered to by the competitors. While I wouldn't go so far as to say that any fisherman might have cheated, it is fair to say that creative "improvisation" was often the order of the day and many of these early contests were won more by cunning than skill.

That changed in 1967, when a brash, young Alabama insurance salesman by the name of Ray Scott decided that not only could an honest fishing derby be held, but it would be popular as well. Gathering 106 of the best bass fishermen he could find, Scott hosted his first tournament — The All American — on Arkansas' Beaver Lake on June 6 of that year.

Unlike other fishing contests, this one attracted the cream of American bass fishermen. The entry fee was an unheard of $100 — big money during the days when $2 fishing derbies had trouble attracting entrants due to their unsavory reputations.

To insure a fair and even contest, competitors were paired two to a boat to keep an eye on each other. With a $2000 first prize up for grabs, as well as the stubborn pride of 106 anglers, the mere thought of impropriety brought icy stares from the contestants. There would be none. And, in the twenty years that followed, there never has been a hint of a cheating scandal in a Ray Scott tournament. Scott wouldn't allow it then and he hasn't changed over the years.

To say the first Ray Scott tournament was a success would be understatement at best. Today, the organization Scott founded shortly after the Beaver Lake tournament, Bass Angler's Sportsman Society, boasts over half a million members, 1700 affiliated club chapters and dispenses some $2.5 million in tournament prize awards annually.

In a major tourney, ounces can be the difference between a check for $25,000 and one for $5000. Many pros use a balance beam to cull fish, making certain the heaviest bass are kept. Shaw Grigsby wins big with a simple tool.

While Bass Angler's Sportsman Society (BASS) is the oldest and still the largest tournament organization, it's not the only one. Tournaments have proven so popular that many BASS events are filled within a few days after the schedule is announced and often have long waiting lists. Several other organizations have stepped in to fill the tournament need, most notably U.S. Bass, and today there is a variety of tournament organizations to choose from.

Some, like BASS, offer big-money national level events, while organizations such as U.S. Bass offer those, as well as affordable local and regional tournaments. All of the better organizations adhere to the same strict standards for conduct introduced by Ray Scott and many have even adopted the BASS tournament rules as their guidelines.

The popularity of these tournaments is undoubtably the result of several factors. For some, the friendly competition and camaraderie are important. Others see it as an opportunity to learn new techniques. For a growing number of anglers, though, it is the chance to actually make a living doing something they love: fishing for bass!

The term "casting-for-cash" aptly describes a growing number of professional bass anglers who derive their incomes largely from their successes in tournament competition. There is money to be made, if you're one of the better tournament anglers. In some cases, a lot of money.

Texas angler Rick Clunn — considered to be one of the best in the sport — has tournament winnings that approach $600,000 over the last decade! More than a few tournament competitors have winnings exceeding $250,000.

When you consider that sponsorship contracts, seminar fees and funds generated through product endorsement by a top pro often exceed his yearly winnings, it's not hard to see that there really is "gold in them thar gills!"

Even anglers who restrict themselves to local tour-

At the end of the fishing day, the fish in the water-filled bags are carried to the waiting area. This is all a part of the procedure aimed at fairness for all.

naments within a day's drive of home can pocket some change. Several friends of mine in Florida hold down full-time jobs and fish tournaments on their weekends off. Some manage to collect up to $20,000 a year. That may not sound like much compared to the top pros, but it does make the boat payment, insurance premiums and leaves some left over for entry fees. In effect, they pay for their fishing by fishing for pay.

Anglers desiring to try their hand at the "cast for cash"

In the waiting area, the fish — still in their bags — are held in a water-filled tank until the judges can get around to counting each fisherman's take for the day and taking measurements that will count in the final scores.

game will find there are two basic tournament formats in common use: the Draw Tournament and the Boat Tournament.

The Draw tournament is the original concept made popular by BASS and it exists today in essentially the same format that was introduced in 1967. This is an individual event in which each angler pays his entry fee and competes against every other angler. Competitors in this event are paired through random drawing or a computer pairing for each of the fishing days.

Once the pairings for the following days fishing are announced at the drawing held each evening the two paired competitors must meet and mutually agree upon whose boat will be used and where they will start fishing the following day. The rules stipulate that each of the competitors sharing the boat has the right to spend one-half of the fishing day in control of the bow fishing position and on the water of his choosing. This right does not, however, have to be exercised and an angler may choose to spend the entire day in the rear of the boat and allow the other competitor to choose the water to be fished.

In the event that the two anglers cannot mutually agree upon whose boat to take, the standard procedure is the old

Each bass is inspected to ensure it's alive. Ounces are taken from the angler not bringing the fish to the scales alive. Check is made on the size and length requirement.

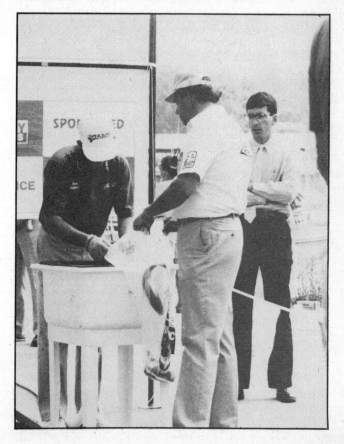

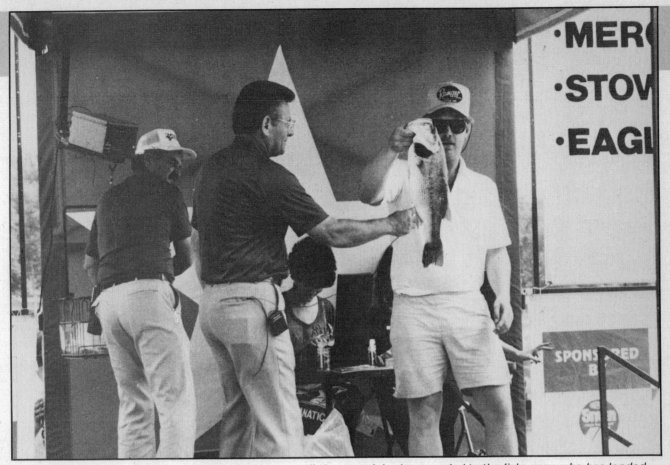

The larger bass are weighed separately, as there usually is a special prize awarded to the fisherman who has landed the biggest individual bass on that particular day. The pro fishermen are highly competitive, after the prizes.

"call it in the air" coin flip, which usually is presided over by a tournament official.

In the event that there is more than one competition day in the tournament (two and three days are common in nationl level events), the pairing procedure will be repeated each evening and no two competitors will be paired together twice during that event.

Scoring for this event is the total weight of an individual angler's catch in pounds and ounces, although there is usually a special cash award going to the angler who lands the largest bass on each tournament day.

The draw format is the one most commonly seen on the national level and is almost standard in big money tournaments.

The Boat Tournament format is often referred to as a "buddy" tournament. Two competitors enter as a team and fish together in the same boat throughout the event. The combined weight of their catch, again in pounds and ounces, will determine the score for the team. This format is gaining popularity on a local and regional level, since it allows husbands and wives, fathers and sons, and even fathers and daughters to compete together as a team, encouraging family participation in the sport.

Finally, the bass are returned to the water alive to battle another day. In most tournaments, up to 95 percent of the fish are returned for the conservation movement.

Left, above: Ray Scott probably did not foresee the full impact his first bass fishing tournament would have. (Above) Florida's Manuel Spencer was a pulp mill employee, who found he could make a year's wages in three-day tournament.

Bass tournaments are offered at all levels. On a local basis, small one-day events may require entry fees as low as $25 and feature a first place award in the $400 to $500 range.

Regional level tournaments often require entry fees of $300 to $450, but reward the winner with cash or merchandise in the $20,000 to $30,000 range. In almost any well run event, there also will be cash and prizes for anglers finishing in the top twenty percent of the field. However, when it comes to the real big bucks, anglers will have to break into one of the major tournaments. Here's a look at how the Big Boys play for pay.

BASS Masters Classic: Hosted by BASS, this is not the richest tournament, but is considered the most prestigious. It is often called The Masters of bass fishing.

Entry in the event is through a series of qualification tournaments that determine the top thirty-five anglers fishing the BASS Tournament Trail. Five "amateurs" from the affiliated BASS Federation chapters also compete, as does the previous year's winner, who is not required to qualify to defend his title. There is no entry fee. All forty-one qualifiers are transported to the tournament site — which changes yearly — at BASS expense and are provided with identically rigged Ranger bass boats.

The winner receives $50,000 for his victory, but can expect to make at least that much through future product endorsements and sponsorships. Rick Clunn, three-time winner, and Bobby Murray, two-time winner, are the only

anglers in the twenty-year history of this event to win more than once.

U.S. Bass World Championship: Hosted by U.S. Bass, this is another qualifying event that takes the top twenty finishers from each of the three regions — west, central and east — and sends all sixty anglers on an all-expenses-paid week of bass fishing for a first place prize of $50,000 in cash and merchandise.

The tournament lake changes yearly. Skeeter Boats provides a fully rigged boat with Mercury engine and trolling motor, plus a Lowrance depthfinder, for the use of each contestant during the event.

An angler is required to fish a six- or seven-tournament series of qualifying events to be eligible to compete. There are, however, some big-bucks tournaments that require only an entry fee.

MegaBucks: (BASS) A $2200 entry fee earns the angler the right to compete in this elimination event which, so far, has been held on the Harris Chain of Lakes in Leesburg, Florida, each spring for the last three years.

Competitors are allowed two days of practice, followed by three days of competition. At that time, the top fifty anglers — determined by pounds and ounces for the three days — fish one day and the top ten anglers are selected based upon their total weight for the four days.

At this point, they all start over again, completely even, in a brand new Ranger bass boat, for two more days of fishing. This segment is held on a lake that was not fished pre-

Bass pro Ken Cook holds aloft the winner's trophy at the 1987 Angler's Dream Tennessee Tournament. With trophy went a check for $50,000. Since 1981, Ken Cook's contest earnings have added up to more than a $350,000 total.

viously in the tournament. Each angler must move through a ten-hole bouyed-off "course," having only one hour per hole. It's a grueling event, but the first place prize is over $100,000 in cash and merchandise. Second place prize is close to $50,000!

U.S. Open: (U.S. Bass) One of the most exhaustive events on the circuit, a $1250 entry fee gives the angler the right to compete for seven days (with a day of rest in the middle) on Nevada's Lake Mead in late July. This event requires not only bass fishing ability, but sound physical conditioning as well. The winner receives $50,000 in cash, but the angler catching the largest bass on each of the competition days take home a fully-rigged Skeeter bass boat

valued at more than $18,000! This is considered the most demanding tournament on the circuit.

Angler's Dream Tournament: (U.S. Bass) An interesting elimination tournament much like MegaBucks, this separates boaters and those without boats; allowing them to compete only against each other. The top five boaters and non-boaters fish equally for a first place prize of $50,000 in cash.

The boater's entry fee is $1000 and entitles him to control the boat fully during each fishing day and to select the waters to be fished. The non-boater's $800 entry fee entitles him to stay in the back of the boat and catch whatever fish he can. One hundred boaters and the same number of non-boaters start, but after two days, the field is cut to fifty of each. Two more days of fishing brings it down to the top five in each category. A final one-day event determines the winner. All anglers start even after each cut. Boaters and non-boaters are paired with different partners each day and on the last day it's anybody's tournament! One large bass could determine the outcome!

One last tournament bears mentioning simply because it allows any angler to fish for big bucks with a fairly small investment.

Red Man All American: (Operation Bass) $100,000 in cash is at stake for the forty anglers who work their way through a grueling series of qualifying events. Beginning with local tournaments charging a $50 entry fee, an angler finishing in the top ten percent of his local division can compete in regional fish-offs. Score well here and he could find himself — or herself — flying to a totally new lake to compete for some serious money!

The first place prize is $100,000, with a significantly smaller amount being split among the remaining anglers. It's virtually a "winner take all" event, unlike the other qualifying tournaments that, at least, reward an angler finishing in the lower spots with a check. Still, for those who make it through the lengthy series of qualifying events, a shot at $100,000 is nothing to sneer at.

Anglers interested in trying their hand at the "cast-for-cash" game will find organizations catering to men, to women or some that allow both to compete equally. Here's a breakdown of the major organizations that sponsor tournaments:

Bass Angler's Sportsman Society, One Bell Road, Montgomery, AL 36117. (Limited to men only)
U.S. Bass, 435 E. Main St., Mesa, AZ 85203. (Open to men and women)
Operation Bass, Route 2 Box 74B, Gilbertsville, KY 42044. (Open to men and women)
Bass'n Gals, P.O. Box 13925, 3600 W. Pioneer Parkway (Suite 6), Arlington, TX 76013. (Limited to women only)
Lady Bass, 129 Avenue A, N.E., Winter Haven, FL 33880. (Limited to women only)

The Bass Anglers Sportsman Society rules are reprinted here (courtesy of BASS) to give anglers an idea of how tightly reputable bass tournaments are controlled. It's not just another fishin' trip!

Every weekend basser feels he could compete successfully on the tournament trail, if only he had the grubstake to get started; but it's not that easy. As in pro golf, few make it to the top of the pyramid in competition.

BASS ANGLERS SPORTSMAN SOCIETY 1987-88 BASSMASTER® TOURNAMENT OFFICIAL RULES AND REGULATIONS

1. RULES CHANGES: Great effort, study and research has gone into the formulation of these rules. The following rules of this tournament will remain unchanged, except for special tournaments conducted by B.A.S.S. Interpretation and enforcement of these rules shall be left exclusively to the Tournament Rules Committee. In the event of a rule violation, the Tournament Rules Committee may impose such sanctions as it deems appropriate, including, without limitation, disqualification, forfeiture of prizes and prohibition from participation in subsequent tournaments. The decision of the judges and tournament officials shall be final in all matters.

2. PARTICIPANTS AND ELIGIBILITY: Participation in this tournament is by invitation only. In order to maintain our high standards of decency and to ensure sexual privacy, this tournament is open only to members of the Bass Anglers Sportsman Society³ who are male and 16 years of age or older. Proof of age to the satisfaction of tournament officials is responsibility of potential competitor. **DURING THE COMPETITION DAYS OF ANY BASS ANGLERS SPORTSMAN SOCIETY TOURNAMENT NO CONTESTANT MAY OPERATE A BOAT UNLESS THAT CONTESTANT HAS SUBMITTED DOCUMENTED PROOF OF A MINIMUM OF $100,000 BOATING LIABILITY INSURANCE TO THE B.A.S.S. TOURNAMENT DEPARTMENT. THIS DOCUMENTED PROOF MUST BE RECEIVED BY US ON OR BEFORE THE APPLICATION DEADLINE DATE.** Any candidate for competition who, in the judgement of the tournament officials, is handicapped in such a manner as to unfairly hinder his partner or endanger the safety and well-being of his partner or himself shall not be eligible. **A PROPERLY COMPLETED AND SIGNED OFFICIAL APPLICATION FORM AND THE ENTRANCE FEE MUST BE RECEIVED AT B.A.S.S. HEADQUARTERS NO LATER THAN THE DEADLINE DATE.** The Tournament Committee reserves the right to discontinue acceptance of applications prior to deadline and also the right to extend the acceptance date. **DEPOSITS ARE NON-REFUNDABLE AND NON-TRANSFERABLE REGARDLESS OF DATE OF CANCELLATION. REFUND OR TRANSFER OF THE BALANCE OF THE ENTRY FEE WILL BE MADE ONLY IF PROPER NOTIFICATION IS MADE TO THE B.A.S.S. TOURNAMENT DEPARTMENT PRIOR TO THE DEADLINE DATE.** A sponsor may pay the entry fee. As a participant in B.A.S.S. tournaments you agree, if you qualify and are invited to

be a contestant in the BASS Masters Classic³ conducted by B.A.S.S., to use during the Classic competition and event any and all official products and equipment so specified and provided by B.A.S.S. **ENTRY DEADLINE DATE FOR EACH TOURNAMENT SHALL BE 21 DAYS PRIOR TO THE FIRST COMPETITION DAY OF EACH TOURNAMENT.**

3. PRE-TOURNAMENT PRACTICE: There will be a practice period immediately preceding the first day of the tournament. The tournament waters shall be off-limits to all competitors commencing at sunup, 14 days prior to the first competition day. The exact dates and times of the practice period and the off-limits period must be obtained from the B.A.S.S. Tournament Department. The competitor must know and observe these dates. **During practice, and during the tournament, a competitor may not have the assistance or advice of anyone for the purposes of locating bass, nor enter the tournament waters with anyone who has been on the tournament waters during the 14-day off-limit period, a professional guide, state or federal wildlife agency employee, or any other person deemed a "local expert" on these tournament waters by the Tournament Committee, unless he is a contestant in the tournament.** Each competitor agrees to report to tournament officials any violation or infraction of these Tournament Rules. The failure to report violations or suggestions to violate these Rules, or false verification of weigh-in forms will be cause for disqualification. **EACH COMPETITOR AGREES TO SUBMIT, BY HIS SIGNATURE ON THIS DOCUMENT, TO A POLYGRAPH TEST SHOULD HE BE ACCUSED OF ANY RULE VIOLATION.** The administration and interpretation of the polygraph test shall be solely the responsibility of the Tournament Committee, and its agents, and shall be used (or not used) in the discretion of the Tournament Committee. Without limiting the foregoing, the Tournament Rules Committee shall have sole discretion to select the place at which such polygraph test shall be administered, the individual who administers such polygraph test, and the scope of the questions which may be asked during such test. The Participant shall be available, at his expense, at the location selected by the Tournament Rules Committee and shall cooperate in all respects with such examination.

4. REGISTRATION: Each competitor must register in person with official B.A.S.S. staff at the time and place prescribed on the schedule of events. Failure to register in person during the prescribed hours shall result in a penalty of one pound off your total catch. No exceptions. **IT SHALL BE EACH COMPETITOR'S RESPONSIBILITY TO CHECK THE SCHEDULE OF EVENTS FOR REGISTRATION TIME AND LOCATION OR OBTAIN TIMES FROM B.A.S.S. TOURNAMENT DEPARTMENT.**

Sponsorship by tackle and boat makers varies according to name value of the angler promoting the firm's product line. Pros like Guido Hibdon, fishing the front casting platform of Ranger 373V, wear sponsor names embroidered on shirts.

5. SAFETY: Safe boat conduct must be observed at all times by tournament competitors. Each competitor is required to wear a Coast Guard approved chest-type life preserver. This perserver must be worn anytime the combustion engine is operating. This preserver must be strapped, snapped or zippered securely and maintained in that condition until the competitor reaches his fishing location and the combustion engine is shut off. Violation of this rule shall be reason for disqualification.

6. SPORTSMANSHIP: Competitors in B.A.S.S. tournaments are expected to follow high standards of sportsmanship, courtesy, safety and conservation. Any infraction of these fundamental sporting principles may be deemed cause for disqualification. Use of alcohol or drugs (other than those purchased over the counter or prescribed by a licensed physician) by any competitor during the tournament will not be tolerated and shall be cause for automatic disqualification for this and all future B.A.S.S. tournaments. Maximum courtesy must be practiced at all times, especially with regard to boating and angling in the vicinity of non-competitors who may be on tournament waters. Any act of a competitor which reflects unfavorably upon the Society's effort to promote fisheries conservation, clean waters, and courtesy shall be reason for disqualification. No alcoholic beverages or other stimulants or depressants, prescription or otherwise, shall be allowed in the boats or in the weigh-in area.

7. TACKLE AND EQUIPMENT: Only artificial lures may be used. No "live bait" or "prepared bait" will be permitted, with the exception of pork strips, rinds, etc. Only ONE casting, spin-casting or spinning rod (8 foot maximum length from butt of handle to rod tip) and reel may be used at any one time. All other types prohibited. Other rigs as specified above may be in boat ready for use, however, only ONE is permitted in use at any given time. All bass must be caught live and in a conventional sporting manner. No dip nets or gaff may be used to boat bass nor be permitted in boat at any time.

8. HORSEPOWER REGULATIONS: MAXIMUM HORSEPOWER FOR ALL OUT-BOARD MOTORBOATS USED IN TOURNAMENT COMPETITION WILL BE 150 HP, not to exceed the horsepower limitations set by the U.S. Coast Guard in their ruling of Nov. 1, 1972. When required, each boat MUST have a U.S. Coast Guard horsepower rating plate attached to the boat by the manufacturer. The horsepower of the outboard engine must NOT exceed the rating specified on this rating plate or the 150 horsepower maximum set by B.A.S.S. Any boat manufactured prior to Nov. 1, 1972 must adhere to the ratings set by the U.S. Coast Guard for similar

boats. Each competitor agrees to submit, by his signature on the official entry form, the boat and outboard motor used in the tournament to an inspection by factory-trained personnel, if there is any reason to suspect the horsepower is in excess of the rating. Normal maintenance to increase the performance of your engine is allowed. Changing or altering standard factory parts of your motor to **increase the horsepower over the factory horsepower rating is forbidden,** and will result in disqualification. Falsifying information on entry forms or altering the horsepower rating numbers on the motor also would be cause for immediate disqualification from Bass Anglers Sportsman Society[3] tournaments.

9. BOAT AND MOTOR: For the safety of all contestants, **ALL BOATS MUST BE EQUIPPED WITH SOME TYPE OF IGNITION KILL SWITCH.** This ignition kill device must be attached to the driver's body any time the combustion engine is operating. Fishing boats may be used that are 14 feet or more in length. A small motor, gas or electric, may be used for slow maneuvering. All **BLADDER** tanks and any other type of **AUXILLARY** gas tanks that are not installed by the boat manufacturer are prohibited. Boats that do not have factory installed gas tanks are restricted to a maximum of 12 gallons of gasoline in tanks that meet U.S. Coast Guard regulations. Trolling as a method of fishing is prohibited. No "barges" or similar cumbersome craft will be permitted. It having been determined that boats equipped with **"STICK STEERING" PRESENT GREATER THAN NORMAL SAFETY HAZARDS, NO BOAT SO EQUIPPED SHALL BE PERMITTED TO BE USED DURING THE TOURNAMENT BY ANY COMPETITOR.** The definition of "stick steering" shall be made by the Tournament Committee. The competitor may use his own boat and motor, if it is allowed under these rules, or rent a boat and motor at the tournament site; such possible rental being the sole responsibility of the competitor. A competitor answering affirmatively the question, "Will you bring a boat and motor?" will be expected to make that boat and motor available for tournament use by himself and his daily partner, if so requested by tournament officials. Those answering the same question negatively will be presumed not to have a boat and motor available and will be paired with one who does when possible. It shall be the responsibility of the fishing partners to mutually agree on whose boat to use and a basis for sharing operational expenses. If the partners are unable to agree, the Tournament Committee shall make such determination, which shall be binding upon the partners.

10. BASIC BOAT EQUIPMENT: Every boat must have all required Coast Guard safety equipment. In addition, it must have a functional bilge pump and **LIVEWELL**

The dream of every pro bass fisherman is to compete in the invitation-only BASS Master's Classic, which is limited to the 35 who boat the most weight in six preliminary contests. Charlie Reed, 51, won in 1986. The tournament is worth big bucks to the winner in endorsements, as well as sponsorships, speaking engagements, appearances.

SPACE, PROPERLY AERATED, TO ADEQUATELY MAINTAIN ALIVE A LIMIT CATCH OF BASS BY BOTH FISHERMEN USING THE BOAT. Tournament officials shall have the sole responsibility for determining whether aeration and capacity is "proper and adequate."

11. BOAT IDENTIFICATION: Each boat MUST be given, prior to each day's start, an inspection check by a tournament official, also a numbered flag, which MUST remain with your boat until turned in each day at the check-in. This flag must be displayed upon the request of tournament officials, and turned in to the officials at each check-in.

12. BOAT OPERATION AND EXPENSE: A full discussion **MUST** be held between the two partners prior to a morning departure as to the schedule of boat operations. This schedule must permit each partner equal time to fish from the front of the boat and to operate the trolling motor, so as to afford each partner the opportunity to fish his selected waters an equal number of hours. Distance traveled to fishing locations must be considered in order not to deprive either partner fishing time while traveling to and from fishing waters. If a contestant waives the above rights, he shall retain the right to select the fishing waters for one-half the tournament day. Any contestant who, in the judgement of the officials, operates the boat in such a manner as to unfairly handicap his partner shall be disqualified. In view of the large expense involved in operating and maintaining a tournament bass boat, it is suggested that the non-owner partner at least share part of cost of gas and oil for the competition day.

13. PERMITTED FISHING LOCATIONS: Tournament waters shall be established by the Tournament Director for each tournament. Each competitor must obtain this information from the B.A.S.S. Tournament Department. Fishing on the tournament waters is permitted anywhere except: Within 50 yards of another competitor's boat which was first anchored or secured in a fixed position. No such boat shall permit selected competitors to fish within the 50-yard circle claimed by him, to the exclusion of any other competitor. Any water within these boundaries posted Off-Limits or No Fishing by state or federal agencies will be **OFF-LIMITS.** Also, the live-bass release area established by the Tournament Director will be **OFF-LIMITS** and will be announced at the Tournament Briefing. Only that water open to **ALL** public fishing will be considered tournament waters. Any waters closed to public fishing will be closed to this tournament's contestants. All angling must be done from the boat. Competitors wishing to change fish habitat by placing any object in the tournament waters may do so if such action does not violate state or federal regulations.

14. CONTESTANTS MUST REMAIN IN BOAT: Contestants must not depart the boat to land fish. Boats must remain in tournament waters during tournament days. Contestants must leave and return to official checkpoint by boat. Both competitors must remain in boat at all times except in case of dire emergency. In such an emergency, competitors may be removed from their boat to: A boat operated by other competitors; or a rescue boat so designated by tournament officials. Partners must remain together at all times, in sight of each other and each other's catch under the conditions cited above, in order for their catch of that day to be scored in the tournament. If a competitor must violate any of the above conditions (to contact a tournament official by phone or other means or to report an emergency or breakdown), both competitors must cease fishing at this point, and their catch must be verified by a tournament official in order to be counted in the tournament. If after the emergency situation is resolved by tournament officials and enough time is left for the competitors to resume fishing, a **RE-START** will be allowed and the competitors will continue and their catch will be counted. This applies only to dire emergency situations. Trailering of boats during tournament hours is prohibited, except by the direction of tournament officials.

15. OFFICIAL CHECKPOINT: There shall be only one official point for check-out in the morning, and check-in in the afternoon, and this point shall be designated at the tournament briefing. At the time of check-out, all competitors and their boats shall be in full conformance with all rules set forth by the Tournament Committee; at check-in, all boats shall identify themselves by means of the numbered flags and proceed immediately to the designated weigh-in area. Partners must stay together, and flags must be turned in at check-in.

16. SCORING: Tournament standings, auxiliary awards and final winners shall be determined by the pound and ounce weight of each competitor's catch during the competition days of the tournament. Only Largemouth, Spotted, Red Eye or Smallmouth bass will be weighed. The limit shall be 7 of the above species and varieties per day, unless the prevailing state limit is less than 7, or a special limit is established for a particular tournament by the tournament officials, in which case the state limit, or special limit, shall be the tournament limit. All competitors are bound by the prevailing statutes and regulations of the various states within which they fish. At no time shall a competitor have reduced to possession more than the limits described above. Tournament officials will conduct checks for violation of

Several organizations sponsor bass fishing tournaments and the professional angler who is successful can make a good living, doing what he likes to do. Nonetheless, he must catch fish to win and the pressure to do so is enormous.

this provision, and in the event a competitor has reduced more than the above-described limits to possession, shall cull the largest bass first, down to the limit described. The official length for bass shall be determined by the Tournament Director and announced at the tournament briefing. In most cases it will be the longest state limit covering the tournament waters. Only bass as described above which measure the official length or more on the longest straight line, shall be weighed-in. Bass presented for weigh-in which fail to measure the official length shall accrue penalties at the rate of one pound for each such bass. This penalty shall be deducted from the total score of the competitor. Any bass that appears to have been mangled, mashed, mauled or otherwise altered will be weighed and credited only at the discretion of tournament officials. Each competitor must present his catch to the weigh-in officials, and the weight of his catch must be certified by the signature of his partner of that day. Bass must not be stringered at any time during the tournament. It has been determined that stringering decreases the chances of a bass's survival, and bass thus handled may be disqualified. Specially designed bags which increase survival rate will be furnished by the Tournament Committee, and these bags must be used for the weigh-in.

17. DON'T KILL YOUR CATCH: Each competitor is expected to keep his bass alive by use of a properly aerated livewell. The few bass which do not survive will be used for scientific study and for charity.

18. PENALTY POINTS: For each legal dead bass presented to weigh-in officials, the competitor shall be penalized two ounces of weight, to be deducted from his daily score. The Tournament Director and his designated appointees shall have sole authority for accessing penalty points.

19. LATE PENALTY: Competitors who are not in the official checkpoint area as described in Rule 15 at the appointed time shall be penalized at the rate of 1 pound per minute to be deducted from the total weight of his catch that day, including any weight to be counted toward a "lunker award," for each one (1) minute he is late. Any competitor more than 15 minutes late shall lose all credit for that day's catch. There shall be no excuse for tardiness, and in no case shall a competitor be allowed to make up "lost time." After proper recognition at the check-in point, competitors will be allowed ample time to proceed to the weigh-in site; however, all fishing must cease upon check-in. After the tournament begins, fishing the tournament waters is prohibited except during the tournament hours. Exact starting and check-in times will be announced at the tournament briefing.

20. TIES: In case of a tie for first place, there will be a sudden-death fish-off between the tied contestants, under the direction and special rules as may be established by the tournament officials. Ties for lesser positions shall be resolved by means selected by tournament officials.

21. PAIRING OF CONTESTANTS: Two contestants will be assigned to each boat. Wherever possible, no contestants from the same city or state will be paired, nor shall two competitors fish together more than one day. Announcement of your first-day fishing partner shall be made at the tournament briefing, which **MUST BE ATTENDED** by each competitor. It shall be the responsibility of each partner to appear at a mutually agreed upon location with sufficient time remaining to check out at the official checkpoint and start on time. Tournament officials shall have no responsibility for finding missing partners. It is suggested that a minimum of 30 minutes is required for preparation to depart to the check-out point. When two contestants check out at the beginning of the day, they must stay together and within sight of each other and each other's catch throughout the day until the weigh-in is completed except in case of dire emergency (See Rule 14). A contestant must not allow any bass caught by him to be counted on the score of another contestant. In such a case, both contestants shall be disqualified from this tournament and from all future tournaments conducted by Bass Anglers Sportsman Society®.

22. None of the above rules shall prohibit a properly designated tournament official from approaching or boarding any competitor's boat at any time during the "warm-up" period or the competition days.

23. PATCHES AND/OR SIGNAGE: B.A.S.S. encourages the use of patches, logo's and other signage to promote sponsors. Realizing we are entering into a television media field that **MAY** sometimes restrict the use of patches, logo's, signage, etc. that promote or advertise products, B.A.S.S. reserves the right to **RESTRICT THE USE OF SUCH SIGNAGE** in such tournaments with as much advance notice as possible to the contestants.

CHAPTER 21

The author questions what bass fishing will be like when this youngster is old enough to own his own bass boat. (Right) Regardless of the degree of involvement, anglers can benefit from modern management practices now in force.

BASS
AND THE
FUTURE

Despite Tremendous Increases In Fishing Pressure, The Bass Is Holding Its Own Quite Well

Anglers at Nevada's Lake Mead proved that fishermen can be a moving force in the restoration of declining areas. They instituted a campaign to restore the fisheries and anglers in other parts of the nation have followed suit.

TWENTY YEARS ago, the bass fisherman was a somewhat disheveled individual who pursued his hobby in solitude or in the company of a few kindred souls. Glamorous, he was not.

His uniform was a faded pair of tobacco-stained coveralls, anchored stylishly by an equally faded ballcap of unknown origin. His chariot was a far cry from today's gleaming marvels and his equipment would make a modern angler consider taking up golf. Still, he caught fish and he had fun. There's a lot to be said for that.

Today's bass angler is quite likely to be an entirely different sort of fellow. For starters, there are a lot more of them. Membership rolls of the Bass Angler's Sportsman Society have about 600,000 card-carrying Bassmasters at the time of this writing.

The modern angler also is likely to be well educated, relatively affluent and possessing more in-depth knowledge of the bass and its habits than his predecessors.

In sharp contrast to the semi-leaky craft of yesteryear, the contemporary angler is likely to start his day in a $20,000 assembly of gleaming fiberglass, raw power and sophisticated electronics. His rods and reels are crafted of materials virtually unheard of in earlier days and the lures he uses are the end result of in-depth research and study.

While early practitioners were likely to be a fairly un-communicative group, modern anglers willingly share knowledge and techniques through a network of clubs, magazines and tournaments.

All of this adds up to a concerted assault by knowledgeable, well equipped anglers that is literally unprecedented in the annals of sportfishing history.

As the most popular gamefish in America, it's fair to ask if the bass can survive its popularity. It appears that it can. Although the bass fishing in some areas has deteriorated over the past two decades, some areas are considerably better. There are locales that now produce bass regularly that offered no bass fishing twenty years ago.

As growing numbers of anglers began pursuing the fish, state game and fish departments were forced, by pressure from user groups, to begin implementing management programs designed to increase the numbers of bass.

This was a major departure from previous policies. Notably in the South, bass were pretty much left on their own. Long growing seasons, a large habitat and minimal pressure required nothing more than preventing the taking of bass for commercial purposes and establishing a daily bag limit. In many cases, these bag limits were liberal and loosely enforced.

But that has changed. For example, the State of Texas recently reduced its daily limit from ten bass to five and

Popularity of bass has prompted growing research that helps understand species. Tag-and-release programs are providing info. (Below) Ranks of new fishermen grow each year thanks to research, management and awareness.

imposed a fourteen-inch minimum size limit on most waters. Serious anglers applauded the move.

"One of the most important things we can do to assure good bass fishing in the future," said Texas pro Tommy Martin, "is to encourage anglers to release bass, instead of dragging a big stringer to the dock. This has been a problem in some areas of Texas, especially on the hydrilla lakes where small bass are numerous and not hard to catch. Every small bass that was taken home and eaten was one that did not spawn and produce more bass. The new size limit and reduced limit is a positive step."

Game and fish departments in many states are giving thought to the use of various size and bag limits to control harvests on specific bodies of water. Rather than a statewide limit, one body of water might be best managed with a fourteen-inch minimum size, while another might require no size limit, if it contained smaller bass that were stunting due to overcrowding. Some small, heavily fished lakes have been brought to excellent levels of productivity through sixteen- and eighteen-inch size limits.

"Each water body," said one fisheries biologist, "is essentially different in its capacities and management needs. With the upsurge in bass popularity, many game departments are seeing more budgetary funds available for specific studies on specific water bodies. The results of these should give us the information we need to more effectively manage them individually."

The battle against pollution of the nation's waterways is one that anglers must win, if they are to enjoy their sport in the future. Great strides have been made and many bodies of water are in better shape than a decade ago.

The classic example of maximum management of a minimal resource is the effort of the California Department of Fish and Game. Through the careful introduction of larger growing strains — both largemouth and spotted bass — they have established one of the finest trophy bass fisheries in the world in a small collection of little lakes in a densely populated region.

Although the San Diego lakes are managed under a strict set of regulations that open them to fishing only a few days each week, few anglers mind, since the lakes regularly produce some of the largest bass caught anywhere in the world.

Even larger bodies of water can benefit from management efforts. Alabama's West Point Lake is a good example. When first impounded, West Point — like any man-made reservoir in its early years of life — produced superb bass fishing. Bag and size limits were liberal and many anglers took advantage of them. Within a few years, the quality of the fishing fell drastically.

"It had been pretty much an accepted principle," ex-

State and federal agencies have enhanced bass fisheries across the nation. Federal budget cuts could damage the program. The research by many universities also is aiding bass propogation.

plained one biologist involved with the lake, "that sportfishing could not generate enough pressure to seriously impact the overall bass population in a large environment. What happened at West Point showed us that was no longer true, given the skill and equipment of today's bass fisherman."

At West Point, tremendous numbers of the more reckless and aggressive smaller bass were caught and kept. When time was reached for that particular class of fish to begin contributing to the overall population replacement through their spawn, there weren't enough left to make a significant contribution.

"An entire year class was virtually eliminated through sportfishing, which impacted the reproductive capabilities of the bass population for several years."

Today, the lake has a sixteen-inch size limit and again offers some of the finest fishing in the South. As pressure on bass continues to grow, anglers can look for more restrictive bag and possession limits on many waters.

Another factor that has improved the fishing on many lakes, especially on older man-made impoundments, is the unplanned spread of hydrilla and milfoil. Although the plants can cause problems at extreme densities, they have proven beneficial in providing protective cover for young bass and baitfish.

"I seriously doubt," says Larry Nixon, the all-time

The damming of many of the nation's rivers to provide flood control and aid navigation has increased the amount of suitable water available for bass. But an increase in the number of anglers can put a strain on resources.

leading money winner on the BASS Tournament Trail, "if many of our Texas lakes could stand the fishing pressure they receive without these plants. They have been beneficial in maintaining a good fish population on lakes like Sam Rayburn and Toledo Bend."

One factor that will largely determine the quality of the fishing on many lakes in future years is in how well these plants are managed and controlled by waterway authorities. Overzealous control (or outright eradication) can damage a fishery seriously, as it did to Lake Conroe.

This is one area where sportsman's groups need to become involved with the political process. The agencies charged with aquatic weed control answer to state and federal lawmakers and derive their operating budgets from them. These lawmakers are supposed to answer to their constituents. A few thousand angry letters from area bass fishermen might have a notable impact on weed control budgets for various state agencies.

One wonders if the devastation wrought upon Lake Conroe by the Asian grass carp could have been avoided by organized fishing groups and other groups, concerned with proper lake management. Had they presented a unified

front to the Texas legislature, the unwise introduction of these exotics might not have taken place and Conroe might still be a topnotch bass lake, as well as a favored wintering ground for ducks.

Introduction of other non-native species to bass lakes also has caused some problems. One of the most controversial has been the widespread stocking of striped bass and white bass/hybrids.

Starting in the late 1960s, many states began stocking the striped bass to provide an additional recreational gamefish and to help control shad populations which, according to current research, make up over ninety percent of the adult striper's diet. It was thought that the originally anadromous striper would not reproduce in a landlocked environment. However, in some bodies of water they have, establishing populations over which biologists now have little control.

Among some bass fishermen, original fears were that the voracious stripers would prey significantly upon young bass. This has not been the case. While some fishing writers have catered to these fears by recounting stories of large striped bass cleaned to reveal a seven-bass limit in

This BASS photo by Charles Beck shows a top tournament angler, Rick Clunn, maneuvering a big bass to the boat. While such scenes are frequent in this day and age, the future of bass fishing depends upon funding, management.

their gullet, scientific research shows this is pure fancy.

As part of an ongoing study into the relationship between black bass and striped bass in the same ecosystem, Dr. William Matthews inspected the stomach contents of 1845 striped bass and found only one of the stripers to contain a bass. Additional research showed virtually no predation under a wide range of conditions. Striped bass and their hybrid cousins prey almost exclusively on soft-rayed fish, like shad.

Bass fishermen still blame stripers for a decline in the bass fishing on some lakes and there could be some truth in those claims.

Striped bass are voracious feeders, consuming more forage per day then does a bass under most conditions. In an ecosystem where the shad is the dominant forage item for upper level predatory fish, every shad a striper eats is one a bass won't get.

Recent studies have revealed little habitat overlap be-

reservoirs that present a diversified food chain. In a system where shad form the major source of food for gamefish, an over-abundance of striped bass may be detrimental to achieving the maximum number of largemouth, smallmouth and/or spotted bass.

Another is to discontinue stocking pure-strain striped bass, which are capable of reproduction in some inland waters, and shift to the white bass/striped bass hybrid, which is not likely to reproduce. With non-reproducing populations, biologists can control populations through the number of hybrids stocked.

Other exotics also have proven popular in some areas. Texas has played with the introduction of redfish, flounder and other non-native gamefish into some of its lakes and has established fishable populations of them. Whether this is detrimental to existing bass populations has yet to be proven, but anglers on Texas' Lake Braunig feel the introduction of redfish has ruined the lake as a bass fishery.

The decision as to whether or not to introduce a non-native gamefish species to a lake with an existing bass population is not one to be taken lightly. In many cases, it can affect native fish adversely. This must be weighed against the benefits that will arise from establishing a fishery other than bass. In some lakes where striped bass and hybrids have been introduced, they have proven popular enough with some anglers that bass fishing pressure has declined significantly. This has resulted in more bass having the time to grow to larger sizes and has made a lot of bass fishermen happy.

One exotic, though, has proven to be a universal disas-

Flooded areas provide stick-ups that offer an excellent habitat for bass. (Right) The future of bass fishing is largely in the hands of America's anglers. The catch-and-release programs, plus funded research, should be a help.

tween bass and stripers; each occupies its own niche in the system. Striped bass inhabit the deeper offshore areas, while most bass are more shallow water-oriented. But shad migrate daily between open waters and the shallows and, on some lakes, the stripers actually may be taking food away from the bass. Lake Mead is one example of a situation where a striper population is offering serious competition for a limited food resource and bass fishing has suffered for it. In other lakes, however, bass and stripers are peacefully co-existing, and indeed both species are prospering.

One key to achieving an acceptable balance between the two species is to introduce striped bass only into those

ter! The rapid spread of tilapia is something that should cause concern among all bass anglers. These robust panfish — which can reach weights of five pounds — do not compete with the bass for food. They are vegetarians and don't prey upon young bass. What they do is destroy bass bedding areas and thus adversely affect the ability of the bass population to sustain itself through natural spawning.

During the decade I have been a trophy bass guide in Central Florida, I have watched tilapia populations increase each year. This is notable in the many spring-fed runs and small canals that Florida largemouths traditionally utilize in January for the first spawns of the year.

Bass flock to these, because the spring runs are warm enough to encourage spawning well before main lake waters warm up. Tilapia flock to them, because these fish cannot tolerate water temperatures much below fifty degrees for any length of time. It becomes a battle between two species for territory and the tilapia have won every time!

One spot in particular stands out in my mind. Silver Glenn Run is a 1½-mile-long spring run on the west shore of Florida's Lake George. It's clean sand and shell bottom once supported a rich and varied assortment of vegetation that provided protection for spawning bass, as well as newly hatched fry. It was one of the most fertile bass spawning areas within miles and became a hotbed of bass activity each winter. It's not any more.

Today, you can cruise the clear waters of the run and seldom see a bass. What you do see are thousands of tilapia digging crater-like nests deep into the bottom. Over the last ten years, these nests have stripped the bottom of

Today's bass angler is better educated, better equipped than those of earlier years and concerned about future. (Left) There still are bass meant to serve as trophies.

much of its vegetation. Unlike a bass which simply fans away a bit of bottom silt to make a bed, tilapia dig right down into the bottom ripping out plants by the roots.

Silver Glen Run resembles a lunar landscape today and few bass even attempt to spawn there. Those that do generally are driven off by schools of big tilapia protecting their own spawning area.

It is difficult to measure the impact that the loss of this prime spawning habitat has had on the local bass population, but when you consider that every one of the spring-fed runs in this area has been similarly overrun with tilapia, it's impossible to say that there has been no negative impact.

Tilapia have infested virtually all Florida waterways.

Research and protection of habitat is having much to do with the growth of larger bass than seen in former years.

How they got there is somewhat clouded. Some say that a small group escaped from a research pond; others say commercial fishermen were responsible. The Florida Game and Freshwater Fish Commission is reluctant to speak on the subject, but is totally reluctant to consider the introduction of any other exotics, so maybe some lessons were learned. Hopefully, those lessons will be learned in other states before they suffer the same affliction as have Florida's waters.

Tilapia currently are being touted as an excellent live bait for striped bass and are even being considered for stocking as a forage fish.

Before anyone starts depositing these fish in public waters, they might want to stop by the Sunshine State and take a look around one winter! If the Florida experience is any indication, these are not the kind of critters you want finning their way around your favorite bass lake.

Even without the threat posed by the introduction of exotic species, the bass still faces enough challenges to require the assistance of concerned anglers, if it is to re-

main as America's Fish. One area of critical concern is in how the water levels of our nation's fisheries are manipulated.

Over 78,000 dams block waterways across our country. Most are designed and created to provide electric power, flood control, to facilitate navigation and to provide drinking water for thirsty cities. These dams — and the lakes they created — are responsible for the bass boom by creating millions of acres of water for bass.

Since that was not the original plan, management of these waterways for the benefit of the bass is not prime concern. Despite their value to the $25 billion fishing industry, the bass' welfare is way down the list of priorities when regulating agencies determine when and how much to manipulate water levels.

Pumpback systems designed to generate electricity more efficiently kill large numbers of young fish each year. Fish barriers that would alleviate the problem can be installed, but it sometimes takes a lot of pressure. The National Wildlife Federation had to team up with the State of

Professional tournament anglers such as Randy Beringer realize the importance of the catch-and-release program, if bass are to thrive for future generations. Many of the top-money tournaments now are encouraging such programs.

Michigan to force a local power company to install such barriers at one of its plants.

Pumping isn't the only problem, nor is it the most serious. Heavy rains or early spring snow melts can expand a reservoir. If the water is held back, bass often move into newly flooded areas to spawn. Should water then be released quickly, the nests are left high and dry and an entire year class can be destroyed. Several years hence, when these fish would be joining the adult spawning population, reproduction problems will occur.

Large scale irrigation needs can alter water levels to the detriment of the fish, as well. Agencies with major dam and water level control powers, like the Corps of Engineers and the Tennessee Valley Authority, have often shared an adversarial relationship with sport fishermen, but things may be changing. Surprisingly, it was the controversy generated

This lake is a classic example of an aging impoundment in decline. Like many older impoundments, shoreline cover has virtually disappeared, leaving few places young bass could hide to escape predation. Also, installation of the Glen Canyon Dam — which forms Lake Powell above it — began to reduce the normal nutrient flow into Lake Mead. The lake, in effect, was starving to death.

It was obvious that the quality of the fishing had declined, so in 1984, a private bass tournament organization and its sponsors decided to do something about it. U.S. Bass had used the lake as the site of its U.S. Open Tournament for several years and they, Lowrance Electronics, Mercury Marine, GNB Batteries and others began to take action.

"The sponsors of the U.S. Bass Tournament Trail had begun to hear the public's feelings that we, as sponsors, needed to put something back into the sport of fishing — leave the lake better than we found it," said Lowrance's Don Siefert. "We agreed and raised $3000 between ourselves and tournament anglers for habitat improvement on Lake Mead."

Approaching Butch Padilla, a Nevada wildlife biologist working on the lake, they asked if they could use the money to purchase some bass for stocking purposes. This is usually seen as the simplest and most direct approach to improve fishing. Unfortunately, professional lake managers have learned it's seldom the best course of action, as Siefert found out.

"What Padilla told us was surprising," Siefert remembers. "He told us stocking more fish would be a waste of our time and money, because the lake suffered from a serious lack of nutrients to support them. Without nutrients there was no vegetation to provide protection for fry and not enough baitfish to feed the adult fish that were there. However, Padilla told us that anything we could do to help improve the lake's habitat could be beneficial.

"We investigated several ways to increase the cover and decided Christmas tree brushpiles would probably be the best bet. From there, we issued a challenge to local fishing clubs: If they would collect the trees, we would cover the expense of getting them installed."

over the endangered snail darter that has forced many reservoir managers to stop ignoring recreational interests in our waterways.

We also continue to fight a battle against pollution of our lakes and rivers, but we may be scoring big points in that area. The concerted effort to clean up America's waterways is paying dividends for bass fishermen. Not only is there a noticeable "watchdog" attitude on the part of governmental agencies tasked with pollution control, but cleanup procedures have restored some waterways that were once thought hopeless. One can find excellent smallmouth bass fishing on the Potomac River and equally good largemouth fishing on the Hudson. A short decade ago, both rivers were virtual open sewers, incapable of supporting gamefish.

There is still a long way to go, but the climate is right. Americans have become environmentally aware and lawmakers have heeded their voices. All of this spells good news for bass — and anglers who pursue them.

The same spirit has been carried over to the private sector. Just take a look at what a few planted Christmas trees have done for Nevada's Lake Mead.

Studies of the relationship between bass and aquatic vegetation may yield the information that can allow lake managers to enhance bass populations by weed control. Such studies now are being conducted for bass populations.

Thanks to publicity from the late Las Vegas outdoor writer Al Ceiri and fellow writer John Kimak, that first year's challenge was answered with 6000 trees.

"Initially," said Siefert, "we intended the trees to be protection for fry and placed them near spawning areas and along migration routes, but we soon began to see some promising side benefits." Divers from local scuba clubs reported that panfish began to gather around the trees almost immediately, and that algae (a base in the food chain) started growing on the planted trees within a short period of time.

By the second year, the project was in full swing and had the support of most of the area's sportsmen. The Lake Mead Enhancement Society — consisting of the area's three bass clubs, two striper clubs, two diving clubs, and a trout fishing club — was formed to oversee future implementation of the project. The second year, planting barges were provided by the Nevada Wildlife Department and the U.S.

Park Service and construction materials were donated by area businesses. That year, 10,000 trees went in, but that was only the beginning!

"Public interest and publicity really began to pay off," explains Siefert, who has been one of the prime shakers and movers of this project. "Since 1984, we had been collecting money quietly through private cash donations, sponsor support (which now included Stren, Skeeter Boats, and Eagle Claw) and cash donations from the U. S. Bass tournament anglers, themselves. We didn't have a great deal, but when Nevada Wildlife saw the strong level of community support, they showed us how to utilize state and federal matching funds through the Wallop-Breaux program. Through the magic of those matching funds the $3000 we started with ultimately grew into $250,000!"

That was far more than was needed to plant Christmas trees, so a research grant was formed to enable the University of Nevada, Las Vegas, to study the feasibility of

Ray Scott (left) has been a moving force in the effort to conserve and protect the nation's bass resources. The philosophy of catch-and-release has been incorporated into his tournaments and passed on to recreational anglers.

introducing nutrients directly into the lake to help promote the growth of plankton that would increase shad populations to support more fish.

In early 1987, over 1000 volunteers converged on Lake Mead to assist in the largest nutrient loading project ever held in the U.S.

Although far from finished, the Lake Mead project has begun to make significant strides in correcting the lake's two major problems: lack of protective cover and nutrients.

Siefert reflects, "When you hear anglers complaining about how their wildlife departments aren't doing anything for the fishing, that's not always true. Butch Padilla is a good example. He knew what was needed and had already done the necessary studies; most wildlife departments have a Butch Padilla. The only problem was that there was no money in the budget to implement them, and that's true

Many of today's most productive bass waters exist on the impoundments where manipulation of the water levels can affect the fishery. However, in some areas of the nation bass fishing actually is better than it was a decade ago.

of many wildlife departments across the country. However, once his organization saw the level of community interest and support and once funds did become available, they were more than willing to get involved."

When the project began in 1984, the Nevada Wildlife budget for Lake Mead was $100,000. Thanks to publicity and community interest generated by the project, the state increased that budget to $400,000 for 1987!

"It's a tremendous example," says Siefert, "of how concerned anglers and outdoorsmen can become a moving force in the management area. The self-help project and interest generated on Lake Mead could be done on many other lakes and similar projects have begun in other states. America's bass fishermen have the capability to improve their sport."

They also have the capability to provide professional fisheries managers with sound scientific studies that will enable them to make informed decisions concerning the most effective management of bass. The easiest way to do this is to become a supporting member of the Bass Research Foundation.

Headquartered at P.O. Box 99, Starksville, MS 39759, the Bass Research Foundation is set up in much the same manner as one of the country's most successful sportsman's groups: Ducks Unlimited. The following, taken from the original By-Laws adopted in 1974, explains their goals:

The primary goal of the Bass Research Foundation is to promote and encourage results-oriented research aimed at improving America's bass fishery resources. The BRF will not be involved in the actual research work, but will act as a funding, coordinating agency.

The Bass Research Foundation will function as a non-profit organization with operational funds being derived from contributions of concerned bass fishermen and members of bass fishing and related industries. The foundation is exempt from Federal income tax under Section 501 (c) (3) of the Internal Revenue Code. All contributions are fully tax deductible.

So far, the BRF has funded studies on a wide-ranging list of subjects that will ultimately benefit America's fish. Among them are; impact of striped bass in a bass fishery; effects of acid rain; feasibility of stocking bass to improve certain fisheries; and many others. One, however, is exceptionally intriguing.

There isn't an angler in America who wouldn't drool at the possibility of fishing a lake where the bass averaged five and six pounds. That doesn't happen often, unless you can wangle access to some private pond, but researchers at the University of Oklahoma may change that!

Using a process called "gynogenesis," biologists are causing female bass to produce more females in their spawn. Then the biologists are changing those female bass into male bass. But while these bass function as males, including the ability to fertilize eggs, they retain the increased growth size of the female!

In theory, these fish will spawn with normal females and the male bass from that spawn will retain the increased growth potential of the fertilizing male.

It's a rare male bass that reaches a weight of five pounds,

but female bass are capable of reaching weights of over ten pounds routinely, in the proper environment. In fact, all of the largest specimens are females.

In this process, the eggs are stripped from the female bass and exposed to ultra-violet light after having been mixed with the sperm of the male bass. This removes the male chromosomes, but retains the female chromosomes and genes. All the fish from that spawn will be females. When the female bass are one to two inches long, they are fed a hormone-laced food that causes sex reversal; the bass become functioning males but retain the female genes.

One drawback in that the process is low-yielding: about one egg in 10,000, but that can be solved simply by increasing the numbers of eggs treated.

The possibility of producing a strain of super bass is intriguing and may ultimately enhance bass fishing across the country.

Biologists in Texas are working along the same lines. They are feeding newly hatched fry hormone-laced food during the time their sex organs are developing, allowing them to dictate the sex of the fry. Since female bass are more hardy, able to survive more adverse conditions — as well as reach larger sizes — this is seen as a potentially valuable stocking tool.

A number of other researchers are exploring ways to increase the average size of bass through genetic engineering and selective breeding. There exists a possibility that strains of larger fish may be available in the near future.

With such efforts under way, it would appear the future of bass fishing is not only bright, but exciting, as well.